50% OFF Online CMA Prep Course

Dear Customer,

We consider it an honor and a privilege that you chose our Certified Medical Assistant Study Guide. As a way of showing our appreciation and to help us better serve you, we have partnered with Mometrix Test Preparation to offer you **50% off their online CMA Prep Course**. Many Certified Medical Assistant courses are needlessly expensive and don't deliver enough value. With their course, you get access to the best CMA prep material, and **you only pay half price**.

Mometrix has structured their online course to perfectly complement your printed study guide. The CMA Prep Course contains **in-depth lessons** that cover all the most important topics, **30+ video reviews** that explain difficult concepts, **1,400+ practice questions** to ensure you feel prepared, and **more than 350 digital flashcards**, so you can study while you're on the go.

Online Certified Medical Assistant Prep Course

Topics Included:

- Clinical Competency
    - Medical Terminology
    - First Aid, CPR, and Emergency Response
    - The Systems of the Body
- General
    - Therapeutic Communication
    - Grief and Loss
- Administrative
    - Financial Bookkeeping
    - Medical Transcription
    - Business Practices

Course Features:

- CMA Study Guide
    - Get content that complements our best-selling study guide.
- Full-Length Practice Tests
    - With over 1400 practice questions, you can test yourself again and again.
- Mobile Friendly
    - If you need to study on the go, the course is easily accessible from your mobile device.
- CMA Flashcards
    - Their course includes a flashcard mode with 350 content cards to help you study.

To receive this discount, visit them at mometrix.com/university/cma/ or simply scan this QR code with your smartphone. At the checkout page, enter the discount code: **TPBCMA50**

If you have any questions or concerns, please contact Mometrix at support@mometrix.com.

Sincerely,

in partnership with

FREE Test Taking Tips Video/DVD Offer

To better serve you, we created videos covering test taking tips that we want to give you for FREE. **These videos cover world-class tips that will help you succeed on your test.**

We just ask that you send us feedback about this product. Please let us know what you thought about it—whether good, bad, or indifferent.

To get your **FREE videos**, you can use the QR code below or email freevideos@studyguideteam.com with "Free Videos" in the subject line and the following information in the body of the email:

a. The title of your product

b. Your product rating on a scale of 1-5, with 5 being the highest

c. Your feedback about the product

If you have any questions or concerns, please don't hesitate to contact us at info@studyguideteam.com.

Thank you!

CMA Study Guide 2025-2026

5 Practice Tests and Certified Medical Assistant Exam Prep Book [9th Edition]

Lydia Morrison

Written and edited by TPB Publishing.

Interested in buying more than 10 copies of our product? Contact us about bulk discounts: bulkorders@studyguideteam.com

ISBN 13: 9781637751978

Table of Contents

Welcome

Dear Reader,

Welcome to your new Test Prep Books study guide! We are pleased that you chose us to help you prepare for your exam. There are many study options to choose from, and we appreciate you choosing us. Studying can be a daunting task, but we have designed a smart, effective study guide to help prepare you for what lies ahead.

Whether you're a parent helping your child learn and grow, a high school student working hard to get into your dream college, or a nursing student studying for a complex exam, we want to help give you the tools you need to succeed. We hope this study guide gives you the skills and the confidence to thrive, and we can't thank you enough for allowing us to be part of your journey.

In an effort to continue to improve our products, we welcome feedback from our customers. We look forward to hearing from you. Suggestions, success stories, and criticisms can all be communicated by emailing us at info@studyguideteam.com.

Sincerely,
Test Prep Books Team

FREE Videos/DVD OFFER

Doing well on your exam requires both knowing the test content and understanding how to use that knowledge to do well on the test. We offer completely FREE test taking tip videos. **These videos cover world-class tips that you can use to succeed on your test.**

To get your **FREE videos**, you can use the QR code below or email freevideos@studyguideteam.com with "Free Videos" in the subject line and the following information in the body of the email:

a. The title of your product
b. Your product rating on a scale of 1-5, with 5 being the highest
c. Your feedback about the product

If you have any questions or concerns, please don't hesitate to contact us at info@studyguideteam.com.

Quick Overview

As you draw closer to taking your exam, effective preparation becomes more and more important. Thankfully, you have this study guide to help you get ready. Use this guide to help keep your studying on track and refer to it often.

This study guide contains several key sections that will help you be successful on your exam. The guide contains tips for what you should do the night before and the day of the test. Also included are test-taking tips. Knowing the right information is not always enough. Many well-prepared test takers struggle with exams. These tips will help equip you to accurately read, assess, and answer test questions.

A large part of the guide is devoted to showing you what content to expect on the exam and to helping you better understand that content. In this guide are practice test questions so that you can see how well you have grasped the content. Then, answer explanations are provided so that you can understand why you missed certain questions.

Don't try to cram the night before you take your exam. This is not a wise strategy for a few reasons. First, your retention of the information will be low. Your time would be better used by reviewing information you already know rather than trying to learn a lot of new information. Second, you will likely become stressed as you try to gain a large amount of knowledge in a short amount of time. Third, you will be depriving yourself of sleep. So be sure to go to bed at a reasonable time the night before. Being well-rested helps you focus and remain calm.

Be sure to eat a substantial breakfast the morning of the exam. If you are taking the exam in the afternoon, be sure to have a good lunch as well. Being hungry is distracting and can make it difficult to focus. You have hopefully spent lots of time preparing for the exam. Don't let an empty stomach get in the way of success!

When travelling to the testing center, leave earlier than needed. That way, you have a buffer in case you experience any delays. This will help you remain calm and will keep you from missing your appointment time at the testing center.

Be sure to pace yourself during the exam. Don't try to rush through the exam. There is no need to risk performing poorly on the exam just so you can leave the testing center early. Allow yourself to use all of the allotted time if needed.

Remain positive while taking the exam even if you feel like you are performing poorly. Thinking about the content you should have mastered will not help you perform better on the exam.

Once the exam is complete, take some time to relax. Even if you feel that you need to take the exam again, you will be well served by some down time before you begin studying again. It's often easier to convince yourself to study if you know that it will come with a reward!

Test-Taking Strategies

1. Predicting the Answer

When you feel confident in your preparation for a multiple-choice test, try predicting the answer before reading the answer choices. This is especially useful on questions that test objective factual knowledge. By predicting the answer before reading the available choices, you eliminate the possibility that you will be distracted or led astray by an incorrect answer choice. You will feel more confident in your selection if you read the question, predict the answer, and then find your prediction among the answer choices. After using this strategy, be sure to still read all of the answer choices carefully and completely. If you feel unprepared, you should not attempt to predict the answers. This would be a waste of time and an opportunity for your mind to wander in the wrong direction.

2. Reading the Whole Question

Too often, test takers scan a multiple-choice question, recognize a few familiar words, and immediately jump to the answer choices. Test authors are aware of this common impatience, and they will sometimes prey upon it. For instance, a test author might subtly turn the question into a negative, or he or she might redirect the focus of the question right at the end. The only way to avoid falling into these traps is to read the entirety of the question carefully before reading the answer choices.

3. Looking for Wrong Answers

Long and complicated multiple-choice questions can be intimidating. One way to simplify a difficult multiple-choice question is to eliminate all of the answer choices that are clearly wrong. In most sets of answers, there will be at least one selection that can be dismissed right away. If the test is administered on paper, the test taker could draw a line through it to indicate that it may be ignored; otherwise, the test taker will have to perform this operation mentally or on scratch paper. In either case, once the obviously incorrect answers have been eliminated, the remaining choices may be considered. Sometimes identifying the clearly wrong answers will give the test taker some information about the correct answer. For instance, if one of the remaining answer choices is a direct opposite of one of the eliminated answer choices, it may well be the correct answer. The opposite of obviously wrong is obviously right! Of course, this is not always the case. Some answers are obviously incorrect simply because they are irrelevant to the question being asked. Still, identifying and eliminating some incorrect answer choices is a good way to simplify a multiple-choice question.

4. Don't Overanalyze

Anxious test takers often overanalyze questions. When you are nervous, your brain will often run wild, causing you to make associations and discover clues that don't actually exist. If you feel that this may be a problem for you, do whatever you can to slow down during the test. Try taking a deep breath or counting to ten. As you read and consider the question, restrict yourself to the particular words used by the author. Avoid thought tangents about what the author *really* meant, or what he or she was *trying* to say. The only things that matter on a multiple-choice test are the words that are actually in the question. You must avoid reading too much into a multiple-choice question, or supposing that the writer meant something other than what he or she wrote.

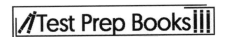

5. No Need for Panic

It is wise to learn as many strategies as possible before taking a multiple-choice test, but it is likely that you will come across a few questions for which you simply don't know the answer. In this situation, avoid panicking. Because most multiple-choice tests include dozens of questions, the relative value of a single wrong answer is small. As much as possible, you should compartmentalize each question on a multiple-choice test. In other words, you should not allow your feelings about one question to affect your success on the others. When you find a question that you either don't understand or don't know how to answer, just take a deep breath and do your best. Read the entire question slowly and carefully. Try rephrasing the question a couple of different ways. Then, read all of the answer choices carefully. After eliminating obviously wrong answers, make a selection and move on to the next question.

6. Confusing Answer Choices

When working on a difficult multiple-choice question, there may be a tendency to focus on the answer choices that are the easiest to understand. Many people, whether consciously or not, gravitate to the answer choices that require the least concentration, knowledge, and memory. This is a mistake. When you come across an answer choice that is confusing, you should give it extra attention. A question might be confusing because you do not know the subject matter to which it refers. If this is the case, don't eliminate the answer before you have affirmatively settled on another. When you come across an answer choice of this type, set it aside as you look at the remaining choices. If you can confidently assert that one of the other choices is correct, you can leave the confusing answer aside. Otherwise, you will need to take a moment to try to better understand the confusing answer choice. Rephrasing is one way to tease out the sense of a confusing answer choice.

7. Your First Instinct

Many people struggle with multiple-choice tests because they overthink the questions. If you have studied sufficiently for the test, you should be prepared to trust your first instinct once you have carefully and completely read the question and all of the answer choices. There is a great deal of research suggesting that the mind can come to the correct conclusion very quickly once it has obtained all of the relevant information. At times, it may seem to you as if your intuition is working faster even than your reasoning mind. This may in fact be true. The knowledge you obtain while studying may be retrieved from your subconscious before you have a chance to work out the associations that support it. Verify your instinct by working out the reasons that it should be trusted.

8. Key Words

Many test takers struggle with multiple-choice questions because they have poor reading comprehension skills. Quickly reading and understanding a multiple-choice question requires a mixture of skill and experience. To help with this, try jotting down a few key words and phrases on a piece of

scrap paper. Doing this concentrates the process of reading and forces the mind to weigh the relative importance of the question's parts. In selecting words and phrases to write down, the test taker thinks about the question more deeply and carefully. This is especially true for multiple-choice questions that are preceded by a long prompt.

9. Subtle Negatives

One of the oldest tricks in the multiple-choice test writer's book is to subtly reverse the meaning of a question with a word like *not* or *except*. If you are not paying attention to each word in the question, you can easily be led astray by this trick. For instance, a common question format is, "Which of the following is...?" Obviously, if the question instead is, "Which of the following is not...?," then the answer will be quite different. Even worse, the test makers are aware of the potential for this mistake and will include one answer choice that would be correct if the question were not negated or reversed. A test taker who misses the reversal will find what he or she believes to be a correct answer and will be so confident that he or she will fail to reread the question and discover the original error. The only way to avoid this is to practice a wide variety of multiple-choice questions and to pay close attention to each and every word.

10. Reading Every Answer Choice

It may seem obvious, but you should always read every one of the answer choices! Too many test takers fall into the habit of scanning the question and assuming that they understand the question because they recognize a few key words. From there, they pick the first answer choice that answers the question they believe they have read. Test takers who read all of the answer choices might discover that one of the latter answer choices is actually *more* correct. Moreover, reading all of the answer choices can remind you of facts related to the question that can help you arrive at the correct answer. Sometimes, a misstatement or incorrect detail in one of the latter answer choices will trigger your memory of the subject and will enable you to find the right answer. Failing to read all of the answer choices is like not reading all of the items on a restaurant menu: you might miss out on the perfect choice.

11. Spot the Hedges

One of the keys to success on multiple-choice tests is paying close attention to every word. This is never truer than with words like *almost*, *most*, *some*, and *sometimes*. These words are called "hedges" because they indicate that a statement is not totally true or not true in every place and time. An absolute statement will contain no hedges, but in many subjects, the answers are not always straightforward or absolute. There are always exceptions to the rules in these subjects. For this reason, you should favor those multiple-choice questions that contain hedging language. The presence of qualifying words indicates that the author is taking special care with his or her words, which is certainly important when composing the right answer. After all, there are many ways to be wrong, but there is only one way to be right! For this reason, it is wise to avoid answers that are absolute when taking a multiple-choice test. An absolute answer is one that says things are either all one way or all another. They often include words like *every*, *always*, *best*, and *never*. If you are taking a multiple-choice test in a subject that doesn't lend itself to absolute answers, be on your guard if you see any of these words.

12. Long Answers

In many subject areas, the answers are not simple. As already mentioned, the right answer often requires hedges. Another common feature of the answers to a complex or subjective question are qualifying clauses, which are groups of words that subtly modify the meaning of the sentence. If the question or answer choice describes a rule to which there are exceptions or the subject matter is complicated, ambiguous, or confusing, the correct answer will require many words in order to be expressed clearly and accurately. In essence, you should not be deterred by answer choices that seem excessively long. Oftentimes, the author of the text will not be able to write the correct answer without offering some qualifications and modifications. Your job is to read the answer choices thoroughly and completely and to select the one that most accurately and precisely answers the question.

13. Restating to Understand

Sometimes, a question on a multiple-choice test is difficult not because of what it asks but because of how it is written. If this is the case, restate the question or answer choice in different words. This process serves a couple of important purposes. First, it forces you to concentrate on the core of the question. In order to rephrase the question accurately, you have to understand it well. Rephrasing the question will concentrate your mind on the key words and ideas. Second, it will present the information to your mind in a fresh way. This process may trigger your memory and render some useful scrap of information picked up while studying.

14. True Statements

Sometimes an answer choice will be true in itself, but it does not answer the question. This is one of the main reasons why it is essential to read the question carefully and completely before proceeding to the answer choices. Too often, test takers skip ahead to the answer choices and look for true statements. Having found one of these, they are content to select it without reference to the question above. The savvy test taker will always read the entire question before turning to the answer choices. Then, having settled on a correct answer choice, he or she will refer to the original question and ensure that the selected answer is relevant. The mistake of choosing a correct-but-irrelevant answer choice is especially common on questions related to specific pieces of objective knowledge.

15. No Patterns

One of the more dangerous ideas that circulates about multiple-choice tests is that the correct answers tend to fall into patterns. These erroneous ideas range from a belief that B and C are the most common right answers, to the idea that an unprepared test-taker should answer "A-B-A-C-A-D-A-B-A." It cannot be emphasized enough that pattern-seeking of this type is exactly the WRONG way to approach a multiple-choice test. To begin with, it is highly unlikely that the test maker will plot the correct answers according to some predetermined pattern. The questions are scrambled and delivered in a random order. Furthermore, even if the test maker was following a pattern in the assignation of correct answers, there is no reason why the test taker would know which pattern he or she was using. Any attempt to discern a pattern in the answer choices is a waste of time and a distraction from the real work of taking the test. A test taker would be much better served by extra preparation before the test than by reliance on a pattern in the answers.

Bonus Content & Audiobook Access

We host multiple bonus items online, including all 5 practice tests in digital format. Scan the QR code or go to this link to access this content:

testprepbooks.com/bonus/cma

The first time you access the tests, you will need to register as a "new user" and verify your email address.

If you have any issues, please email support@testprepbooks.com.

Introduction to the CMA Exam

Function of the Test

The Certified Medical Assistant (CMA) Exam is offered by the Certifying Board of the American Association of Medical Assistants (AAMA) as part of their program for credentialing medical assistants. Individuals taking the CMA Exam fall into one of three categories: 1) prospective or recent graduates of accredited medical assisting programs; 2) graduates applying more than twelve months after graduating from an accredited medical assisting program; or 3) candidates who previously passed the exam and are seeking recertification. Scores are generally used only for the certification process.

The exam is intended to impartially, objectively, and fairly measure a thorough, broad, and current understanding of healthcare delivery. It is taken by individuals seeking certification or recertification as medical assistants nationwide. In 2015, 17,324 individuals sought initial CMA Certification. Of that cohort, 10,573 test takers passed, yielding a 62% pass rate.

Test Administration

Individuals wishing to take the exam must apply through the AAMA. In the application, the individual must select their preferred 90-day testing window. If the application is approved, the individual must contact Prometric – the testing center that administers the exam. The individual must then select a test date, time, and location, and complete the exam within the assigned window.

Upon arrival at the test center, the test taker must furnish the appropriate identification. The test center will offer test takers lockers for personal items and then set each test taker up at a computer. Test takers are offered an optional tutorial to familiarize themselves with the test taking software. The tutorial lasts a maximum of fifteen minutes.

Individuals seeking certification for the first time are allowed three attempts to pass the exam. In accordance with the Americans with Disabilities Act, test takers with documented disabilities may request accommodations by submitting a Request for Special Accommodations form, which is available from the AAMA.

Test Format

The CMA Exam consists of 200 questions, 180 of which are scored and 20 of which are pretest questions. The pretest questions are included for evaluation of potential questions for future exams and are not scored, but the test taker is not informed as to which of the 200 total questions are pretest questions. The test is administered in four sessions of 40 minutes each; the total examination time is 2 hours and 40 minutes. Test takers may also take up to 20 minutes as break time between sections if they so choose.

The content of the exam falls into three major categories: General, Administrative, and Clinical. Within those categories, test takers receive questions on a wide variety of topics such as medical terminology,

anatomy, physiology, and record keeping. The questions from the various categories are interspersed amongst each other throughout the exam.

Section	Category	# of Qs	Percent of Exam
1	General	50	28%
2	Administrative	45	25%
3	Clinical	85	47%
Total		**180**	**100%**
Unscored		**20**	**NA**

Scoring

Scores are based on the total number of correct answers provided by the test taker, with no penalty for wrong answers beyond the missed opportunity to get another answer correct. This raw score is standardized and converted to a scaled score. The Certifying Board sets the passing score at a level that indicates the minimum competency for an entry level medical assistant and adjusts it as appropriate. The current minimum passing score is 430.

The test taker receives an immediate pass/fail notification upon completion of the exam, before leaving the testing center. Official score reports containing a percentile rank in each of the three major subject areas are distributed four weeks after exam completion.

Study Prep Plan for the CMA Exam

1 **Schedule -** Use one of our study schedules below or come up with one of your own.

2 **Relax -** Test anxiety can hurt even the best students. There are many ways to reduce stress. Find the one that works best for you.

3 **Execute -** Once you have a good plan in place, be sure to stick to it.

One Week Study Schedule

Day 1	Clinical Competency
Day 2	Procedures/Examinations
Day 3	General
Day 4	Administrative
Day 5	Practice Test #1
Day 6	Practice Test #2
Day 7	Take Your Exam!

Two Week Study Schedule

Day 1	Clinical Competency	Day 8	Administrative
Day 2	Safety and Infection Control	Day 9	Scheduling Appointments and Health Information Management
Day 3	Procedures/ Examinations	Day 10	Practice Test #1
Day 4	Specimen Collection Techniques	Day 11	Practice Test #2
Day 5	Pharmacology	Day 12	Practice Test #3
Day 6	General	Day 13	Practice Test #4
Day 7	Communication	Day 14	Take Your Exam!

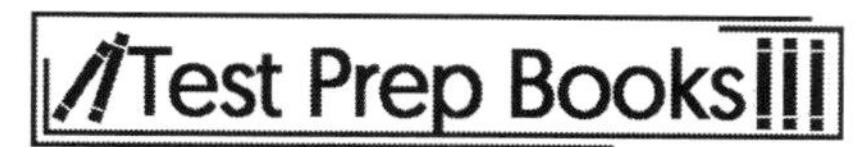

One Month Study Schedule

Day 1	Clinical Competency	Day 11	Pharmacology	Day 21	Answer Explanations
Day 2	Interviewing Techniques	Day 12	Immunization Resources	Day 22	Practice Test #2
Day 3	Processing Provider Orders	Day 13	General	Day 23	Answer Explanations #2
Day 4	Safety and Infection Control	Day 14	Federal and State Regulations	Day 24	Practice Test #3
Day 5	Safety Resources	Day 15	Communication	Day 25	Answer Explanations #3
Day 6	Safety and Emergency Procedures	Day 16	Therapeutic/Adaptive Responses	Day 26	Practice Test #4
Day 7	Procedures/ Examinations	Day 17	Administrative	Day 27	Answer Explanations #4
Day 8	Wound Care	Day 18	Authorizations and Resources	Day 28	Practice Test #5
Day 9	Specimen Collection Techniques	Day 19	Scheduling Appointments and Health Information Management	Day 29	Answer Explanations #5
Day 10	Laboratory Panels and Selected Tests	Day 20	Practice Test #1	Day 30	Take Your Exam!

Build your own prep plan by visiting:
testprepbooks.com/prep

As you study for your test, we'd like to take the opportunity to remind you that you are capable of great things! With the right tools and dedication, you truly can do anything you set your mind to. The fact that you are holding this book right now shows how committed you are. In case no one has told you lately, you've got this! Our intention behind including this coloring page is to give you the chance to take some time to engage your creative side when you need a little brain-break from studying. As a company, we want to encourage people like you to achieve their dreams by providing good quality study materials for the tests and certifications that improve careers and change lives. As individuals, many of us have taken such tests in our careers, and we know how challenging this process can be. While we can't come alongside you and cheer you on personally, we can offer you the space to recall your purpose, reconnect with your passion, and refresh your brain through an artistic practice. We wish you every success, and happy studying!

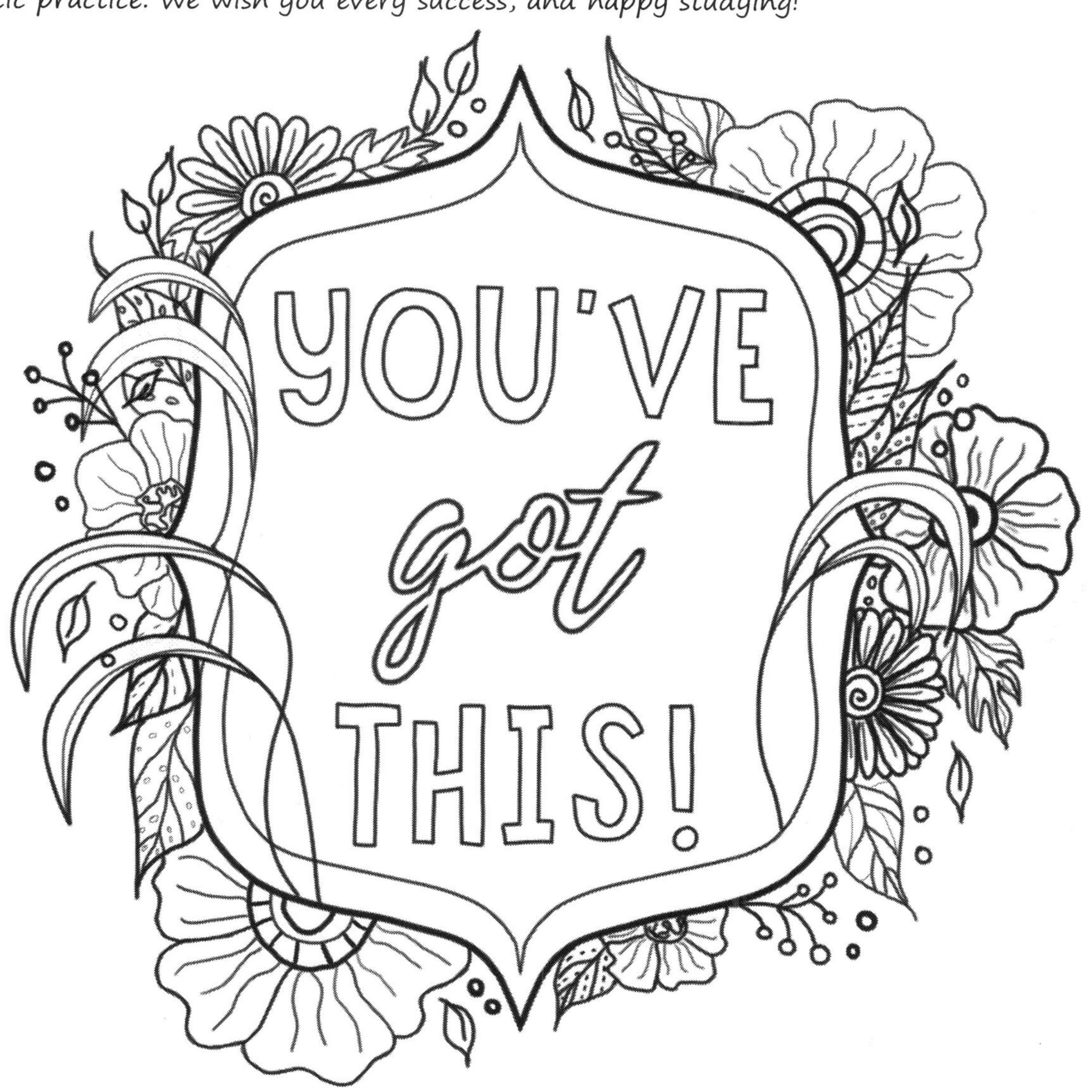

Clinical Competency

Clinical Workflow: Patient Intake and Discharge

Vital Signs

Blood Pressure

Technique

To obtain an accurate **blood pressure** measurement, the provider will:

- Assist the patient to a seated position.
- Expose the upper arm at the level of the heart.
- Apply the appropriately sized cuff.
- Palpate the antecubital space to identify the strongest pulsation point.
- Position the head of the stethoscope over the pulsation point.
- Slowly inflate the cuff to between 30 and 40 mm Hg above the patient's recorded blood pressure (BP). If this information is unavailable, the cuff may be inflated to between 160 and 180 mm Hg.
- Note the point at which the pulse is initially audible, which represents the systolic BP.
- Slowly deflate the cuff and record the point at which the pulse is initially audible as the systolic BP.
- Record the point at which the sounds are no longer audible as the diastolic BP.

Equipment

The **stethoscope** is a Y-shaped, hollow tube with earpieces and a diaphragm that transmits the sound to the earpieces when the provider places the diaphragm against the patient's body.

The **sphygmomanometer** includes the cuff, the mercury-filled gauge, or manometer that records the patient's pressure, and the release valve that regulates the air pressure in the cuff.

Pulse Points

Technique

To assess the **pulse** the provider will:

- 1. Expose the intended pulse point.
- 2. Palpate the area for the strongest pulsation.
- 3. Position the middle three fingers of the hand on the point.
- 4. Count the pulse for one full minute.

The provider will identify the pulse points that include the **radial artery** in the wrist, the **brachial artery** in the elbow, the **carotid artery** in the neck, the **femoral artery** in the groin, the **popliteal artery** behind the knee, and the **dorsalis pedis** and the **posterior tibialis arteries** in the foot.

The provider will assess the pulse rate by counting the number of pulsations per sixty seconds. In addition to the pulse rate, the provider will document the regularity or irregularity and strength of the pulsations.

Height/Weight/BMI

Technique

To record an accurate **height**, the provider must instruct the patient to:

- 1. Remove all footwear.
- 2. Stand straight with the back against the wall.
- 3. Remain still until the height is recorded.

To record an accurate **weight**, the provider must first zero the scale and then instruct the patient to:

- 1. Remove all heavy objects from the pockets.
- 2. Stand on the scale facing forward.
- 3. Remain still until the weight is recorded.

The **BMI** (**body mass index**) is equal to:

- 1. Imperial English BMI Formula: $weight\ (lbs) \times 703 \div height\ (in^2)$
- 2. Metric BMI Formula: $weight\ (kg) \div height(m^2)$

For example:

The BMI of a patient who weighs 150 pounds and is 5'6" is equal to:

$$150 \times 703 = 105{,}450 = \ 24.2 \text{ or } 24.0$$

$$66 \times 66 = 4{,}356$$

Equipment

Bodyweight scales may be mechanical or digital. Some digital scales also provide detailed metabolic information including the BMI in addition to the weight. Other scales can accommodate patients who are confined to bed.

Body Temperature

There are five possible assessment sites for **body temperature**, including oral, axillary, rectal, tympanic, and temporal. The route will depend on the patient's age and the agency policies. Assessment of oral temperatures requires the provider to verify that the patient has had nothing to eat or drink for five minutes before testing in order to avoid inaccurate readings.

Thermometers may be digital with disposal covers for the probe, wand-like structures that use infrared technology and are moved across the forehead to the temporal area, or handles with disposable cones that measure the tympanic temperature.

Pulse Oximetry

When every hemoglobin molecule in the circulating blood volume is carrying the maximum number of four oxygen molecules, the **oxygen saturation** rate is 100 percent. The normal oxygen saturation level is 95 percent to 100 percent, and levels below 90 percent must be treated.

The provider measures oxygen saturation noninvasively by the application of a **pulse oximetry** device, which the provider will attach to the patient's finger. The device may be used for continuous or intermittent monitoring of the saturation rate.

The **pulse oximeter** is a foam-lined clip that attaches to the patient's finger and uses infrared technology to assess the oxygen saturation level, which is expressed as a percentage.

Respiration Rate and Pattern

The **respiratory rate** is counted, and the breathing pattern is assessed. The provider should ensure that the patient is unaware that the breathing rate is being counted by leaving the fingers resting on the radial pulse site while the respiratory rate is assessed.

Pain Scale

The common measure of pain is the **pain scale**, rated one to ten. The CMA assesses pain by asking the patient what aggravates the pain, alleviates it, the location, quality, and onset. The CMA should ask about when exacerbations occur, what signs and symptoms accompany an exacerbation, how the pain affects overall functioning ability, how intense it becomes, and its temporal characteristics.

A simple tool to determine what type of medication is helpful for different pain levels is the World Health Organization ladder:

- Step 1. Mild pain (intensity 1 to 3): acetaminophen; NSAIDS; adjuvant medications, such as tricyclic antidepressants and muscle relaxants
- Step 2. Moderate pain (4 to 6 intensity): combination opioids, such as hydrocodone and acetaminophen or oxycodone and acetaminophen, plus continued adjuvant drugs
- Step 3. Severe pain (7 to 10 intensity): opioids, such as morphine and hydromorphone, plus continued adjuvant drugs.

Pediatric Measurements/Growth Chart

The growth chart is a systematic assessment of a child's growth pattern that can be compared to gender-specific norms.

The head circumference, height, and body weight are measured in children from birth to three years of age. In children older than three, the BMI is measured in addition to height and weight.

The head circumference is measured from birth to three years of age. The provider will measure the head circumference by placing a flexible measuring tape around the widest circumference of the child's head, which most commonly is above the eyebrows and the top of the ears. The provider will weigh infants lying down without clothes or diapers, and older children on mechanical or digital scales. To assess an infant's height, the provider will lay the child on a flat surface with the knee straightened and extend the flexible tape from the top of the infant's head to the bottom of the foot. The provider will position older children with their backs to a wall for an accurate measurement of their height.

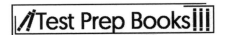

Recognize/Document/Report Age-Specific Normal and Abnormal Vital Signs

Age	Temperature Degrees Fahrenheit	Pulse Range	Respiratory Rate Range	Blood Pressure mmHg
Newborns	98.2 axillary	100-160	30-50	75-100/50-70
0 - 5 years	99.9 rectal	80-120	20-30	80-110/50-80
6 - 10 years	98.6 oral	70-100	15-30	85-120/55-80
11 - 14 years	98.6 oral	60-105	12-20	95-140/60-90
15 - 20 years	98.6 oral	60-100	12-30	95-140/60-90
Adults	98.6 oral	50-80	16-20	120/80

Medical Terminology

Word Parts

Knowing the basic structure of a word, including its root, prefix, and suffix, will give the CMA the clues they need to determine the word's meaning. Many medical terms originate from Greek or Latin words.

Roots/Combining Forms

A word's **root**, or its **combining form**, is the most basic part of the word. A prefix or suffix may be added to change the meaning of the word. Common root words in medical terminology and what they refer to include:

- acous- hearing
- adip- fat
- angi- cardiovascular
- bronch- bronchus
- cerebr- cerebrum
- cyst- bladder
- derma- skin
- enceph- brain
- enter- intestine
- femor- thigh bone
- gastr- stomach
- hepat- liver
- hyster- uterus
- lact- milk
- laryng- larynx
- mamm- breast
- my- muscle
- nephr- kidney
- ocul- eye
- oste- bone
- ot- ear
- pancreat- pancreas
- pneum- air, lung

- ren- kidney
- retin- retina
- somat- body
- splen- spleen
- thrombo- clot
- tympan- eardrum
- ven- vein
- vesic- bladder

Prefixes

A **prefix** is a group of letters that can be added to the beginning of a word to alter its meaning. The following is a list of common prefixes in medical terminology and their meanings:

- a/an- without, not, such as analgesic
- ab- from, away from, such as abnormal
- ante- before, in front of
- anti- opposing
- bi- double, two, twice, both
- co- together, with
- di- twice, two
- extro/extra- beyond, outside of, outward
- hemi- half
- hyper- above, excessive, beyond
- infra- below, beneath
- inter- between
- macro- large
- micro- small
- post- after, following, behind
- pre/pro- in front of, before, preceding
- semi- half
- trans- through, across
- tri- three
- ultra- excessive, beyond

Suffixes

The opposite of a prefix is a **suffix**. The suffix is the group of letters attached to the end of a root word that alters its meaning. The following is a list of common medical suffixes and their meanings:

- -ac: pertaining to, such as cardiac
- -al: pertaining to, such as abdominal
- -alge: pain, such as myalgia, a term for muscle pain
- -ate, -ize: subject to, use
- -ent, -er, -ist: person, agent
- -genic: produced by
- -gram: written record
- -graph: instrument used to record

- -graphy: process of recording
- -ism: condition or theory
- -itis: inflammation
- -ologist: one who studies, specialist
- -ology: study of, process of study
- -oma: tumor
- -pathy: disease, disease process
- -phobia: morbid fear of, intolerance
- -scope: instrument used to do a visual examination
- -scopy: process by which an exam is performed visually

Diagnostic Procedures

The following is a list of some common diagnostic procedures that a CMA will encounter in their practice:

- **X-ray**: a test using a high-energy electromagnetic wave to visualize internal structures of the human body; useful for diagnosing broken bones and respiratory conditions such as pneumonia

- Mammography: a visualization of the breast tissue to screen for abnormalities, such as cancerous tumors

- Complete blood count: Obtained from a blood sample, this test measures the amount of red blood cells, white blood cells, and hemoglobin and can be used to diagnose various medical conditions such as anemia, leukemia, and the presence of an infection.

- Prothrombin Time (PT test): This blood test measures the amount of time it takes a patient's blood to clot and can help determine the effectiveness of blood-thinning medicine such as warfarin.

- Magnetic Resonance Imaging (MRI): This diagnostic tool gives practitioners an image of the inside of the body, like an x-ray, but with much more detail.

- Computer Axial Tomography (CT/CAT scan): a radiological diagnostic tool that can use contrast or not to produce images of the inside of the body; useful for visualization of fractures, kidney stones, tumors, and many other uses

- Echocardiography (ECHO): a type of ultrasound that visualizes the chambers of the heart as well as surrounding structures; used to diagnose heart conditions and evaluate overall function

- Colonoscopy: a visualization, using a "scope" or tiny camera at the end of a long tube, of the colon; most often used to screen for colorectal cancer, remove polyps, and diagnose other colonic conditions

- Bone density study: a test like an x-ray that is used to visualize bones and assess bone loss

- Prostate-Specific Antigen (PSA): This test is used to screen for prostate cancer or other diseases of the male prostate gland; an elevation could indicate a pathology is at work.

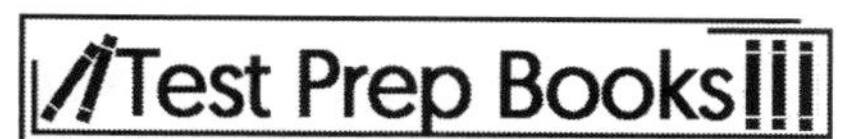

- Electrocardiogram (EKG or ECG): A test in which electrodes placed on the patient's chest pick up the electrical activity of the heart; abnormalities can be detected using this noninvasive test, such as heart dysrhythmias and myocardial damage.

- Bronchoscopy: a visualization of the internal passages of the lung, usually performed by a pulmonologist, using a long tube with a camera at the end called a "scope"; used for tissue sampling or biopsy and to diagnose conditions such as lung cancer.

Surgical Procedures

The following is a list of some common surgical procedures that a CMA will encounter in their practice:

- **Mastectomy**: removal of the entire breast; used for treating breast cancer

- Hysterectomy: removal of a woman's uterus, potentially for uterine cancer, fibroids, or endometriosis, among other reasons

- Dilation and curettage (D&C): procedure where a woman's cervix is dilated and the uterine lining is scraped out using a spoon-like device called a curette; used for miscarriages and any other time the contents of the uterus need to be evacuated

- Carotid endarterectomy: procedure in which blockages are removed from the carotid arteries located in the neck, usually for prevention of stroke

- Breast biopsy: removal of breast tissue, usually a lump, to screen for cancer and other conditions

- Appendectomy: removal of the appendix in the treatment of appendicitis, an inflammation of the appendix

- Cataract surgery: removal of cataracts from the lens of the eye using ultrasound waves, sometimes involving the removal of the entire lens depending on the severity of the disease

- Cholecystectomy: removal of the gall bladder; can be for a cancerous gall bladder, one prone to gallstones, or infection

- Cesarean section (C-section): delivery of a baby through a lower abdominal incision when vaginal delivery is deemed an unsafe option; can be an elective or emergent procedure

- Coronary artery bypass (CABG): also known as open-heart surgery, a procedure in which the patient's chest is opened at the sternum and grafting of leg veins is performed to repair or bypass clogged or narrowed arteries supplying the cardiac muscle with blood; for patients with a history of atherosclerotic disease

- Wound debridement: removal of dead tissue from a wound to promote healing

Interviewing Techniques

Motivational interviewing (MI) is a communication technique that focuses on altering the patient's behavior. It is often used as a counseling tool for patients with substance use disorders, behavioral alterations, smoking, and obesity. There is a subset of skills used in MI that facilitate the progress in each of the MI phases. The **OARS** skills are a set of verbal and non-verbal interview techniques, which can be tailored to the specific needs of the MI process. The acronym OARS stands for **open-ended questions**, **affirmations**, **reflections**, and **summaries**. **Open-ended questions** encourage two-way conversation because they are not generally answerable with a simple "yes" or "no." Questions beginning with the word "why" can potentially elicit a defensive patient response and should be avoided. **Affirmations** acknowledge the patient and convey a message of empathetic understanding. These statements can also build a patient's self-efficacy which positively affects motivation. **Reflections**, or reflective listening, improve the interviewer's understanding of the patient's narrative. Periods of reflection after the patient speaks slow the pace of the conversation so that it is not simply a series of questions and answers. **Summaries** provide a review of the substance of the conversation and an opportunity for closure by the interviewer and the patient.

The OARS skills are used with each process of MI to maximize the outcomes. If the work of the MI process is slowed down or is unsuccessful at any point, the provider returns to the initial process and reestablishes it. MI is not a linear process; it is responsive to the flow of the conversation, which depends on the skill of the interviewer and the use of the OARS techniques. The four processes of MI include engaging, focusing, evoking, and planning. **Engaging** is the process of establishing a rapport, assessing and reducing any defensive behavior, and creating a collaborative environment for the discussion of change. The interviewer is able to assess the focus of the patient's conversation, in other words, is the patient actually engaged in the work of MI. If the patient is resistant to participating in the process of MI, the interviewer often finds that empathy is effective in re-establishing the interviewer-patient relationship.

The second process of MI is **focusing**. Communication experts advise that it may take several sessions before the interviewer can direct the conversation to the issue at hand. The potential for success at this stage is enhanced when the patient has already reached a state of contemplation for the desired change. The process of **evoking** focuses on the discussion or "**change talk**" for two behaviors: identification of the specific steps necessary for the desired change and the steps required for an ongoing commitment to the changed behavior. There are two forms of change talk: **preparatory** refers to the desire to change, and **mobilizing** addresses commitment and action. The **planning** process may be optional, but when it is included in MI, it identifies the "how" for the planned change.

Documentation of Care

Subjective Data

Subjective data is supplied by the patient.

- The **chief complaint** is the reason for the medical visit or hospital admission.
- The present illness is a detailed description of the symptoms related to the chief complaint.
- The past medical history identifies all of the patient's previous conditions and illnesses.
- The family history includes all diseases that have affected the patient's family. Genetically linked illnesses may be identified.

- The social and occupational history identifies lifestyle and work activities that may influence the patient's health, such as occupational exposure to biohazardous agents.
- The review of systems is a series of questions that are related to individual body organs or systems and identify the patient's specific concerns.

Objective Data

Objective data is observed by the provider. The data may be obtained through observation, physical assessment, or diagnostic testing.

Making Corrections

The process of **making corrections** in healthcare documentation must comply with agency policies. In general, the original text must remain visible with the erroneous information indicated with a single line through the text. The entry containing the revised information must be initialed and dated, and the use of "whiteout" and erasers is prohibited.

Treatment/Compliance

All treatments and the patient's compliance with those plans will be documented in the health history. This information is necessary for the evaluation of the effectiveness of the treatment plan.

Patient Screenings/Wellness Assessments

Cancer Prevention and Screening

Cancer screening tests relevant to several organ systems have effectively decreased the incidence and mortality of cancer in those systems. Common screening tests include the **Papanicolaou** (**PAP**) test for cervical cancer, colonoscopy for colon cancer, and **mammography** for breast cancer. Recently, screening for lung cancer with advanced **computed tomography** (CT) technology in patients with a history of smoking has been proposed, in an effort to identify lung cancers at an earlier stage that may be treated more successfully. Conversely, the research indicates that there is insufficient evidence to support any relationship between decreased disease incidence and morbidity and the **prostate-specific antigen test** (**PSA**) measurements for prostate cancer, or the annual full-body skin assessments by a dermatologist. In addition, there are no screening tests available for ovarian cancer.

Prevention/Screening of Sexually Transmitted Infections

Sexually transmitted diseases (**STD's**), including chancroid, chlamydia, genital herpes, gonorrhea, hepatitis C, HIV, and syphilis, are caused by intimate contact. The scope of treatment ranges from oral antibiotics for chlamydia to long-term antiviral treatment for HIV and hepatitis C infections. Complications are common when the initial infection is not treated.

Nicotine Risks and Cessation

Smoking by direct contact or through secondhand exposure can result in lung cancer and other obstructive lungs diseases such as COPD and emphysema. **Smoking cessation** programs are offered by many private and governmental agencies, and providers monitor the use of prescription medications that assist with cessation efforts.

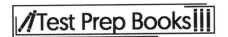

Recognition of Substance Use/Addiction

Abuse of recreational or prescription drugs may be evidenced by changes in behavior, appetite, and sleep patterns. Affected students may neglect course work and ignore family responsibilities. Providers work with parents and educators to identify at-risk individuals.

Osteoporosis Screening

Osteoporosis is the "thinning" of the bone, which most commonly affects postmenopausal women. The degree and progression of the changes associated with osteoporosis can be measured by the bone-density exam, which compares a patient's test results with the results of younger patients who are disease free.

Domestic Violence Screening and Detection

The efficiency of **domestic violence screening** and detection is often hampered by the reluctance of the abused individual to report the abuse. Institutions and insurance companies have included routine assessment questions related to a patient's perceptions of personal safety; however, the widespread acceptance and effectiveness of these measures are not known.

Suicide Awareness and Response

A **suicide risk assessment** should be performed when patients verbalize suicide ideation or poor coping skills. The patient should be asked if they have a suicide plan and the means to carry it out. The SAD PERSONAS suicide risk assessment can be used to assess a patient's suicide risk. Eleven major areas (sex, age, depression, previous attempt, ethanol abuse, rational thinking loss, social supports lacking, organized plan, no spouse, availability of lethal means, sickness) are assessed and scored. The higher the score, the higher the risk.

Depression Screening

Depression is a general term that can be characterized by a loss of interest in daily activities and feelings of hopelessness. **Major depressive disorder** is diagnosed based on clusters of symptoms, including sleep disturbances, depressed mood, feelings of guilt, and decreased energy. According to the DSM-5, there are a number of specific criteria that must be met in order to diagnose a patient with major depressive disorder. Patients who verbalize withdrawal from social activities and experience changes in sleeping and eating patterns are a cause for concern. Safety is an important assessment in a patient diagnosed with major depressive disorder because of the risk of suicide. Some of the risk factors associated with suicide include a specific plan to carry out the suicide, social isolation, and previous suicide attempts. Assessing for suicide risk is a priority and counselors should be familiar with all of the risk and protective factors associated with it.

Processing Provider Orders

Diabetic Teaching

Diabetic teaching and **home care**: Prior to discharge, the patient will participate in a comprehensive program in order to learn about diabetes, self-care for diabetes, and the process of home monitoring.

Home blood sugar monitoring provides improved control of the patient's blood by more frequent assessment of the blood glucose level and more timely intervention of abnormal levels. The provider will assess the patient's ability to follow the treatment plan.

Instructions on Use of Mobility Equipment and Assistive Devices

The provider must instruct the patient on the proper use of **patient mobility equipment** and **assistive devices**. Depending on the specific injury or condition, the patient may use assistive devices such as crutches, walkers, or canes to maintain mobility during the recovery period or for longer periods of time. Patients must receive appropriate safety instruction in the correct use of any device in order to maintain safety.

Pre-/Post Procedure/Treatment Instructions

Pre-/post-op care instructions are designed to minimize preoperative surgical delays and complications and to promote the patient's recovery following discharge. Providers, commonly advanced practice nurses, conduct preoperative assessments and educational sessions, while community-based nurses provide care once the patient is discharged.

Patient-Administered Treatments and Medications

Patient-administered medications are medications that are self-administered. The provider must assess the patient's ability to comprehend the details of the medication information and safe administration and provide resources to ensure the patient's ongoing safety.

Home Monitoring

The research relevant to the use of **home blood-pressure monitoring** systems indicates that patients who closely monitor their blood-pressure readings are better able to control the lifestyle factors associated with **hypertension**. Some of these lifestyle factors include dietary intake of salt, smoking behavior, and participation in aerobic exercise.

Alternative Medicine/Massage/Acupuncture

Alternative medicine includes complementary treatments that may not be offered by healthcare providers, including massage, acupuncture, herbs, meditation, and homeopathy.

Nutrition Counseling

Basic Nutritional Elements

Carbohydrates

Carbohydrates are organic (containing carbon) compounds that are converted into energy for the body. They may be simple, such as refined table sugar, or complex, such as pasta, rice, and fiber.

Fats

Fats are lipid-containing compounds that are necessary for cell wall integrity, energy storage, and protection of all body organs against injury. **Cholesterol** is a body fat that exists in two forms: **low-density lipoprotein** (**LDL**) and **high-density lipoprotein** (**HDL**). LDLs are associated with the formation and progression of **atherosclerosis**, which is a build-up of lipid cells in the vasculature that results in hypertension and cardiovascular disease. Fats are also classified by the configuration of the hydrogen bonds and are classified as **saturated fats**, which are solid at room temperature, or **unsaturated fats**, which are liquid at room temperature. Research indicates that replacing saturated fats with unsaturated fats in the diet facilitates the removal of excess cholesterol from the body. Fats are contained in dairy and animal products, nuts, and vegetable oils. Current recommendations include a consuming a balanced diet that provides unsaturated fats and limited animal fats.

Proteins

Proteins are also organic compounds that contain carbon, hydrogen, and oxygen and form amino acids, the building blocks of the protein molecule. There are nine essential amino acids that must be consumed because the body cannot synthesize them. A **complete protein** consists of all nine essential amino acids, while an **incomplete protein** is deficient in one or more of the essential amino acids. Proteins are essential for all intracellular processes and as enzymes that facilitate all chemical reactions in the body. Nutritional sources of protein include animal products, dairy products, beans, and tofu.

Minerals/Electrolytes

Mineral/electrolytes are metals and nonmetals, including sodium, potassium, chloride, phosphorus, magnesium, calcium, and sulfur. They are necessary for fluid balance, transmission of nervous impulses, bone maintenance, blood clotting, healthy teeth, and protein synthesis and cardiac-impulse conduction. Minerals and electrolytes are generally consumed in adequate amounts from a balanced diet.

Vitamins

Vitamins are organic compounds that are necessary for blood clotting, immune function, maintenance of teeth, and the action of enzymes. There are two classes of vitamins. **Fat-soluble vitamins**, including A, D, E, and K, can be stored in excess in the body in the event of excessive intake. **Water-soluble** vitamins, including B-complex and C, are not stored in the body and ingested amounts greater than body requirements will be excreted in the urine. Vitamins are present in fruits, vegetables, fish, organ meats, and dairy.

Fiber

Dietary fiber is composed of complex carbohydrates and other plant substances that are not broken down by the digestive enzymes. Fiber can be water soluble or insoluble, and both forms contribute to the normal function of the gastrointestinal system. **Soluble fiber** that is present in oatmeal, blueberries, nuts, and beans facilitates the excretion of cholesterol, controls abrupt increases in blood glucose levels, and contributes to normal bowel function. The **insoluble fiber** that is present in whole grains, the skin and seeds of many fruits, and brown rice improves bowel function and also contributes to a feeling of fullness following food intake, which can lead to modest weight loss.

Water

Making up about 75 percent of the body, **water** is a vital necessity to human life. Water feeds cells and organs, creates a lubricant around the joints, and regulates body temperature. It is also important to digestion, as water moves food through the intestines.

Function of Dietary Supplements and Herbs

Dietary supplements and herbs contain various nutrients that are intended to compensate for inadequate dietary intake of those elements. These products should be used with care by anyone who also takes prescription medications because adverse interactions between the two are common.

Special Dietary Needs

Weight Control

Weight control requires a balanced diet that is calorie controlled and combined with adequate aerobic exercise. Current research indicates that the consumption of sugar and white flour, rather than dietary fats, is the greatest dietary threat to successful weight management.

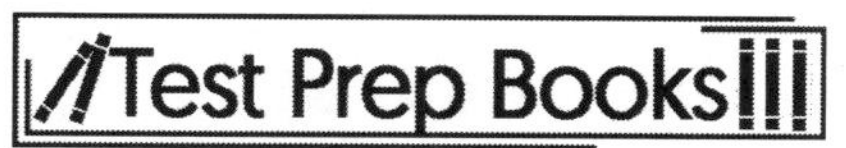

Diabetes

Diabetes requires a balanced diet that is carbohydrate controlled. Diabetes may be due to a lack of insulin production by the pancreas or cellular insensitivity to the insulin that is present in the bloodstream. The controlled intake of carbohydrates limits the amount of insulin that is necessary to protect the body against the side effects of chronically elevated blood glucose levels.

Cardiovascular Disease/Hypertension

Cardiovascular disease most often is accompanied by excess fluid volume that is manifested by hypertension and edema. The condition requires a balanced diet that is sodium controlled, with adequate fluid intake.

Hypertension is associated with fluid volume excess, which means that excess dietary sodium and fluid should be avoided.

Cancer

Cancer may affect multiple body systems, which means that the diet should be balanced with additional calories to meet energy needs.

Food Sensitivity/Intolerance

Lactose sensitivity/intolerance results from the deficiency of the enzyme lactase, which is necessary for the breakdown or digestion of lactose, a sugar found in dairy products. This deficiency can result in stomach bloating, nausea, vomiting, and diarrhea following the ingestion of dairy products.

Gluten-free diets must be free of wheat, barley, and rye in any form. This means that, in addition to bread, all processed foods must be avoided. **Gluten intolerance** may be a symptom of celiac disease, which affects the absorption of food in the small intestine, or an allergic response to wheat gluten; however, it is most commonly due to the lack of a necessary digestive enzyme. Possible manifestations include stomach bloating, diarrhea, fatigue, and weight loss.

Food allergies can be related to one or several foods for a given patient. The allergic responses can range from mild to life threatening. The diet must be balanced and free of the allergens.

Kidney Disease

While acute injury and failure of the kidney can often be corrected, **chronic kidney disease** is a slow, progressive, and irreversible decline in function of the kidney. The most common causes of CKD are diabetes, hypertension, and diseases of the glomerulus. Metabolic syndrome, in which the patient has both diabetes and hypertension, is a major factor in CKD development.

Over time, these causative factors slowly destroy vital cells in the renal tissue. Renal function first becomes insufficient and then fails altogether, which is called **end-stage renal disease** (ESRD).

As the kidney fails, waste products build up in the body. Creatinine and urea are markers for kidney decline, though they are not the only waste products that cause the symptoms of **uremia**, or “urine in the blood.” Sodium, water, potassium, and other fluid and electrolyte imbalances will occur as a result of CKD.

The kidney is responsible for releasing **erythropoietin**, a hormone that stimulates the production of red blood cells. When kidneys fail, as is the case in CKD, erythropoietin release is decreased as well, resulting in decreased erythropoiesis, or RBC production. Thus, anemia results. Patients with CKD often must be treated for anemia along with many other conditions.

A patient with CKD will present with weight loss, anorexia, nausea, vomiting, and stomatitis. They may have a yellow-brown tint to their skin, as well as itchiness and crystallization of their sweat called uremic frost.

Treating a patient with CKD is a complicated matter, as so many other systems are involved as a result of the kidneys failing. Management of diabetes and hypertension is crucial, as these are often the underlying causes. Heart failure and anemia must be addressed. Patients should quit smoking, keep cholesterol levels, glucose levels and blood pressure within normal limits, and eat a reduced-salt diet to protect the kidneys. Patients with CKD should have a pharmacist carefully considering all medications to help look for drugs that are nephrotoxic such as many antibiotics (vancomycin) and analgesics (NSAIDS). Dialysis will likely be an option in the future of the CKD patient to replace the function of the kidney.

Food Label Interpretation

Food labels include valuable information about a food item's nutritional content. The main component on the label is the number of calories, an energy source. Depending on the patient's needs, the calories per serving will determine how much should be served. For example, a half cup of prepared oatmeal is approximately 150 calories. If the patient eats a cup of oatmeal, 300 calories must be recorded in the medical record. Among the most commonly listed nutritional components are total fat content, cholesterol, sodium, carbohydrates, and protein. Each food label includes the quantity of each component, usually in grams, and the percentage of daily value it equals. Daily value percentages are based on a healthy adult diet established by the U.S. Food and Drug Administration. It is also important to note that the remaining ingredients listed on the label are arranged based on weight, with the heaviest ingredient listed first.

Eating Disorders

Eating disorders are psychologically induced alterations in nutrition. The most common disorders include anorexia nervosa, bulimia, and binge-eating disorder. **Anorexia nervosa** is seen most commonly in young women and is manifested by a fear of gaining weight and refusal to eat. The effects of this self-imposed starvation can vary from mild nutritional deficits to cardiac failure and death. **Bulimia** is also related to the fear of gaining weight and is manifested by the intake of large amounts of food followed by self-induced vomiting or purging, fasting, and depression. Bulimic patients can sustain significant damage to the mouth and teeth as a result of the effects of gastric acids associated with the vomiting. Binge eating occurs in men and women and is manifested by the regular episodes of the consumption of large amounts of food that are followed by feelings of depression. These individuals are often obese and relate these episodes to being out of control. In general, these diseases are difficult to resolve, and relapses are common.

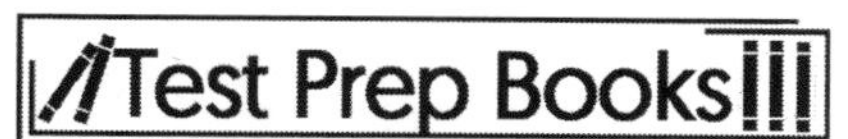

Safety and Infection Control

Infectious Agents

Infectious agents can alter the function of any body system, and they stimulate the immune system.

- **Bacteria** are unicellular organisms that are either essential to normal body function or harmful to the body, and therefore capable of triggering an immune response.
- Viruses contain only a core of DNA or RNA and a protein coat. Common viruses include the flu viruses, acquired immune deficiency syndrome (AIDS), and chicken pox, which can lead to shingles.
- Fungi, which include yeasts and molds, are multicellular organisms that can cause local infections such as athlete's foot.
- Protozoa are single-celled parasites that can affect the lungs, skin, and gastrointestinal system. Manifestations and treatment are specific to the individual organisms.
- A parasite is any agent that lives in or on a host and causes harm to the host.

Infection Cycle/Chain of Infection

Chain of infection

Infectious agent

Reservoir

Portal of Exit

Mode of Transmission

Portal of Entry

Susceptible Host

In order to promote patient safety, the provider must be aware of the elements of the process or **chain of infection**, and employ all means necessary to prevent the transmission of the infectious agent. An infectious agent is any pathogen that is capable of transmitting an infection to a susceptible host. Once infected, the susceptible host becomes a reservoir for the infectious agent, where the agent is able to survive, grow, and multiply. The portal of exit is the route used by the infectious agent to move from a reservoir to another susceptible host. This route is often predicted by the body system that is affected by the pathogen; for example, the respiratory tract is often the portal of exit for influenza viruses. The mode of transmission identifies the manner by which the infectious agent makes contact with the host, and the provider must recognize that food, water, and insects are all possible modes of transmission, in addition to direct and indirect contact. The portal of entry is the host body system that serves as the initial point of contact with the infectious agent. The susceptible host is the individual who is infected by the pathogen, and the susceptibility to a given infectious agent will be influenced by genetics, immune function, and the individual's general health status at the point of contact.

Body's Natural Barriers

Along with the immune system, the skin, mucous membranes, tears, and stomach acids all act as natural barriers to inhibit the transmission of **infectious agents**.

Modes of Infectious Transmission

- **Direct contact** requires skin-to-skin contact between an infected person and a host who is susceptible to the infectious agent.
    - Indirect contact occurs when the susceptible host contacts an object that has been previously handled by the infected person.
    - Airborne infections are spread through the air by small particles from coughing and sneezing.
    - Droplet infections occur from coughing and sneezing, but the particles are heavier droplets that fall and settle on objects.
    - The susceptible host may inhale infectious agents that are in the environment.

Standard Precautions and Exposure Control

Standard precautions are standardized protocols that identify safe practices aimed at the prevention of infection by pathogens that exist in the blood and body fluids. These guidelines apply to all patients.

Occupational Safety and Health Administration (OSHA)

OSHA is an agency that was developed under the Occupational Safety and Health Act in 1970 under President Nixon's administration. OSHA works to ensure the health and safety of American workers through regulations, laws, and their enforcement.

Personal Protective Equipment

The purpose of **personal protective equipment** is to decrease the incidence of infection in healthcare workers. The equipment should be appropriate to the situation and degree of contamination. In addition, the equipment should be used consistently and correctly.

Gowns cover the entire body and have long sleeves that fit snugly around the wrists. Clean gowns may be used for patients in isolation, while sterile gowns are required for all invasive procedures. If contamination with fluids is anticipated, a fluid-repellent material should be chosen.

Gloves protect the hands and should be changed between individual tasks or if damaged to prevent cross contamination from one area to another area. Handwashing is also necessary after gloves are removed. Once gloves have been contaminated, they must be removed and discarded.

Masks must fit firmly over the bridge of the nose and the mouth. If contamination of other areas of the face is possible, as when irrigating wounds, a face shield that covers the entire face to the forehead is indicated. Specialized particulate masks must be used for airborne organisms such as tuberculosis.

Caps should fit snugly, covering the hair in order to protect the healthcare worker from contamination and to protect the patient during invasive procedures.

Eye protection from droplet infection and splashing of secretions cannot depend on personal eyeglasses or contact lenses. Depending on the anticipated contamination, a full shield may be chosen in the place of standard safety glasses and a mask.

Hand Hygiene

Hand hygiene is essential to maintaining medical asepsis. There are two acceptable methods: handwashing and the use of alcohol-based hand rubs.

All providers must wash their hands before and after patient contact, when handling any of the objects that enter the patient's environment, and when leaving the patient-care area.

Alcohol-based hand rubs are able to kill germs more effectively than soap and water and according to some authorities may be less irritating to the skin; however, soap and water are still the most effective when it comes to removing germs from the skin, though not necessarily killing them.

Post-Exposure Protocol/Eyewash Station

The **post-exposure plan** is a set of written guidelines that must be followed when a healthcare worker is exposed to an infectious pathogen as the result of a sharps injury, patient behavior, or failure of the personal protective equipment. The exact steps of the plan will be appropriate to the specific infectious agent. All exposures will be followed by a medical examination and serial laboratory tests to monitor for the presence of infection. **Vaccinations** aimed at limiting the incidence of disease may be appropriate in some circumstances. Individual institutions are responsible for educating all employees about the post-exposure plan, as well as monitoring the implementation of the plan following any incident that involves exposure of an employee to an infectious agent. Healthcare facilities must have an eye wash station that meets Occupational Safety and Health Administration (OSHA) standards. After an exposure, the station should be activated via a clearly marked lever. The eyelids should be held open for water to flow inside the eye for a period of 15 minutes. The affected person should roll them around to ensure that the water rinses all surfaces. Contact lenses, if worn, should be removed during the process.

Sharps/Needle Safety

Sharps include hypodermic needles, surgical scalpels, lancets, and all other devices that can puncture the intact skin. These devices may be destroyed by heat, oxidation of the stainless-steel needles, or by passing an electrical current through the needles.

Medical Asepsis

Medical asepsis is considered a "clean" technique that is aimed at reducing the number of infectious agents in a patient's environment.

Sanitization

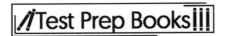

Sanitization is the process of cleaning utensils and the environment with soap and water to attain general cleanliness.

Disinfection

Disinfection refers to the use of more-potent cleaning agents to destroy infectious organisms, which exist on inanimate objects that exist in the patient-care environment.

Cleaning

The CMA understands that the **sanitation** of the reception room must be a priority for aesthetic purposes as well as infection control purposes. All surfaces and furnishings must be cleaned with approved cleaning agents per agency protocol. In addition to regularly scheduled maintenance, the providers ensure that there are resources in place to respond immediately to any incident that may occur in the reception area.

Biohazard Disposal/Regulated Waste

Biohazard waste is identified as any material that has been contaminated by body fluids or blood, which can potentially harm individuals or the environment. Disposal methods include the use of the incinerator, autoclave, or microwave in addition to chemical disinfection or irradiation. The disposal of biohazard waste is generally regulated by the **Department of Health** in the individual states, which means that healthcare workers must be aware of applicable state laws.

Blood/Body Fluids/Body Tissue Disposal

Blood and **body fluids** are designated as biohazardous or medically regulated waste. At the bedside, these wastes are placed in the appropriate collection bags, which are identified as hazardous waste and subsequently destroyed by incineration.

Spill Kit

A **spill kit** contains all of the equipment and information that is necessary to safely clean an area after an accidental spill or leakage of a biohazardous material.

Safety Resources

Safety Signs, Symbols, Labels

In a healthcare environment, it is imperative that appropriate signs be hung in areas where any potential hazards or dangers may lie to keep people safe. Knowing what common safety signs, symbols, and labels look like will help the CMA safely navigate through their environment. Commonly seen signs include the following categories:

Wet floor sign: This sign will be placed by housekeeping most commonly after mopping a floor to warn of a slip hazard.

No smoking sign: Most healthcare facilities are smoke-free areas, so the no smoking sign will be something the CMA will be familiar with.

Caution: A caution sign warns of a potential hazard. This hazard may pose the risk of a minor to moderate injury to the healthcare worker. Caution signs are usually yellow and black.

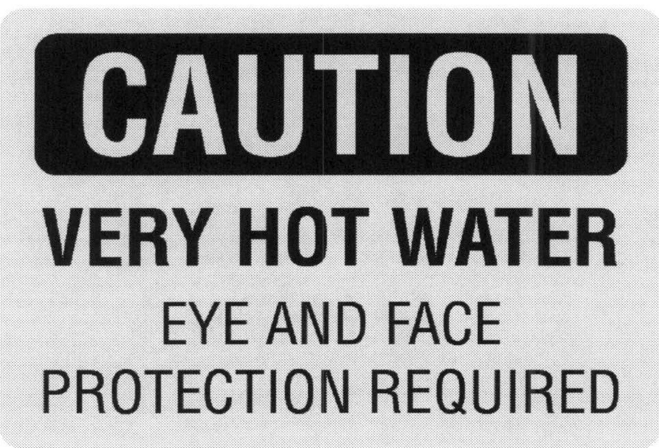

Warning: In between caution and danger signs are warning signs, indicating the potential for serious injury or even death. These signs are usually formatted as black letters on an orange background.

Biological hazard: This type of hazard originates in a living thing, such as bacteria, viruses, or insects.

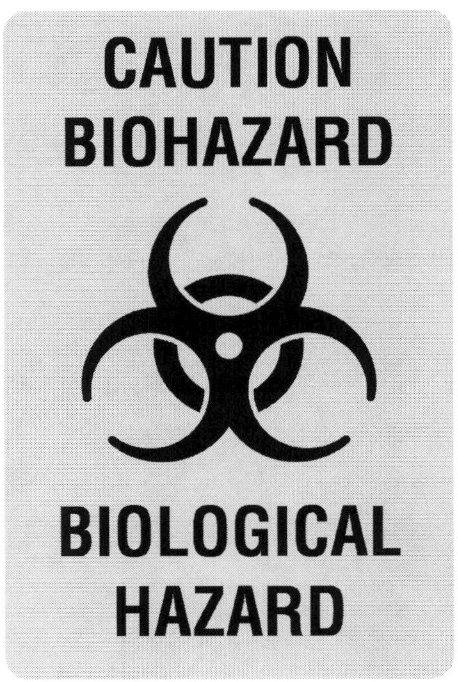

Danger: This type of safety sign indicates an immediate hazard that could cause death or serious injury.

Safety Data Sheets

Safety data sheets contain detailed information for all substances that are designated as biohazardous, including the appropriate use of personal protective equipment, first aid protocols, and disposal requirements. Institutions are required to publish an **SDS** for any substance that is corrosive or may cause cancer, damage to an unborn fetus, or damage to the ovaries and testes.

Safety and Emergency Procedures

Workplace Safety/Emergency Preparedness/Evacuation

All healthcare agencies will create a plan that identifies the personnel, actions, and resources required to respond to any emergency. The provider will participate in the implementation of the plan as necessary. The provider will assist agency employees to implement the evacuation plan for all patients and staff.

Crash Cart Supplies/Equipment

The provider will verify that all supplies recommended for emergency resuscitation according to advanced cardiac life support protocols (ACLS) are available for use. The contents of the crash cart must be specific to the patient population (e.g., adult care unit supplies will differ from pediatric care unit supplies). In addition, the provider will verify that all sterile supplies have valid sterility dates.

Fire Prevention/Regulations/Extinguisher

All healthcare workers, including CMAs, must have a basic amount of training in **fire safety** and prevention. The basic concepts of fire safety include the following:

Fire hazards: Cigarette or any other type of smoking is a serious fire hazard. Most healthcare facilities are smoke-free, but some have designated areas where smoking is allowed. Patients on supplemental oxygen should not be allowed to smoke, as oxygen is highly flammable. Faulty or improperly used equipment could pose a fire hazard. The CMA should keep a lookout for frayed wires, split cords, or overloaded extension cords, as these all pose a fire hazard.

Responding to a fire: The CMA should know the facilities' procedure for responding to a fire, including the emergency plan; location of fire alarms, fire extinguishers, and emergency oxygen shutoff valves; and how to move the patients and staff to safety using emergency exits.

RACE: The acronym "RACE" refers to the following steps to be taken when responding to a fire in a healthcare facility:

- R: Remove anyone directly threatened by the fire, patients being the priority, removing them far from the location of the fire (outside of the building if necessary).
- A: Activate the emergency response system when a fire is discovered, usually by pulling the emergency fire alarms.
- C: Confine the fire by closing all facility doors.
- E: Extinguish the fire only if it is small enough for an extinguisher to handle; otherwise, Evacuate and let the authorities handle it.

Fire extinguisher use: Every healthcare employee needs to know how to operate a fire extinguisher using the "**PASS**" acronym:

- P: Pull the pin.
- A: Aim at the base of the fire.
- S: Squeeze the trigger.
- S: Sweep side to side.

Emergency Management, Identification, and Response/Basic First Aid

The provider will use basic first aid to respond to the following emergencies, and will access emergency care as appropriate.

Emergency	Basic First Aid Response
Abrasion	Clean the wound and make sure patient has had tetanus shot
Avulsion	Reset limb through splinting or casting
Bleeding/pressure points	Apply firm pressure to the site with a clean cloth
Burns (minor)	Rinse with cool water, apply aloe, cover with clean dressing
Cardiac and respiratory arrest	CPR (depending on training), activate emergency medical services (EMS)
Chemical Exposure	Gather information; wash area; induce vomiting unless caustic
Foreign body obstruction	Heimlich maneuver, back blows, abdominal thrusts
Choking	Heimlich maneuver, back blows, abdominal thrusts
Diabetic ketoacidosis	Recognize manifestations, activate EMS
Insulin shock	Recognize manifestations, offer sugar if alert, activate EMS
Bone fractures	Treat bleeding, immobilize the limb, apply ice
Poisoning	Position on left side, identify substance, call 1-800-222-1222
Seizures	Position on side, protect the head
Shock	Elevate the feet, maintain body warmth, CPR as necessary
Cerebral vascular accident (CVA)	Recognize manifestations, activate EMS
Syncope	Elevate legs 12 inches; loosen restrictive clothing
Vertigo	Maintain safety, access care to treat the cause
Wounds	Control bleeding, cover with clean material, access emergency care (ER)
Punctures	Tetanus shot, sterile bandaging, topical or oral antibiotics
Cold exposure	Remove wet clothing, blankets for gradual warming, fluids if alert
Heat exposure	Activate EMS, cold packs to pulse points, cool environment
Joint dislocations	Immobilize the limb, apply ice, access ER care for dislocation
Asthmatic attack	Rescue meds, activate EMS if no improvement
Hyperventilation	Calm victim, use paper bag, activate EMS with c/o chest pain
Animal bite (minor)	Control bleeding, clean site, apply antibiotic ointment and cover
Insect bite	Remove stinger, assess for anaphylaxis, clean site and cover
Concussion	Activate EMS, assess breathing and level of consciousness
Laceration	Clean the wound and cover with a sterile bandage; stitch if required

Body Mechanics/Ergonomics

Ergonomics studies people in their work environments and how work is most efficiently performed. It is commonly used to refer to safe lifting techniques. Healthcare workers are especially prone to back and knee injuries because of improper lifting techniques or too much lifting when assisting patients who cannot lift their own weight. The proper lifting technique involves the following: bending at the hips and knees, not at the back; avoiding awkward positions or twisting when lifting; holding the load as close to the body as possible; keeping a wide base of support; and always maintaining good posture.

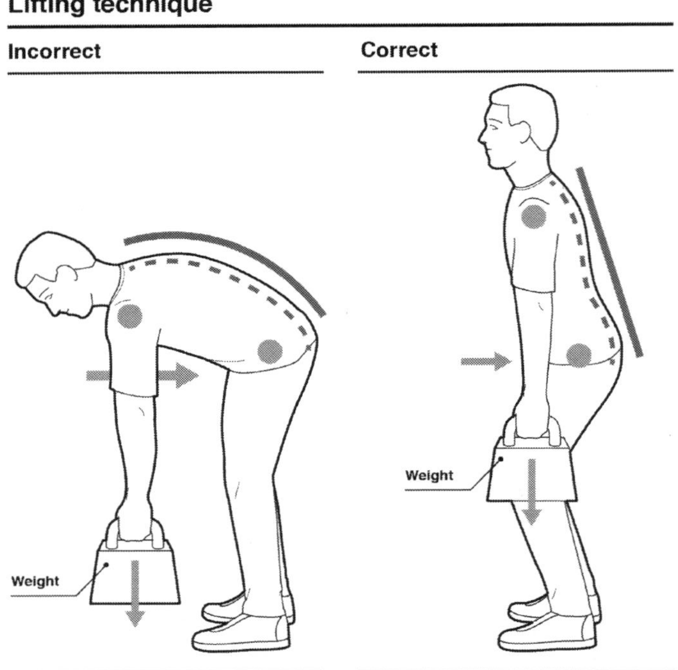

Risk Management, Quality Assurance, and Safety Procedures

Risk management teams work in hospitals to prevent adverse events from happening to healthcare workers. Healthcare workers such as CMAs face a variety of hazards in their workplace, from blood-borne pathogens and infectious diseases to exposure to radiation and other harmful substances. Preventing accidents and promoting the health and safety of healthcare workers is a high priority for risk managers to ensure that a high quality of healthcare is provided to the patients.

Reporting Unsafe or Unlawful Activities and Behaviors

The CMA may witness a colleague participating in an unsafe behavior such as substance abuse. Healthcare workers are especially prone to substance abuse due to the high-stress work environment and relatively easy access to painkillers and other prescription drugs. It may be conflicting and feel like a betrayal, but a CMA must report this type of behavior to a supervisor. Substance abuse not only is part of a dangerous addiction, but it also poses a serious threat to patient safety.

Conflicts of Interest

Any **conflict of interest** witnessed by the CMA in their facility needs to be reported to the appropriate supervisor. This could include doing clinical research on a product while receiving funding from the product's owners, giving preferential treatment to a certain pharmaceutical brand or medical equipment company, accepting gifts from vendors, or owning stock in a company upon whose product one is performing clinical research, among many others.

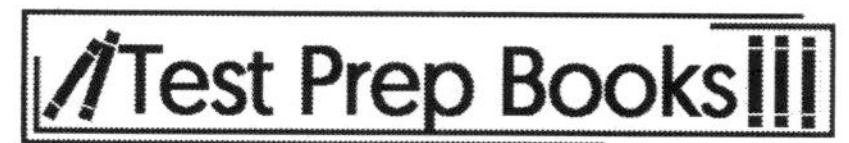

Incident Reporting/Patient Safety Variance Reporting

Incident reporting is a way in which patient safety can be monitored in healthcare systems. The CMA can voluntarily report any event involving patient safety, recording what circumstances surrounded the event, actions that led up to the event, and what took place after the incident occurred. An example of an incident report is a patient fall report. Patient falls are, unfortunately, a common occurrence in the healthcare environment. This type of incident report is a way to look at the fall and look for ways to prevent it from happening in the future. A drawback to incident reporting is their subjective nature, prone to bias and a limited point of view. Any event in a healthcare setting that deviates from standard policies and procedures should be reported. **Safety variance reporting** includes events such as patient falls, medical equipment failures, or failures to follow protocol. The purpose of a variance report is to collect data and analyze the factors that led to the event. Variance reports track data and help to prevent the occurrence of similar events. The report should be objective, with clear facts and observations made during the event.

Procedures/Examinations

Prepare Patients for Examinations, Procedures, and Treatments

Examination Methods

- **Auscultation** refers to listening to the sounds of body organs or processes, such as blood pressure, using a stethoscope.
- **Palpation** refers to using the hand or fingers to apply pressure to a body site to assess an organ for pain or consistency.
- **Percussion** refers to tapping on a body part to assess for rebound sounds. It may be used to assess the abdomen or the lungs.
- **Mensuration** refers to the measurement of body structures, such as measuring the circumference of the newborn's head.
- **Manipulation** refers to using the hands to determine motion and flexibility of a body part or to correct a defect such as realigning the bones after a fracture.
- **Inspection** refers to the simple observation of the color, contour, or size of a body structure.

Body Positioning

The provider will use proper draping to maximize the patient's privacy and to facilitate the planned procedures.

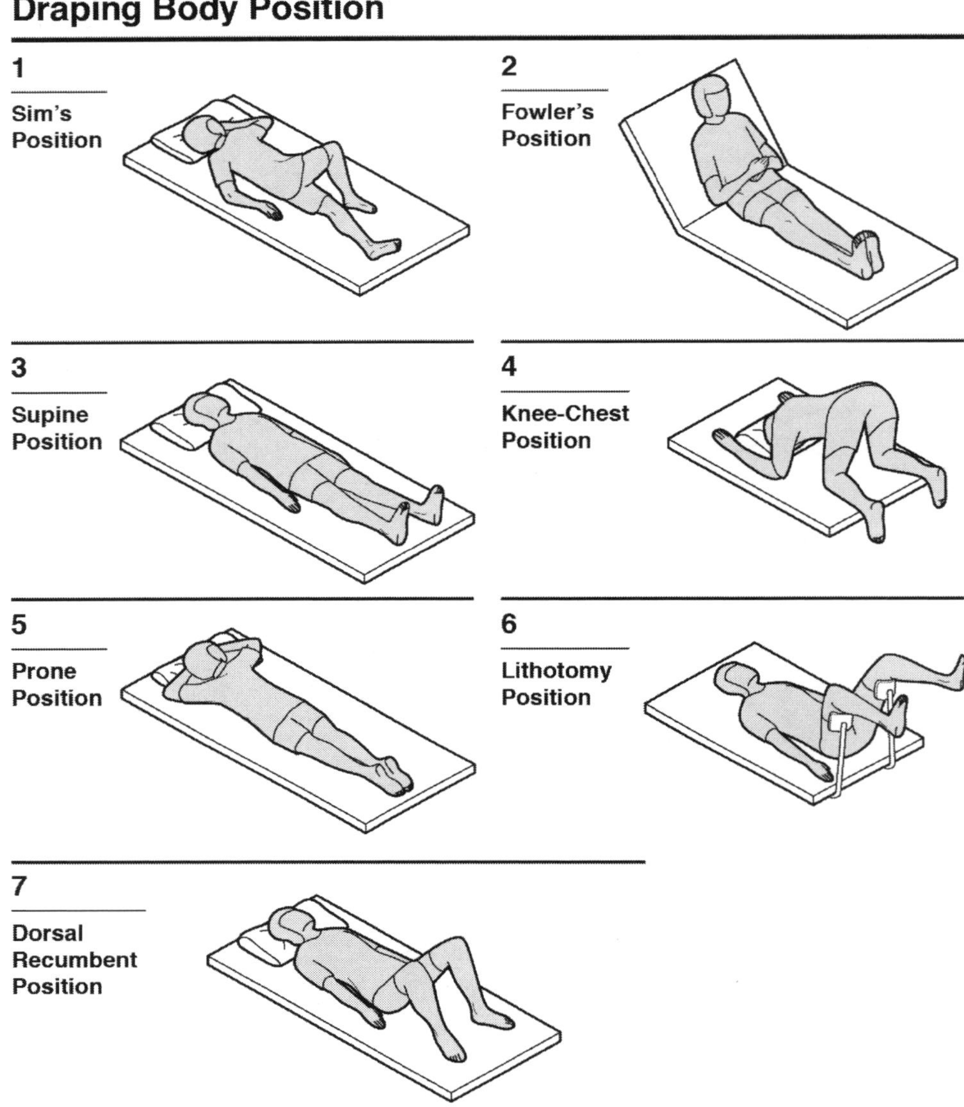

Pediatric Examinations

The purpose of the **pediatric exam** is to assess the child's growth and development and to provide family counseling regarding behavioral issues, nutrition, and injury protection. In addition, providers screen children for specific conditions at various ages to ensure that appropriate treatment is not delayed. For instance, newborns are tested for phenylketonuria and hearing loss. Children between three and five years old are tested for alterations in vision, and school-aged children are screened for obesity.

Obstetric/Gynecologic Examinations

Pelvic Exam/ Papanicolaou (PAP) Smear

The **pelvic exam** is done to assess the organs of the female reproductive system. The ovaries and the uterus are assessed by palpation, and the cervix is assessed by inspection. The PAP smear sample is a screening test for cervical cancer. The sample, obtained from the opening of the cervix, is transferred to glass slides for processing.

Prenatal/Postpartum Exams

The provider performs the **prenatal pelvic exam** to assess the development of the fetus and the status of the maternal reproductive system. The pelvic exam is done at the first visit, but is not repeated with every visit. In a normal pregnancy, it may not be repeated until the third trimester. The provider performs the postpartum exam to assess the return of the maternal reproductive organs to the nonpregnant state.

Supplies, Equipment, Techniques, and Patient Instruction

Eye Irrigation

The purpose of the **eye irrigation** is to remove drainage or foreign bodies from the eye. The provider must be aware that alternative protocols are necessary for major trauma or exposure to toxic materials. The provider will instruct the patient to perform frequent handwashing, refrain from touching the eye, report eye drainage/pain/alterations in vision, and avoid airborne contaminants.

The provider will assemble the necessary equipment, which includes the irrigating solution and syringe, sterile normal saline, appropriate personal protective equipment (PPE), a curved basin, and a waterproof towel.

The provider will assist the patient to a seated or supine position with the head turned to the affected side, and then position a waterproof towel under the patient's head. After removing any secretions from the eyelid and eyelashes with normal saline and gauze, the provider will use the nondominant hand to hold the eye open to expose the conjunctiva. The provider will position the curved basin against the patient's cheek and, holding the syringe tip at least 1 inch from the eye, irrigate the eye from the inner to the outer canthus. Once the eye is free of all drainage, the provider will dry the area with sterile gauze and adhere a protective covering, if ordered. The provider will assist the patient to a position of comfort and document the procedure.

Ear Irrigation

The purpose of the **ear irrigation** is to remove impacted cerumen or small foreign bodies from the ear.

The provider will instruct the patient to refrain from inserting anything into the ear, to report drainage/pain/alterations in hearing, and to use a washcloth to clean the outer ear.

The provider will assemble the necessary equipment, which includes the irrigating syringe, sterile normal saline warmed to body temperature, appropriate PPE, a curved basin, cotton balls, and a waterproof towel.

The provider will assist the patient to a seated or supine position with the head turned to the affected side, and then position a waterproof towel under the patient's head. After positioning the curved basin against the side of the head, the provider will remove secretions from the outer ear and pinna with normal saline and gauze. To expose the auditory canal in infants, the provider will pull the pinna down and to the rear of the head, and in older children and adults the provider will pull the pinna up and to the rear of the head. After verifying that the canal is not occluded by the syringe tip, the provider will direct the flow of the solution to the top of the canal and allow the irrigating fluid to flow back into the basin. Once all secretions have been removed, the provider will dry the area with gauze and loosely insert a cotton ball to absorb any additional drainage. The provider will then assist the patient to lie on the affected side to promote drainage and document the procedure.

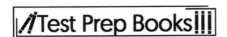

Suture/Staple Removal

The purpose of the procedure is to remove the suture materials from a healing wound.

The provider will instruct the patient to report any drainage, increased pain, or fever, and to keep the wound clean. If steri-strips are ordered to secure the wound after the removal of the staples/sutures, the provider will instruct the patient to leave them in place because they will gradually separate from the skin seven to ten days after application.

The provider will gather the necessary equipment that includes sterile normal saline, sterile gauze, staple/suture removal kit, sterile gloves, appropriate PPE, and waterproof pads.

The provider will expose the wound, remove the existing dressing, clean the wound as ordered, and assess the integrity of the incision. The provider will begin at one end of the incision, removing only every other staple/suture initially, by inserting the tip of the removal instrument between the skin and the staple, and gently closing the instrument, which will force the edges of the staple up and out of the wound (see image below). To remove the sutures, the provider will use forceps to pick up the free thread of the suture to raise the suture material above the surface of the skin, and then insert the blade of the scissors (the blade with the circular depression) under the suture material to cut the suture (see image below). Once the integrity of the wound is verified, the provider will remove the remaining staples/sutures, apply steri-strips as ordered, and document the procedure and the condition of the wound.

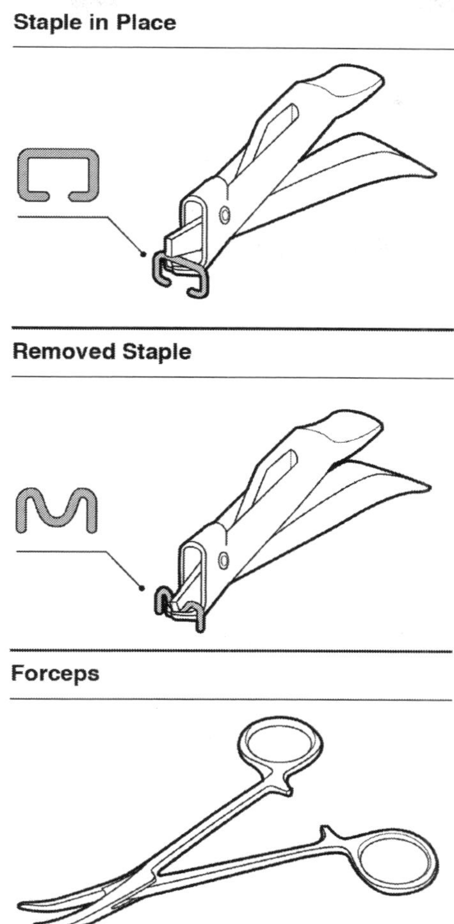

Cast Care/Splints/Slings

Care of an injured extremity may require the use of a cast, splint, or sling. Patients who have a cast have limited mobility of the affected extremity. Casts are made from fiberglass or plaster with internal padding, so it is important to keep the cast dry. Skin irritation may occur if water is trapped underneath the cast. The patient's affected extremity should be wrapped with a waterproof cover when the patient performs personal hygiene. Splints, which are removable, are used to immobilize an extremity. If an extremity has a complex fracture and swelling is expected, splints are placed on it. During routine skin care, if it's necessary to remove a splint, it is important to maintain proper limb alignment. Slings hold an affected extremity in a neutral position. Dislocations of the shoulder are a common reason for using a sling. The sling maintains the shoulder in an internally rotated position. When performing care, it is important to limit excessive range of motion, as well as lifting, pulling, or pushing with the affected extremity.

Surgical Assisting

Surgical assisting refers to the procedures in the surgical suite that may be assigned to certified assistants. Some of these activities include suturing, suctioning, clearing the operative field of blood, and maintaining traction on retractors.

Surgical Asepsis

Surgical asepsis is a process that eliminates any viable infectious agents from the immediate environment.

Surgical Scrub

Providers in the surgical suite will perform a **surgical scrub**, which is a handwashing technique aimed at reducing infectious agents to a minimum from the fingernails, hands, and forearms. The process involves a timed, five-minute systematic scrub with antimicrobial soap that begins with the hand and then progresses to the forearm. Once the scrub is complete, the hands are kept above the elbows to prevent contamination from areas of the body not included in the scrub. The provider then dries the skin thoroughly with a sterile towel.

Surgical Tray Prep/Sterile Field Boundaries

Surgical tray prep is the collection and preparation of all of the surgical instruments and equipment necessary for a specific surgical procedure performed by a specific surgical team.

Sterile field boundaries relate to the operative field, the surgical staff, and the operative instruments. The boundaries of the operative field include the surgical site and the proximal areas of the sterile drapes. All members of the surgical team are dressed in sterile gowns, sterile gloves with appropriate masks, eye protection, and head coverings; however, once a member of the team approaches the operative site, only the front of the gown from the waist to the mid chest and the arms to the elbows is considered sterile. In addition, only the inside of the sterile packaging for instruments is considered sterile.

Antiseptic Skin Prep

The **antiseptic skin prep** is required to remove all possible organisms and debris from the surgical site and to prevent contamination of the wound or postoperative infection. The provider washes the skin with soap and water to remove any dirt and debris, and then applies **bactericidal agents** according to agency policy.

Wound Care

Wound care is required for patients with all types of wounds: intentional or unintentional, acute or chronic. Wound care helps to remove surface bacteria and prevent infection of the surrounding tissue. Performing wound care ensures proper healing and regeneration of tissue. The type of wound care is dependent on the location, complexity, and classification of the wound.

Chronic or Non-Healing Wounds

Wounds can be classified as either acute or chronic. The classification is determined by the time it takes a wound to heal. **Chronic wounds** remain in the inflammatory stage of wound healing for a prolonged period of time and take longer than 30 days to complete the healing process. Wounds of this type also lack approximated edges and have a greater risk of infection. A patient's medical history may also contribute to a delay in the wound healing process. For example, if a patient with a medical history of diabetes and venous insufficiency has a foot ulcer, the wound may take months to heal, if at all, due to poor circulation and hyperglycemia.

Bandaging and Dressing Changes

Wounds that are not closed with staples or sutures have a greater risk of infection. The majority of open wounds have a dressing placed over them to protect them from bacteria and microorganisms. The dressing must be changed and the wound should be cleaned according to the provider's order. Dressing changes can be sterile or aseptic, depending on the type and location of the wound. Dressing methods vary, but the most commonly used supplies include rolled gauze, gloves, medical tape, scissors, normal saline for cleansing, and an absorbent pad to cover the wound.

Post-Op Incision Care

When patients undergo surgery, the CMA may be tasked with monitoring and recording the output of **postoperative incisions**. A postoperative incision is usually closed with sutures or staples. A common complication after surgery is bleeding, so the CMA should ensure the incision dressing remains dry and intact. Some incisions have drains or tubes to collect excess fluid from the wound. It is important to record the output and report it to the nurse as soon as it is documented. Patients who are being discharged should be educated on the signs of symptoms of a wound infection such as fever, redness, and inflammation.

Ostomy Care

Care of a patient with an ileostomy or colostomy includes emptying and changing the appliance and promoting adequate skin care and nutrition. The appliance should be drained when it is one-third full to prevent leakage or odor. The appliance should be changed according to the manufacturer or when it is no longer functional. Most appliance pouches are replaced every three to seven days. It is important to record intake and output, especially for a patient with an ileostomy. High output should be reported promptly to the nurse or provider to prevent dehydration. Skin care around the stoma is vital to prevent breakdown or infection.

Instruments

Surgical Instruments

Classification	Instrument Use
Cutting/Grinding/Dissecting	Remove by cutting with scissors or a knife Smooth irregular surfaces in bone Remove tissue from the body
Clamping	Control blood loss Bypass blood flow from the surgical site
Grasping/Holding	Move structures to gain access to surgical site Stabilize structures for dissection
Probing	Assess distal anatomy
Dilating/Enlarging	Restore anatomical lumen Increase access to the operative site
Retracting	Increase visibility of the operative site by displacing adjacent organs
Suctioning	Maintain surgical site, free of excess fluid Remove surgical debris and irrigation fluid

Sterilization Techniques/Autoclave

Sterilization eliminates all transmissible organisms from inanimate objects. The **autoclave** is an efficient, cost-effective method of sterilization that utilizes moist heat to destroy organisms; however, it is not appropriate for heat-sensitive materials.

Before autoclaving, the provider will thoroughly clean all of the items to be processed and verify that all instruments are in the open position to ensure that all surfaces are exposed to the heat. The provider must be aware that different types of metals cannot be processed together, and carbon steel instruments must be wrapped in special towels to avoid the oxidation that can occur if the instruments come in contact with the stainless-steel trays of the autoclave.

To ensure sterility, the provider will include a sterilization indicator with each instrument or package.

Anatomy and Physiology

Human Growth and Development

Along with psychological development, there are specific physical stages of growth and development that each patient must go through. Depending on where the CMA practices, whether with a pediatric, geriatric, or general population, knowing these patterns and milestones will help guide decisions regarding the patient's care.

Normal Developmental Patterns/Milestones Across the Life-Span

In the first year of life, the human baby goes from being completely helpless to being able to walk, talk, and feed themselves. Here is a short list of important milestones to watch out for in the first year, as well as milestones for up to five years of age:

- **2 months:** Begins to smile, uses hand sucking to self-soothe, looks at parents, makes cooing noises, notes faces, becomes fussy when bored, and holds head up while on tummy.
- **4 months:** Spontaneously smiles and laughs, babbles, reaches for toys, and pushes legs down when held in standing position on a hard surface.
- **6 months:** Recognizes familiar faces, makes consonant sounds, puts objects in mouth, and rolls over both ways.
- **9 months:** Exhibits fear of strangers, understands the word "no," plays peek-a-boo, and gets into sitting position and sits without support.
- **1 year:** Displays nervousness around strangers and cries when parents leave, waves "hi" or "bye," puts things in and out of a container, and may take steps or even walk.
- **18 months:** Has temper tantrums, points to objects they want, says single words, understands functions of basic objects such as a phone, and carries toys while walking.
- **2 years:** Copies the behavior of others, knows names of familiar body parts such as "nose," begins sorting colors and shapes, and kicks a ball.
- **3 years:** Shows concern for crying friend, follows two- or three-step instructions, does three- to four-piece puzzles, runs easily, and climbs.

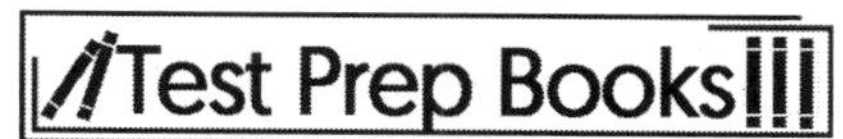

- **4 years:** Enjoys group play and storytelling, names colors and numbers, and stands on one foot for up to 2 seconds.
- **5 years:** Mimics friends; enjoys singing, dancing, and acting; speaks more clearly; counts to ten or higher; and stands on one foot for 10 seconds or longer.

Structural Units (Cells, Tissues, and Organs)

The structural units of the human body include the cells, tissues, organs, and organ systems. The **cell** is the basis for all life. The function of a specific cell type will dictate its structure; however, all cells have certain subunits or organelles in common. The nucleus directs all cellular activities and contains the DNA-specific chromosomes for the individual. The cell membrane provides a barrier between the cellular contents and the environment and regulates the substances that cross the membrane in either direction. The cytoplasm is the intracellular fluid where all cellular reactions occur. The mitochondria are responsible for energy production. The ribosomes create the proteins that are necessary for all bodily functions. The smooth endoplasmic reticulum creates lipids, which are necessary for cellular structure. The centrioles are responsible for cellular division and reproduction. The lysosomes synthesize and store digestive enzymes.

Tissues are groups of cells that perform specific functions. The four types of tissues are epithelial, muscle, connective, and nervous. Epithelial tissue covers the exterior surface of the body, lines the interior surfaces, and forms some glands. Muscle tissue is capable of movement as a result of electrical stimulation. There are three specialized types of muscle tissue: skeletal or voluntary muscle; smooth or involuntary muscle, found in hollow internal organs such as the bladder, lungs, and blood vessels; and cardiac muscle. Connective tissue connects all body systems and provides structural support. The skin, ligaments, and tendons are all composed of varying forms of connective tissue. Nervous tissue also responds to an electrical stimulus and can generate nerve impulses that result in voluntary and involuntary bodily functions.

An **organ** is a coordinated structure of various tissue types that performs a specific function for the body. An **organ system** is composed of two or more organs that contribute complementary functions to support the vital functions of the body. For example, the heart, lungs, and circulatory system work together to provide for oxygenation.

Anatomical Divisions, Body Cavities

Body Cavities	
Cavity	**Contents**
Dorsal Cavity (Posterior)	Brain
	Spinal Cord
Ventral (Anterior)	Includes the organs of the: Thoracic Cavity, Abdominal Cavity, and Pelvic Cavity
Thoracic Cavity	Heart, Lungs, and Thymus
Abdominal Cavity	Stomach, Liver, Gall Bladder, Spleen, Small Intestine, Kidneys, Large Intestine, Adrenal Gland
Pelvic Cavity	Urinary Bladder, Sigmoid Colon, Male and Female Reproductive Organs

Anatomical Positions and Directions

The basic anatomical position refers to the body standing straight, forward facing, with the upper extremities at the side and the palms forward facing. Specific body positions may be necessary to accommodate the patient's condition or planned interventions. In the **supine** position, the patient lies flat with straight knees and arms at the side. A variation of the supine position is the Fowler's position, which includes elevation of the head to approximately 30 to 45 degrees. In the **prone** position, the patient lays on the stomach with straight knees and the arms at the side or under the head. The dorsal recumbent and lithotomy positions are similar because in each position the patient lies flat with knees flexed and their feet either flat on the bed or resting in stirrups. The **knee-chest** and standing positions are also similar. The patient is bent at the waist, either standing or with knees resting on the bed. In the left-lateral or **Sim's** position, the patient lies on the left side with the right knee flexed. In the Trendelenburg position, the patient lies flat with the head lowered.

The **anterior position** indicates the front of the body. The **posterior position** is the opposite of anterior, meaning toward the back. Superior is toward the head, and inferior is toward the feet. Medial is closer to the midline of the body. **Lateral** is away from midline toward the side of the body. **Proximal** means closer to the center of the body. Distal means further from the center of the body. Superficial refers to the surface of the body. **Deep** is the opposite of superficial, meaning it is closer to the body core. Bilateral refers to two structures, with one on each side of the body. Ipsilateral means the same side of the body, and contralateral means the opposite side of the body.

Body Planes and Quadrants

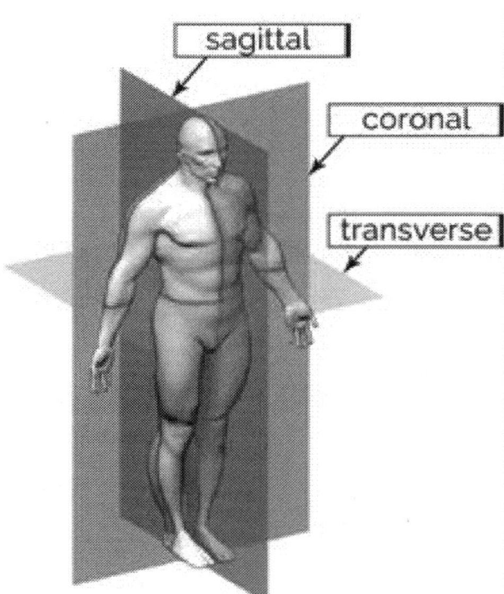

The **coronal plane** divides the body into the anterior, or **frontal**, and **posterior**, or **dorsal**, sections. The **sagittal plane** divides the body into left and right sections. The **transverse plane** divides the body into top and bottom sections.

For purposes of assessment, the abdomen is divided into four anatomical quadrants, as noted in the figure below to the right.

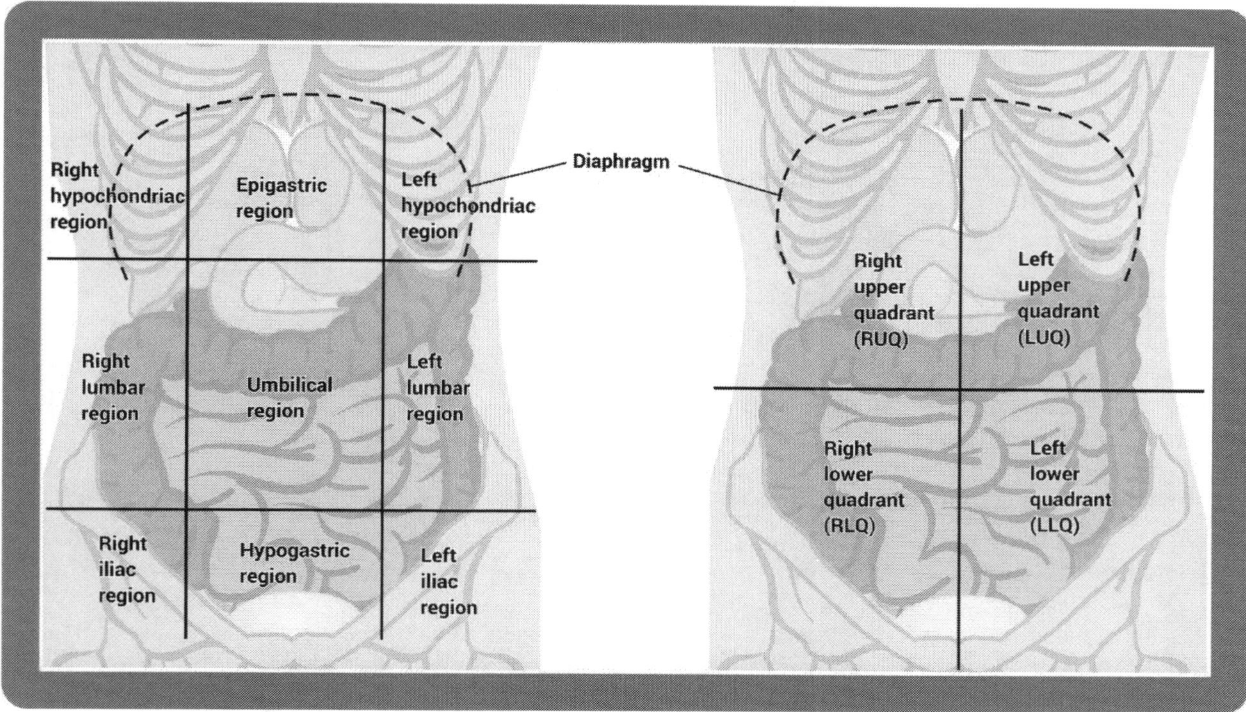

Body Systems, NORMAL Structure and Function

Integumentary

The skin or **integumentary** body system is the largest organ of the body in surface area and weight. It is composed of three layers, which include the outermost layer or **epidermis**, the **dermis**, and the **hypodermis**. The thickness of the epidermis varies according to the specific body area. For example, the skin is thicker on the palms and the soles of the feet than on the eyelids. The dermis contains the hair follicles, sebaceous glands and sweat glands. **Melanin** is the pigment that is responsible for skin color.

The main function of the skin is the protection of the body from the outside environment. The skin regulates body temperature, using the insulation provided by body fat and the secretion of sweat, which acts as a coolant for the body. **Sebum** lubricates and protects the hair and the skin, and melanin absorbs harmful ultraviolet radiation. Special cells that lie on the surface of the skin also provide a barrier to bacterial infection. Nerves in the skin are responsible for sensations of pain, pressure, and temperature. In addition, the synthesis of Vitamin D, which is essential for the absorption of calcium from ingested food, begins in the skin.

Vernix caseosa is a thick, protein-based substance that protects the skin of the fetus against infection and irritation from the amniotic fluid from the third trimester until it dissipates after birth. Several childhood illnesses, such as measles and chicken pox, are associated with specific skin alterations. Acne related to hormonal changes is common in adolescents, and the effects of sunburn are observed across the life span. In the elderly, some of the protections provided by the skin become less effective; decreases in body fat and altered sweat production affect cold tolerance, loss of collagen support results in wrinkling of the skin, and decreased sebum secretions lead to changes in hair growth and skin moisture content.

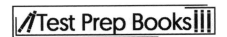

Musculoskeletal

The **musculoskeletal system** consists of the bones, muscles, tendons, ligaments, and connective tissues that function together, providing support and motion of the body. The layers of bone include the hard-exterior compact bone, the spongy bone that contains nerves and blood vessels, and the central bone marrow. The outer compact layer is covered by the strong periosteum membrane, which provides additional strength and protection for the bone. **Skeletal muscles** are **voluntary muscles** that are capable of contracting in response to nervous stimulation. Muscles are connected to bones by tendons, which are composed of tough connective tissue. Additional connective tissues called ligaments connect one bone to another at various joints.

In addition to providing support and protection, the bones are important for **calcium storage** and the production of blood cells. Skeletal muscles allow movement by pulling on the bones, while joints make different body movements possible.

The two most significant periods of bone growth are during fetal life and at puberty. However, until old age, bone is continually being remodeled. Specialized cells called **osteoclasts** break down the old bone, and **osteoblasts** generate new bone. In the elderly, bone remodeling is less effective, resulting in the loss of bone mass, and the incidence of **osteoporosis** increases. These changes can result in bone fractures, often from falling, that do not heal effectively. Muscle development follows a similar pattern with a progressive increase in muscle mass from infancy to adulthood, as well as a decline in muscle mass and physical strength in the elderly.

Nervous

The two parts of the **nervous system** are the **central nervous system**, which contains the brain and spinal cord, and the **peripheral nervous system**, which includes the ganglia and nerves. The cerebrospinal fluid and the bones of the cranium and the spine protect the brain and spinal cord. The nerves transmit impulses from one another to accomplish voluntary and involuntary processes. The nerves are surrounded by a specialized myelin sheath that insulates the nerves and facilitates the transmission of impulses.

The nervous system receives information from the body, interprets that information, and directs all motor activity for the body. This means the nervous system coordinates all the activities of the body.

The fetal brain and spinal cord are clearly visible within six weeks after conception. After the child is born, the nervous system continues to mature as the child gains motor control and learns about the environment. In the well-elderly, brain function remains stable until the age of eighty, when the processing of information and short-term memory may slow.

Cardiovascular, Hematopoietic, and Lymphatic

The **cardiovascular system** includes the heart, the blood vessels, and the blood. The heart is a muscle that has four "chambers," or sections. The three types of blood vessels are: the arteries, which have a smooth muscle layer and are controlled by the nervous system; the veins, which are thinner than arteries and have valves to facilitate the return of the blood to the heart; and the capillaries, which are often only one-cell thick. Blood is red in color because the **red blood cells** (**RBCs**) contain hemoglobin, which is a red pigment as well a protein that transports oxygen.

The deoxygenated blood from the body enters the heart and is transported to the lungs to allow the exchange of waste products for oxygen. The oxygenated blood then returns to the heart, which pumps the blood to the rest of the body. The arteries carry oxygenated blood from the heart to the body; the veins return the deoxygenated blood to the heart, while the actual exchange of oxygen and waste products takes place in the capillaries.

The **fetal cardiac system** must undergo dramatic changes at birth as the infant's lungs function for the first time. Cardiovascular function remains stable until middle age, when genetic influences and lifestyle choices may affect the cardiovascular system. Most elderly people have at least some indication of decreasing efficiency of the system.

The **hematopoietic system**, a division of the lymphatic system, is responsible for blood-cell production. The cells are produced in the **bone marrow**, which is soft connective tissue in the center of large bones that have a rich blood supply. The two types of bone marrow are red bone marrow and yellow bone marrow.

The **red bone marrow** contains the stem cells, which can transform into specific blood cells as needed by the body. The yellow bone marrow is less active and is composed of fat cells; however, if needed, the yellow marrow can function as the red marrow to produce the blood cells.

The red bone marrow predominates from birth until adolescence. From that point on, the amount of red marrow decreases, and the amount of yellow marrow increases. This means that the elderly are at risk for conditions related to decreased blood-cell replenishment.

The **lymphatic system** includes the spleen, thymus, tonsils, lymph nodes, lymphatic vessels, and the lymph. The spleen is located below the diaphragm and to the rear of the stomach. The thymus consists of specialized lymphatic tissue and lies in the mediastinum behind the sternum. The tonsils are globules of lymphoid tissue located in the oropharynx. The lymphatic vessels are very small and contain valves to prevent backflow in the system vessels. The vessels that lie in close proximity to the capillaries circulate the lymph. Lymph is composed of infectious substances and cellular waste products in addition to hormones and oxygen.

The main function of the lymphatic system is protection against infection. The system also conserves body fluids and proteins and absorbs vitamins from the digestive system.

The **spleen** filters the blood in order to remove toxic agents and is also a reservoir for blood that can be released into systemic circulation as needed. The thymus is the site of the development and regulation of **white blood cells (WBCs)**. The tonsils trap and destroy infectious agents as they enter the body through the mouth. The lymphatic vessels circulate the lymph, and the lymph carries toxins and cellular waste products from the cell to the heart for filtration.

There is rapid growth of the **thymus gland** from birth to ten years. The action of the entire system declines from adulthood to old age, which means that the elderly are less able to respond to infection.

Respiratory

The **respiratory system** consists of the airway, lungs, and respiratory muscles. The airway is composed of the pharynx, larynx, trachea, bronchi, and bronchioles. The lungs contain air-filled sacs called **alveoli**, and they are covered by a visceral layer of double-layered **pleural membrane**. The **intercostal muscles** are located between the ribs, and the diaphragm separates the thoracic cavity from the abdominal cavity.

On inspiration, the airway transports the outside air to the lungs, while the expired air carries the carbon dioxide that is removed by the lungs. The alveoli are the site of the exchange of carbon dioxide from the systemic circulation with the oxygen contained in the inspired air. The muscles help the thoracic cavity to expand and contract to allow for air exchange.

The respiratory rate in the infant gradually decreases from a normal of thirty to forty breaths per minute, until adolescence when it equals the normal adult rate of twelve to twenty breaths per minute. Pulmonary function declines after the age of sixty because the alveoli become larger and less efficient, and the respiratory muscles weaken.

Digestive

The **digestive system** includes the mouth, pharynx, esophagus, stomach, small intestine, large intestine, and sigmoid colon. The entire system forms a twenty-four-foot tube through which ingested food passes. **Digestion** begins in the mouth, where digestive enzymes are secreted in response to food intake. Food then passes through the esophagus to the stomach, which is a pouch-shaped organ that collects and holds food for a period of time. The **small intestine** begins at the distal end of the stomach. The lining of the small intestine contains many **villi**, which are small, hair-like projections that increase the absorption of nutrients from the ingested food. The **large intestine** originates at the distal end of the small intestine and terminates in the rectum. The large intestine is four feet long and has three segments, including the ascending colon along the right side, the transverse colon from right to left across the body, and the descending colon down the left side of the body, where the sigmoid colon begins.

The enzymes of the mouth, stomach, and the proximal end of the small intestine break down the ingested food into nutrients that can be absorbed and used by the body. The nutrients are absorbed by the small intestine. The large intestine removes the water from the waste products, which forms the stool. The muscle layer of the large intestine is responsible for peristalsis, which is the force that moves the waste products through the intestine.

The function of the digestive system declines more slowly than other body systems, and the changes that most often occur are the result of lifestyle issues or medication use.

Urinary

The **urinary system** includes the kidneys, ureters, bladder, and urethra. The kidneys are a pair of bean-shaped organs that lie in the peritoneal cavity just below and toward the rear of the liver. The **nephron** is the functional unit of the kidney, and there are about 1 million nephrons in each of the two kidneys. The **ureters** are hollow tubes that allow the urine formed in the kidneys to pass into the bladder. The **urinary bladder** is a hollow mucous lined pouch with the ureters entering the upper portion, and the urethra exiting from the bottom portion. The urethra is a tubular structure lined with mucous membrane that connects the bladder with the outside of the body.

In addition to the formation and excretion of the waste product urine, the nephron of the kidney also regulates fluid and electrolyte balance and contributes to the control of blood pressure. The ureters allow the urine to pass from the kidneys to the bladder. The bladder stores the urine and regulates the process of urination. The urethra delivers the urine from the bladder to the outside of the body.

The lifespan changes in the urinary system are more often the result of the effects of chronic disease on the system, rather than normal decline.

Reproductive

The major organs of the **female reproductive organs** include the uterus, cervix, vagina, ovaries, and fallopian tubes.

The **uterus** is a hollow, pear-shaped organ with a muscular layer that is positioned between the bladder and the rectum. The uterus terminates at the cervix, which opens into the vagina, which is open to the outside of the body. The **ovaries**, supported by several ligaments, are oval organs 1- to 2-inches long that are positioned on either side of the uterus in the pelvic cavity. The **fallopian tubes**, which are 4 inches long and .5 inches in diameter, connect the uterus with the ovaries.

The **male reproductive organs** include the penis, scrotum, testicles, vas deferens, seminal vesicles, and the prostate gland. In addition to the urethra, the **penis** contains three sections of erectile tissue. The **scrotum** is a fibromuscular pouch that contains the **testes**, the spermatic cord, and the epididymis. The pair of testes is suspended in the scrotum and each one is approximately 2 inches by 1 inch long. The vas deferens is a tubular pathway between the testes and the penis, and the **seminal vesicles** are small organs located between the bladder and the bowel. The prostate gland surrounds the proximal end of the urethra within the pelvic cavity.

The main function of the male reproductive system is the production of **sperm**. Unlike the female, beginning at puberty, several million immature sperm are produced every day in the testes. The sperm are transported through the vas deferens to the penis, and the prostate gland and seminal vesicles contribute fluids that support the activity of the sperm after ejaculation.

At puberty, egg maturation, menses, and sperm production begin, and the secondary sex characteristics appear. Female fertility declines at thirty years of age, and the maturation of eggs in the ovaries ceases at menopause, which occurs at fifty years of age. Sperm production continues from puberty until death; however, after sixty years of age the ability of the sperm to travel to the fallopian tube to fertilize an egg is decreased.

Endocrine

The glands of the **endocrine system** include the pituitary, thyroid, parathyroid, adrenal, and reproductive glands, as well as the hypothalamus, the pancreas, and the pineal body. The function of the system is to synthesize and secrete **hormones** that control body growth, **sexual function**, and **metabolism**, which is the production and use of energy by the body. The **thyroid gland**, located on either side of the trachea, regulates energy production, or the rate at which the body uses ingested food to support body functions. The **parathyroid**, located on the upper margin of the thyroid gland, regulates calcium levels by the activation of Vitamin D, which increases intestinal absorption of calcium, and by regulating the amount of calcium that is stored in the bones or excreted by the kidneys. The **adrenal glands**, located on the upper margin of the kidneys, consist of the adrenal cortex and the adrenal medulla.

The hormones secreted by the adrenal cortex are necessary for life and include: **cortisol**, or **hydrocortisone**, which regulates the breakdown of proteins, carbohydrates, and fats for energy production and the body's response to stress; corticosterone, which works with cortisol to regulate the immune system; and aldosterone, which contributes to blood-pressure control. The **adrenal medulla**

secretions, including **adrenaline**, regulate the body's reaction to stress known as the fight-or-flight response. The ovaries secrete **estrogen** and the testes secrete **testosterone**, which regulate sexual maturation and function. The **pancreas**, located in the right upper quadrant of the abdomen, secretes the insulin that regulates blood sugar, in addition to other hormones that regulate water absorption and secretion in the intestines. The **pineal gland**, located in the center of the brain, secretes **melatonin**, which regulates the **circadian rhythm** or sleep cycle.

The nervous system connects each of these glands to the **hypothalamus** and the **pituitary gland**. The hypothalamus senses alterations in hormone secretions in all of these organs and conveys those messages to the pituitary gland, which then stimulates each specific organ to either increase or decrease secretion of the relevant hormone. This feedback system is necessary for **homeostasis**.

Sensory

The **sensory organs** include the eyes, ears, nose, tongue, and skin, and they contain special **receptor cells** that transmit information to the nervous system. The **eyes** receive and process light energy. The **ears** process sound waves and also contribute to the maintenance of equilibrium. The **nose** senses odors and the **tongue** senses taste. The **skin** responds to **tactile stimulation**, including pain, hot, cold, and touch. Internal organs also sense pain and pressure. The brain is responsible for processing all of these sensations.

The senses of touch and smell are active in the fetus and continue to mature after birth. Touch is especially important for infants. The elderly experience a decline in the acuity of all of the senses; however, eyesight and hearing are most commonly affected due to the effects of chronic diseases such as hypertension and diabetes.

Body Systems, ABNORMAL Structure and Function, Recognition and Etiology

Integumentary

The function of the **integumentary system** may be affected by:

- Allergic responses, including eczema
- Infections resulting from bacteria, fungi, and viruses (herpes virus)
- Vasculature alterations, including venous stasis ulcers
- Genetic defects, including psoriasis
- Autoimmune disorders, including scleroderma
- Cancers, including basal cell, squamous cell, and melanoma

Musculoskeletal

The function of the **musculoskeletal system** may be affected by:

- Alterations in bine integrity, resulting in osteoporosis
- Fractures that result from injury or disease

Nervous

The function of the **nervous system** may be affected by:

- Acute injury, resulting in concussion and other catastrophic injuries
- Alterations in cognition, evidenced by Alzheimer's disease
- Alterations in movement, evidenced by Parkinson's disease

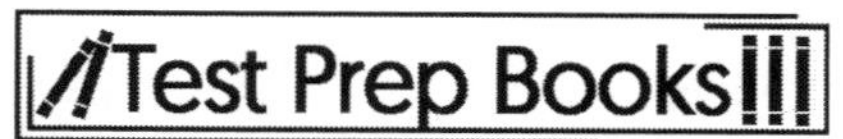

- Alterations in circulation, resulting in stroke
- Genetic defects, including Huntington's chorea
- Cancer, evidenced by brain tumors

Cardiovascular, Hematopoietic, and Lymphatic

The function of the **cardiovascular system** may be affected by:

- Decreased oxygen supply, resulting in myocardial infarction and angina
- Alterations in the blood vessels, resulting in hypertension

The function of the hematopoietic system may be affected by:

- Cancer, resulting in leukemia
- Alterations in red-blood-cell production, resulting in anemia

The function of the lymphatic system may be affected by:

- Cancer, resulting in lymphoma and Hodgkin's disease
- Infection

Respiratory

The function of the **respiratory system** may be affected by:

- Airway obstruction, resulting in chronic obstructive pulmonary disease (COPD) and emphysema
- Infections, resulting in pneumonia
- Allergic responses, resulting in asthma

Digestive

The function of the **digestive system** may be affected by:

- Inflammation, resulting in Crohn's disease and ulcerative colitis
- Autoimmune disease, evidenced by lupus erythematosus
- Cancer, resulting in colorectal tumor

Urinary

The function of the **urinary system** may be affected by:

- Infection, resulting in bladder infection and kidney infection
- Alterations in blood vessels, resulting in kidney failure
- Cancer

Reproductive

The function of the **reproductive system** may be affected by:

- Infection, resulting in vaginitis and prostatitis
- Genetic alterations, evidenced by sterility and endometriosis
- Cancer

Endocrine

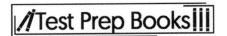

The function of the **endocrine system** may be affected by:

- Alterations in metabolism, resulting in diabetes
- Alterations in fluid volume regulation, resulting in hypertension and Cushing's syndrome
- Cancer

Sensory

The function of the **sensory system** may be affected by:

- Alterations in perception, evidenced by deafness, blindness, and pain perception

Specimen Collection Techniques

Methods of collection

Blood

For a **venipuncture process**, the provider will:

- Identify the patient, review the order, and label the collection tubes.
- Assess the nondominant hand to identify a vein that is straight and palpable.
- Wash hands and apply PPE.
- Clean the selected site with an alcohol swab per agency policy.
- Inspect the test-specific vacuum tubes and needles to verify that:
  1. The tube is securely sealed and vacuum has been maintained.
  2. Appropriate additives such as anticoagulants or other fixatives that may be required to maintain the sample are present in the tube.
  3. The chosen needle size is appropriate to the selected vein.
- Complete the venipuncture per agency policy.
- Apply pressure and a sterile dressing to the venipuncture site.
- Submit the sample for processing per agency policy.

The provider will use a **capillary/dermal puncture** to obtain blood from small children or when only a small volume of blood is necessary as in finger-stick puncture for blood glucose analysis.

Urine

The provider can collect a random **urinalysis** any time the patient voids.

To obtain a **midstream/clean catch urine sample**, the provider will instruct the patient to first clean the urinary meatus with the appropriate antiseptic solution, void without collecting the initial volume, and then deposit the remaining output into the container.

Before beginning the collection of a timed twenty-four-hour collection, the provider must obtain a storage container containing any necessary preservative from the laboratory, and confirm the accommodations for refrigeration of the sample if required. The first time the patient voids, the provider will discard the specimen and record the time. All urine collected in the following twenty-four-hour period will be collected by the provider and stored in the prepared container at the prescribed temperature.

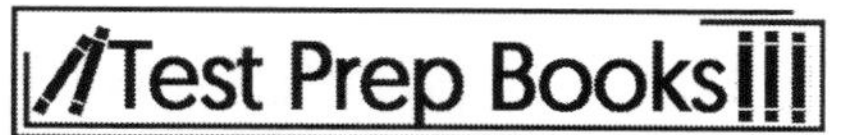

Catheterization may be used to obtain a sterile specimen. The provider will pass the sterile catheter into the bladder to drain the urine into a sterile container, which must then be labeled and transported to the lab according to agency policy.

The **pediatric urine collector** is a plastic pouch attached to a foam adhesive backed base. The provider will verify that the skin around the urinary meatus is clean, dry, and free of powder or lotions. The provider will adhere the adhesive section of the collection device over the urinary meatus and replace the patient's diaper.

Fecal Specimen

The provider will place the **fecal specimen** in a clean, leak-proof, properly labeled container, and promptly transport the sample to the laboratory for processing.

Sputum Specimen

The **sputum specimen** must contain sputum, not saliva, and it is best obtained early in the morning.

Swabs

The provider will verify the order, identify the patient, and use proper handwashing technique and appropriate personal protective equipment for each of the following procedures.

Throat Swab

After assisting the patient to a seated position in a chair or bed, the provider will use sterile swabs to remove the sample from the back of the throat while avoiding contact with the uvula and tongue. The provider will then break the tips of the swabs and secure them in the labeled collection sleeve, transport the sample to the lab according to agency policy, and document the sample collection time and site.

Genital

The provider will position the patient according to the site being sampled. The provider will use sterile swabs to sample the top of the vaginal vault for a vaginal swab, the center of the cervical os for a **cervical swab**, or the urinary meatus for a urethral swab. The provider will then break the tips of the swabs and secure them in the labeled collection sleeve, transport the sample to the lab according to agency policy, and document the sample collection time and site.

Wound

The provider will position the patient according to the site being sampled. The provider will remove and discard the existing dressing, use sterile swabs to obtain the sample from the center of the wound, then break the tips of the swabs and secure them in the labeled collection sleeve. Once the swabs are secured, the provider will dress the wound, ensure that the sample is delivered to the laboratory, and document the wound assessment and the sample collection time and site.

Nasopharyngeal

The provider will position the patient in a seated position with the head tilted back. After verifying the patency of the nares, the provider will insert the sterile swab 3 to 4 inches into the nasopharynx, rotate the swabs to obtain the sample, remove the swabs, break the tips of the swabs to secure them in the labeled collection sleeve, transport the specimen to the laboratory, and document the collection site and time.

Prepare, Process, and Examine Specimens

Proper Specimen Labeling

Provider errors related to specimen collection are a threat to patient safety. Most recently, the use of two patient-specific identifiers has been mandated as the standard for all patient specimens. The provider must verify the patient's name and date of birth or other unique identifier per agency policy for all specimens that are submitted for processing.

Sources of Specimen Contamination

Collected samples may be **contamination** by extraneous body secretions and other environmental debris or infectious agents. Deviations in sterile technique are also a possible source of specimen contamination.

Specimen Preservation

The provider should be aware of all conditional requirements for the collection of a particular specimen.

Refrigeration

Samples collected over an extended period of time, such as twenty-four-hour urine collections or fecal samples may require a dedicated **refrigeration** source for the duration of the testing period. In general, most culture specimens must be refrigerated if there is an anticipated delay in processing; however, culture samples of cerebrospinal fluid and blood must be processed without delay, and should not be refrigerated.

Fixative

Fixatives are chemical substances that are added to preserve test specimens for processing. The solutions are specific to the type of testing, which means that histological testing of tissue biopsies may require different fixative solutions than chemistry testing of venous blood. The provider must be certain that all laboratory requirements are met for specimen collection and submission.

Centrifuge

The **centrifuge** is a laboratory device that rapidly spins samples, which results in the separation of the less dense elements from the heavier elements according to the sedimentation principle. The process of **differential centrifugation** can separate cellular organelles from the individual cell, while **isopycnic centrifugation** can be used to isolate DNA strands. Sucrose gradient centrifugation can be used to refine viruses and other small cellular inclusions.

Microscope

A **microscope** is used to view substances, structures, or organisms that are not visible without magnification. The optical or light microscope, the first to be developed, uses light and a series of lenses to magnify an image up to four hundred times the actual size. The **electron microscope** aims a beam of high-speed electrons at a sample, which interacts with the sample to form an image. The scanning electron microscope interacts with the surface of the sample, while the transmission electron microscope interacts with the full thickness of the sample in order to produce an image. Electron microscopes can magnify a structure up to 10 million times the actual size.

Wet Mount (Saline and KOH) Slides

The **microbiologic slides** are pieces of glass that provide the base for microscopic samples. A dry mount refers to a sample placed on a slide with a cover slip. A wet mount slide contains a sample that is suspended in a small amount of liquid—such as water or glycerin—to increase the refraction of the light, and a cover slip.

Laboratory Quality Control/Quality Assurance/Clinical Laboratory Improvement Act (CLIA) Requirements

Testing protocols are test-specific, standardized instructions for laboratory processes.

The provider will retain all testing records for completed laboratory analyses, which may be used to measure the degree of consistency with control values. Daily performance logs track the personnel completing the analyses and the test results on a daily basis.

All laboratory personnel are required to meet all manufacturer requirements for daily equipment maintenance protocols for laboratory instruments, in addition to documenting those activities in the maintenance log.

All laboratory personnel are responsible for conducting and documenting the calibration or verification of the quantitative measurement of all instruments.

Daily control testing refers to the daily process of comparing random testing results to a control.

All laboratory personnel must monitor temperature controls to prevent the destruction of collected specimens due to the effects of alterations in temperature on the specimen or lab chemicals.

Reagent storage refers to the maintenance of laboratory reagents within the proper temperature range. Reagents are most commonly maintained in cold storage or frozen.

Tests waived by the **Clinical Laboratory Improvement Amendments** (**CLIA**) as identified by the Food and Drug Administration (FDA) are a group of tests that are cleared for home use and in healthcare agencies that have a certificate of waiver and a documented quality assurance plan. Healthcare agencies that hold certificates of waiver for testing will be subject to periodic evaluations. In addition, nonclinical community agencies may apply for a certificate for waived rapid HIV testing or work with a clinical site that has a certificate of waiver for the test. The waived tests include only tests that are technically simple to perform and carry a low risk of harm to the patient even if they are performed incorrectly. **Common waived-test** categories identified in the list of more than 1,400 test systems include:

- Drug abuse screening
- Ovulation calculation
- Pregnancy
- HIV
- Electrolytes and liver function
- Blood glucose
- Fecal occult blood
- Cholesterol and lipid profile
- Lyme disease

- Basic metabolic panel including calcium

Laboratory Panels and Selected Tests

Urinalysis

- **Physical urinalysis**: The provider will perform a visual assessment of the color and turbidity of the urine sample.
- **Chemical urinalysis**: The provider will use the reagent strip to assess the specific gravity, the pH, and the presence and quantity of protein, glucose, ketones, hemoglobin, and myoglobin, leukocyte esterase, bilirubin, and urobilirubin.
- **Microscopic urinalysis**: The provider will separate the urine sediment from the fluid volume to microscopically identify the presence of RBCs, WBCs, epithelial cells, bacteria, yeasts, and parasites.

Hematology

- **Hematocrit** (**HCT**): The provider will assess the RBC count as defined by the hematocrit—amount of red blood cells in the blood—by placing the anticoagulated blood sample into the microhematocrit centrifuge and documenting the results.
- **Hemoglobin**: The provider will assess the amount of the hemoglobin protein that is present in the red blood cells by placing the anticoagulated blood sample into the microhematocrit centrifuge and documenting the results.
- **Erythrocyte Sedimentation Rate** (**ESR**): The provider will assess the ESR, which is a nonspecific indicator of inflammation, by placing the anticoagulated sample in the Westergren tube and recording the height of the settled RBCs after one hour.
- **Automated Cell Counts**: The provider will use the automated device to assess RBC, WBC, and platelet counts by preparing the sample, obtaining, and documenting the results.
- **Coagulation testing/international normalized ratio** (**INR**): The provider will calculate the INR, which is used to assess blood-clotting levels in patients being treated with Warfarin, according to laboratory protocol after verifying that the sample was not drawn from a heparinized line.

Chemistry/Metabolic Testing

Glucose

The provider will identify the **blood glucose** sample, which measures the amount of glucose in the circulating blood volume, after fasting or not fasting, before processing and documenting the results.

Kidney Function Tests

Kidney function is assessed by measuring the levels of metabolic waste products, including **blood urea nitrogen** (BUN) and creatinine, and by calculating the **glomerular filtration rate** (GFR), which corresponds with the clearance of waste products from the blood by the kidneys. The provider will process the sample to obtain the BUN and creatinine levels. The provider will then use the creatinine level and the patient's age, body size, and gender to calculate the GFR according to the agency-approved equation for GFR. There are four equations that may be used to calculate the GFR in adults that include

the **Modification of Diet in Renal Disease** (MDRD), the Study equation (IDMS-traceable version), and the **Chronic Kidney Disease Epidemiology Collaboration** (CKD-EPI) equation.

Liver Function Tests

Elevated levels of **alanine transaminase** (ALT) and **aspartate aminotransferase** (AST), two liver enzymes, indicate acute/chronic hepatitis, cirrhosis, or liver cancer. Decreased levels of these enzymes may be due to Vitamin B-12 deficiency. **Albumin**, a protein synthesized by the liver that is necessary for the maintenance of osmotic pressure in the vasculature, is decreased in liver failure due to cirrhosis or cancer. The liver processes **bilirubin**, a waste product resulting from the normal destruction of old red blood cells, for excretion by the gastrointestinal system; however, elevated levels may be due to liver failure or transfusion reactions. The provider will verify a ten-minute centrifuge time, process the sample, and document results.

Lipid Profile

Excess dietary intake of animal fats can result in elevated total cholesterol and low-density lipoprotein (**LDL**) or "bad cholesterol" levels, while elevated high-density lipoprotein (**HDL**) or "good cholesterol" levels are the result of appropriate nutrition or the effect of cholesterol-lowering medications. Elevated triglycerides levels may result from diabetes, obesity, liver failure, or kidney disease. The provider will verify that the fasting sample was obtained before the administration of **N-Acetylcysteine** (NAC) or Metamizole, if indicated. The provider will then process the sample per protocol within two hours of the venipuncture and document the results.

Hemoglobin A1c

A **Hemoglobin A1c** test measures the percentage of hemoglobin molecules that are coated or glycated with glucose. Hemoglobin molecules are located in the red blood cell, which has a lifespan of 110 to 120 days; therefore, the hemoglobin A1c test measures the average blood sugar for a four-month period. The normal A1c level is less than 5.7 percent; levels between 5.7 percent and 6.4 percent indicate prediabetes and levels greater than 6.5 percent indicate diabetes. Elevated HGB A1c levels must be confirmed with additional testing before treatment is initiated. The provider will inform the patient that fasting is not required, process the sample, and document results.

Electrolytes

Electrolytes are minerals that, when dissolved, break down into ions. They can be acids, bases, or salts. In the body, different electrolytes are responsible for specific cellular functions. These functions make up larger, critical system-wide processes, such as hydration, homeostasis, pH balance, and muscle contraction. Electrolytes typically enter the body through food and drink consumption, but in severe cases of imbalance, they may be medically-administered. They are found in the fluids of the body, such as blood.

Thyroid Function

When patients are diagnosed with hypothyroidism, they may also be referred to as having an underactive thyroid, which results in the underproduction of T4 and/or T3 hormones. Symptoms include depression, excessive fatigue, chills, dry skin, lowered heart rate, gastrointestinal problems such as constipation, and unexplained weight gain. Hypothyroidism is commonly caused by Hashimoto's disease, another autoimmune disease that affects thyroid function. This disease is usually treated with synthetic thyroid hormone replacement therapy, which involves taking a daily dose of the T4 hormone. T3 supplementation is rare, as it is derived from T4. Hypothyroidism can also be caused by the presence of too much iodine. The thyroid uses iodine to make T4 and T3 hormones. If there is too much iodine in the blood, the pituitary gland releases less TSH. The low levels of TSH can later result in the thyroid not producing enough T4 and/or T3 hormones. In some cases of hypothyroidism, surgery is required.

Specialized Testing

Mononucleosis

The immune system produces **heterophile proteins** in response to the presence of the Epstein-Barr virus (EBV), the causative agent of **mononucleosis**. Specific tests include the analysis of the **viral capsid antigen** (VCA), the **early antigen** (EA), or the EBV **nuclear antigen** (EBNA). **The Monospot test** detects antibodies that are not specific for mononucleosis, leading to false positive and false negative results. In addition, the Monospot test may be insensitive to the heterophile antibodies produced by children with mononucleosis. The provider will freeze the sample if processing is delayed beyond twenty-four hours after preparation.

Rapid Group A Streptococcus

Identification of the beta-hemolytic bacterium **Streptococcus pyogenes**, the most common cause of acute pharyngitis in adults and children, is obtained by using isothermal nucleic acid amplification technology. The provider will transfer the sample to the testing device adhering to proper wait-times, process the sample, and document the results.

C-Reactive Protein (CRP)

CRP is an indicator of inflammation that is released into the bloodstream in response to tissue injury or the onset of an infection. The provider will verify that all reagents and the serum sample are at room temperature, assess the processed sample for agglutination, and document the results.

HCG Pregnancy Test

Serum levels of **human chorionic gonadotropin** hormone detect the presence of a pregnancy. Elevated levels may indicate a normal pregnancy, either single or multiple, chorionic cancer, or a hydatidiform mole. The provider will centrifuge the clotted sample for ten minutes at room temperature, and document the results.

H. Pylori

There are three testing methods for the **Helicobacter pylori** organism, including histological examination and culture of samples obtained by endoscopic biopsy, the urea breath test (UBT) that measures CO_2 levels on exhalation, and the fecal antigen test that identifies antibodies to the organism. The provider will verify that the patient has avoided antibiotics and bismuth preparations for two weeks prior to the testing. The provider will process all samples according to the specific test requirements and document the results.

Influenza

Influenza testing methods include the **Rapid Influenza Diagnostic Test** (RIDT), the **Real Time Polymerase Chain Reaction**, and the viral culture, which identify the genetic material of the virus in secretions obtained from a nasal or throat swab. The provider will process all samples according to the specific test requirements and document the results.

Genetic/Hereditary

A **genetic risk assessment** estimates an individual's risk for the development of chronic and rare diseases that are genetically linked. This assessment only identifies a statistical probability, not cause and effect, because diseases that result from variants in multiple genes as opposed to a single gene increase the complexity of estimating the risk. There is a wide variation in the degree to which the genetically-linked diseases contribute to the possibility of expression of the disease in the offspring. For instance, the genetic risk associated with the development of melanoma is 21 percent whereas the risk associated with type 1 diabetes is 88 percent. There are two categories of risk: absolute risk and relative risk. **Absolute risk** means that if the patient has a one in ten chance of developing a disease in their lifetime, that person has a 10 percent risk for that disease. **Relative risk** compares the risk for two groups for the same disease. For instance, the risk of breast cancer is higher for descendants of Ashkenazi Jews who emigrated from Eastern Europe than for the average female population in the United States.

There are family patterns that increase the risk for the development of diseases including having multiple first-degree relatives with the same condition, having a relative diagnosed with the condition before the age of 55, having a relative with a disease that is more common in the opposite gender, and having more than one genetically linked disease in the family. The genetic pedigree, which is a visual representation of the patient's family tree, may be used to assess the patient's genetic risk factors. Providers must also support patients and families as they decide whether or not to access formal genetic testing. The Genetic Information Nondiscrimination Act (GINA) and the Health Insurance Portability and Accountability Act (HIPAA) of 1996 provide some protection against discrimination due to the findings of the testing. There also can be ethical questions related to reproductive planning and family dynamics. The patient should be encouraged to seek professional counseling when considering genetic testing. The patient should also understand that direct-to-consumer genetic tests may or may not provide reliable information for the patient's unique circumstances and that none of the commercial products provides counseling.

Tuberculosis Tests/Purified Protein Derivative Skin Tests

Tuberculosis tests/purified protein derivative (PPD) skin tests are screening tests for the presence of **Mycobacterium tuberculosis**. The provider will use a **tuberculin (TB) syringe** to inject 0.1 ml of tuberculin purified protein derivative, the TB antigen, into the interior portion of the forearm. The solution forms a small, round elevation or wheal that is visible on the skin surface. The patient must return to the agency for evaluation of the site between forty-eight and seventy-two hours after the injection. The provider will assess the site and document the size of any visible induration or palpable swelling. The provider will not include any reddened areas in that measurement. The provider will refer all results that exceed 5 mm for additional testing and treatment.

Cardiovascular

Electrocardiography

Perform Standard 12-Lead

- Verify the order and obtain all equipment before approaching the patient.
- Explain the procedure to the patient and assist him/her to a supine position.
- Expose the limbs and the chest, maintaining appropriate draping to preserve patient's privacy.
- Clean the electrode sites with alcohol and remove excess body hair according to agency policy.
- Attach electrodes to appropriate anatomical positions.

- Attach machine cables to the electrodes.
- Enter the patient data and calibrate the machine as necessary.
- Request that the patient does not move or speak.
- Obtain an artifact-free tracing.
- Remove the electrodes and residual conductive gel.
- Return the patient to a position of comfort.
- Submit the tracing for interpretation.

The accuracy of the tracing is dependent on correct lead placement; therefore, the provider will position the chest leads as follows:

- V_1 - right sternal border at the level of the fourth intercostal space
- V_2 - left sternal border at the level of fourth intercostal space
- V_3 - centered between V_2 and V_4
- V_4 - the midclavicular line at the level of the fifth intercostal space
- V_5 - horizontal to V_4 at the anterior axillary line
- V_6 - horizontal to V_4 at the midaxillary line

The provider must attach the limb leads to the extremities, not the torso. In addition, the provider must avoid large muscle groups, areas of adipose tissue deposit, and bony prominences when placing the limb leads on the four extremities.

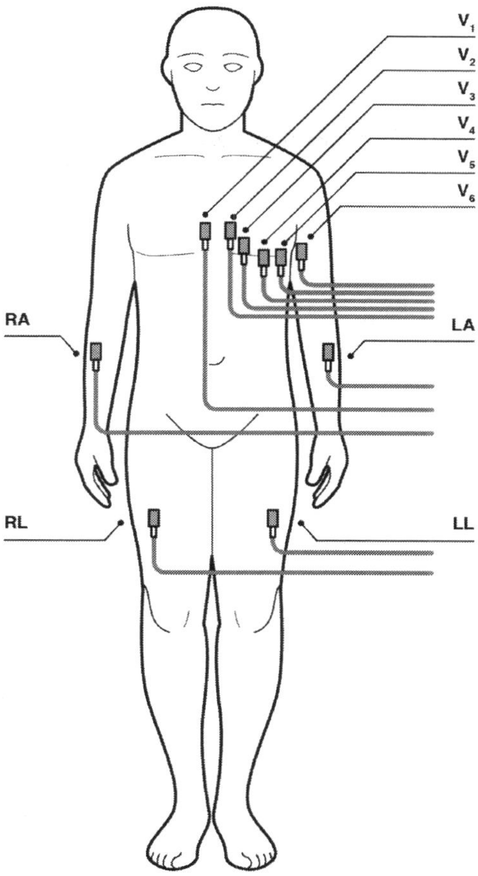

In order to ensure an accurate tracing, the provider will:

- Explain the procedure to the patient.
- Expose the chest as necessary.
- Clip or shave excess hair as consistent with agency policy.
- Wipe the skin surface with gauze to decrease electrical resistance.
- Remove excess oils with alcohol wipe if necessary.
- Verify that the electrode is intact with sufficient gel.
- Attach the electrodes as appropriate.
- Complete the tracing.

Recognize and Eliminate Artifacts

An **artifact** is an error produced in the results of a test. Artifacts can emerge for many reasons, including improper technique, faulty or miscalibrated equipment, or as a normal occurrence in a test that must be accounted for during analysis.

Artifacts during an ECG are most often the result of patient movement while the tracing is being recorded. The provider must be able to differentiate between the artifact and lethal arrhythmias. An ECG artifact is most often evidenced by a chaotic wave pattern that interrupts a normal rhythm, as shown in the figure below.

EKG Artifact

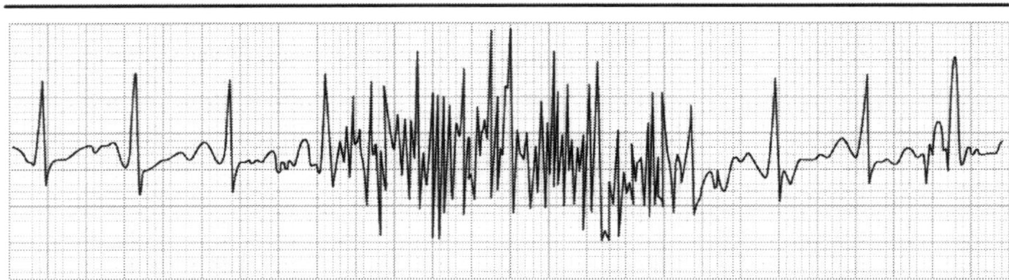

Recognize Rhythms, Arrhythmias

Normal Sinus: The rhythm originates in the **sinoatrial** (SA) node as indicated by the presence of an upright p wave in lead 2. A p wave precedes every QRS complex, and the rhythm is regular at sixty to one hundred beats per minute.

Normal Sinus Rhythm

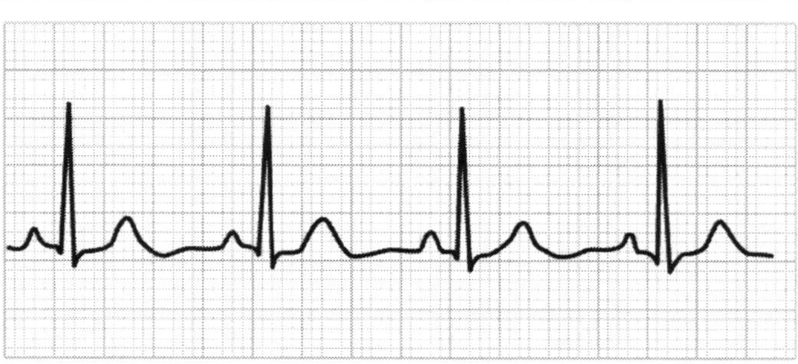

Sinus Tachycardia: The rhythm originates in the SA node as indicated by the presence of an upright p wave in lead 2. A p wave precedes every QRS complex, and the rhythm is regular at a rate greater than one hundred beats per minute.

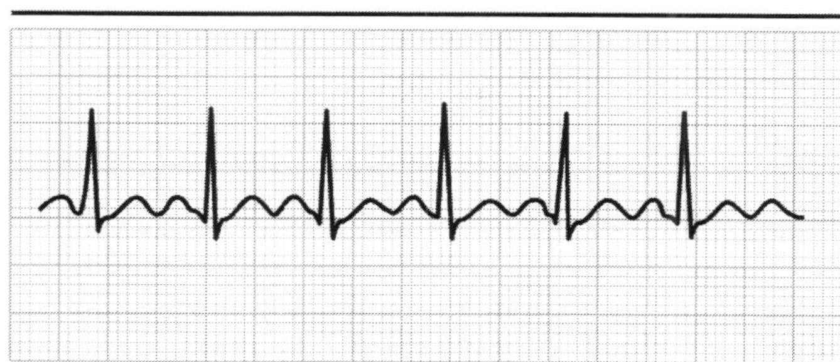

Sinus Bradycardia: The rhythm originates in the SA node as indicated by the presence of an upright p wave in lead 2. A p wave precedes every QRS complex, and the rhythm is regular at less than sixty beats per minute.

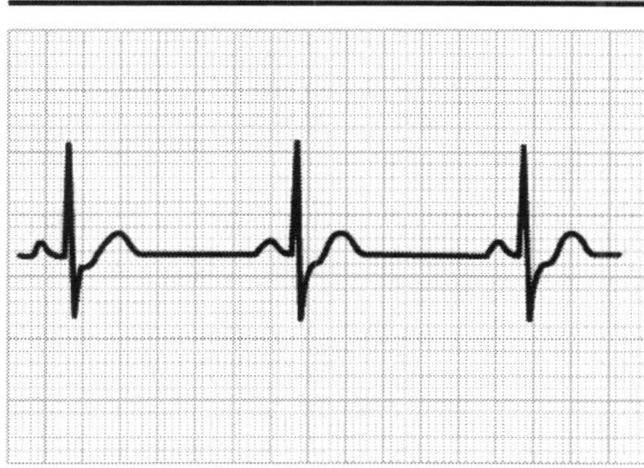

Atrial Fibrillation: Irregular electrical impulses around the heart create disorganized electrical waves in the atria that cause the AV node to fire at irregular intervals. Individual p waves are not visible due to the rapid rate, and the QRS complexes are generally wider than the QRS complexes in the sinus rhythms.

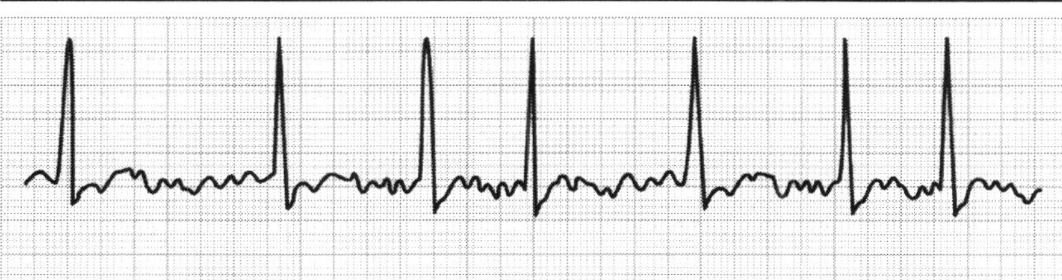

Complete Heart Block: The SA node generates a p wave that is not transmitted to the ventricles. The ventricles respond to an impulse from an alternative site, and the resulting complex has no association with the p wave. This condition requires immediate intervention.

Complete Heart Block

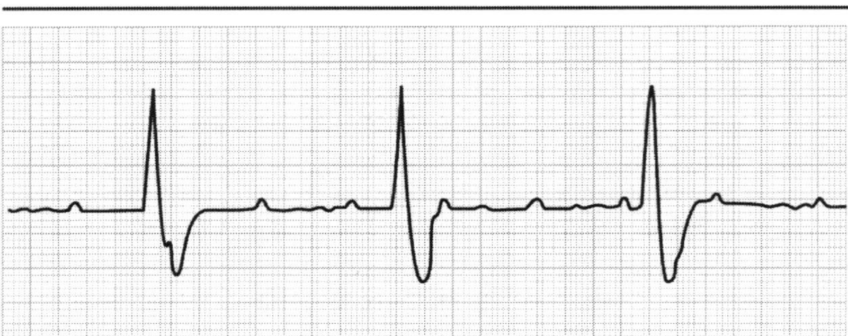

Ventricular Fibrillation: There is only erratic electrical activity resulting in quivering of the heart muscle. Immediate intervention is necessary.

Ventricular Fibrillation

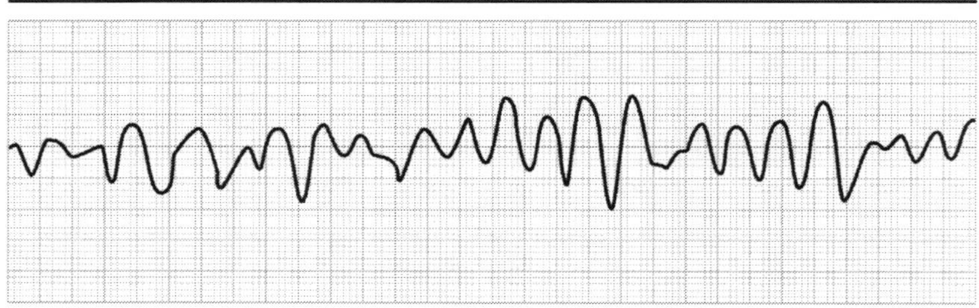

Recognize Rhythms, Arrhythmias

The provider can use a six- to ten-second strip of cardiac activity to identify the heart rate and rhythm. The ECG paper is standardized to measure time from left to right, with each small box equal to four-tenths of a second, which means that each large box is equal to one-fifth of a second and the time elapsed between the black ticks is three seconds. The provider calculates the heart rate by dividing 300 by the number of large squares between two QRS complexes. In the figure below, the heart rate is 300/4 = 75. Alternatively, the provider can identify the heart rate by counting the number of QRS complexes in a ten-second EKG strip and multiplying that result by ten.

The provider will assess the rhythm by comparing the distance between complexes 1 and 2 with the distance between complexes 2 and 3.

Cardiac Rhythm Strip

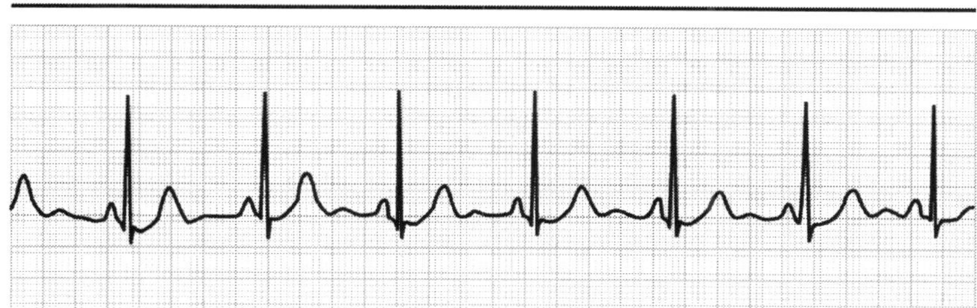

Holter/Event Monitors

The **Holter monitor** is a portable device that is used for monitoring the EKG/ECG. The monitor may be used for routine cardiac monitoring or for diagnosing cardiac conditions that may not be evident on a single EKG/ECG tracing. The provider will attach the leads to the patient's chest, verify the patient's understanding of the process, and provide the patient with a diary with instructions to record all activity and physical symptoms for the duration of the testing period.

Holter monitor with EKG reading

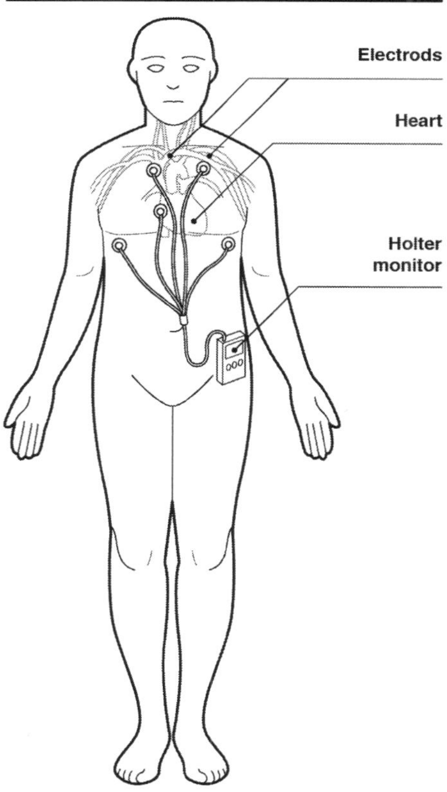

Cardiac Stress Test

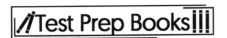

The provider uses the **cardiac stress test** to identify the patient's cardiac response to the stress of exercise. The cardiac activity is recorded after the patient's heart rate reaches a target rate that is equal to 220 minus the patient's age. There are two forms of the test, which include the treadmill test and the pharmacologic test. Patients who are physically able walk on the treadmill until the target heart rate is achieved. Patients who are unable to tolerate the exercise will receive medications to raise the heart rate to the desired level. The provider will reverse the effects of these medications as soon as the appropriate tracings are obtained

Vision

Color Vision

The most commonly used test for color blindness is the **Ishihara Color Vision Test**, which is a series of circular images that are composed of colored dots. The identification of the numbers embedded in the colored plates is determined by the patient's ability to identify the red/green numbers and background. There are currently online variations of this test in addition to color testing forms that the provider may use for younger children who are not yet able to identify numbers.

Visual Acuity and Distance

Snellen Chart

The **Snellen chart** contains eleven rows of letters that differ in size from row to row and is viewed from a distance of twenty feet. The resulting numbers, 20/100 for example, indicate that the patient can see objects at a distance of 20 feet that are visible to a person with normal eyesight at a distance of 100 feet.

E Chart

The **E chart** contains nine rows of letters that differ in size from row to row depicting the letter E in alternating positions. The chart is useful for children and others who are not familiar with the English alphabet. The scoring is similar to the Snellen chart.

Jaeger Card

The **Jaeger card** uses six paragraphs in differing font sizes ranging from 14 point to 3 point Times New Roman font to test near vision. The J1 paragraph at 3 point Times New Roman font is considered to equal 20/20 vision per the Snellen chart.

Ocular Pressure/Tonometry

The provider uses a tonometer to touch the surface of the patient's anesthetized cornea in order to record the pressure inside the eye.

Visual Fields

Visual fields are defined as the total horizontal and vertical range of vision when the patient's eye is centrally focused. The provider may use this test to detect "blind spots" or scotomas.

Audiometric/Hearing

Pure Tone Audiometry

The patient's **pure-tone threshold** is identified as the lowest decibel level at which sounds are heard 50 percent of the time.

Speech and Word Recognition

The **speech-awareness threshold** (SAT), or **speech-detection threshold** (SDT), is defined as the lowest decibel level at which the patient can acknowledge the stimuli. The test utilizes spondees—two-syllable words that are spoken with equal stress on each syllable—as the stimuli for this test.

The **speech-recognition threshold** (SRT), or less commonly speech-reception threshold, measures the lowest decibel level at which the patient can recognize speech at least 50 percent of the time. This test also may be used to validate pure-tone threshold measurements, to determine the gain setting for a patient's hearing aid, or to provide a basis for suprathreshold word recognition testing.

Suprathreshold word recognition is used to assess the patient's ability to recognize and repeat one-syllable words that are presented at decibel levels that are consistent with social environments. Human-voice recordings are used to present the words, and the patient's responses are scored. The provider may use the results of this test to monitor the progression of a condition such as **Meniere's disease**, to identify improvement afforded by the use of hearing aids, or to isolate the part of the ear that is responsible for the deficit.

Tympanometry

The provider uses a **tonometer** to assess the integrity of the **tympanic membrane** (ear drum) and the function of the middle ear by introducing air and noise stimuli into the ear. The provider then assesses the resulting waveform and records the results.

Allergy

Scratch Test

During a **scratch test**, the provider applies a small amount of diluted allergen to a small wound created in the patient's skin in order to identify the specific allergens that elicit an allergic response in the patient. The allergist will select up to fifty different allergens for testing, which means that the provider will make fifty small incisions or scratches in the patient's skin arranged in a grid system to facilitate the interpretation and reporting of the test results. The provider will observe the patient closely for a minimum of fifteen minutes following the introduction of the allergen for the signs of an anaphylactic reaction, in addition to signs of a positive reaction. The provider will document all positive results that are evidenced by a reddened raised area that is pruritic.

Intradermal Skin Test

The provider may use **intradermal injections** of the allergen to confirm negative scratch tests, or as the primary method of allergy testing. Using a 26- or 30-gauge needle, the provider will inject the allergen just below the surface of the skin. The provider must closely observe the patient and record results based on the appearance of raised, reddened wheals that are pruritic.

Patch Test

A **patch test** is used to determine whether skin inflammation occurs as result of an allergen. Various substances such as fragrances, preservatives, or latex are infused into a patch. The patch is then applied to the skin for a period of 48 hours. When the patch is removed, any skin reaction is assessed to determine whether the patient has an allergy.

Radioallergosorbent Test (RAST)

Specific allergy testing measures the concentration of immunoglobulin E (IgE) antibodies in the blood. IgE is an immunoglobulin that releases antibodies in response to an allergen. A **radioallergosorbent test** is done using a blood serum sample; this test measures the amount of IgE antibodies in response to specific allergens such as food, dust, drugs, and mold. The allergens being tested must be specified for analysis.

Respiratory

Pulmonary Function Tests (PFTs)

Pulmonary function tests evaluate the two main functions of the pulmonary system: air exchange and oxygen transport. The specific tests measure the volume of the lungs, the amount of air that can be can be inhaled or exhaled at one time, and the rate at which that volume is exhaled. The tests are used to monitor the progression of chronic pulmonary disorders, including asthma, emphysema, chronic obstructive lung disease, and sarcoidosis.

Spirometry

Spirometry is one of the two methods used to measure pulmonary function. The provider attaches the mouthpiece to the spirometer and instructs the patient to form a tight seal around its edge. The provider will then demonstrate the breathing patterns that are necessary for successful evaluation of each of the pulmonary measurements. The spirometry device calculates each of the values based on the patient's efforts.

Peak Flow Rate

Peak flow rate is defined as the speed at which the patient can exhale. This measure is commonly used to evaluate pulmonary function in patients with asthma.

Diagnostic Imaging (MRI, CT Scan, Nuclear, and Ultrasound)

Various imaging procedures are performed on patients to assist in diagnosing medical conditions. Which diagnostic test is used depends on the anatomical location and the required visualization of the internal images. **Magnetic resonance imaging (MRI)** is a precise diagnostic test that uses radio waves and magnetic fields to provide details of soft tissues and organs. MRIs can also be functional, producing an image of the blood flow to specific locations inside the body. MRIs produce three-dimensional images that can be viewed from different angles to aid the healthcare provider in diagnosing patient conditions. Common conditions that require MRI diagnostic imaging include tumors, infections, seizure activity, and cognitive disorders. Patients should be instructed to remove jewelry and any accessories that contain metal. The test commonly takes a long time, usually between 30 to 90 minutes.

Computerized tomography (CT) scans are detailed x-ray images of bones, blood vessels, and soft tissues. Cross-sectional images are processed by a computer to allow layered visualization of internal structures. A contrast dye may be injected, taken by mouth, or administered rectally into the patient to help emphasize areas of concern. CT scans are non-invasive and are commonly ordered for conditions such as masses, internal bleeding, or excess fluid. If contrast material is to be used, the patient should be assessed for allergies, a cross-allergy to shellfish, and any current medications.

Nuclear imaging uses small quantities of radioactive material that aids in visualizing the functionality of organs, bones, and tissues. The patient is given a radioactive tracer via the oral or parenteral route. The radioactive material settles into specific parts of the body and is later detected by specialized cameras. Types of nuclear imaging studies include bone density and positron emission tomography (PET) scans. A bone density scan is a common screening tool to measure bone mass, strength, and density. A PET scan can detect abnormal metabolic processes inside the body, such as cell activity of malignant tumors.

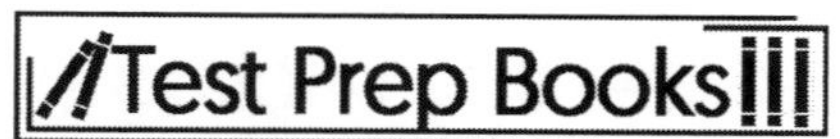

An **ultrasound**, also referred to as a sonograph, is an imaging test that uses high frequency sound waves to create images from inside the body. Ultrasounds can be done on various parts of the body and help visualize blood flow, tissues, tumors, and cysts. One of the most common uses of ultrasound imaging is to detect and monitor pregnancy. Sound waves produce fetal images that can be observed on an ultrasound machine.

Differentiate Between Normal and Abnormal Laboratory and Diagnostic Test Results

Certified medical assistants (CMAs) are responsible for preparing and filing information in patient charts. Results from diagnostic or laboratory centers may be faxed or delivered to the facility. It is important for the CMA to recognize flagged alerts on lab reports. Lab reports include the normal range (expected result) of analyzed tests; results that are out of range are flagged as low, high, or abnormal. For example, a patient's report states the platelet count is 120,000/mm^3. The normal platelet count is between 150,000 and 450,000/mm^3. The laboratory report would flag, use bold font, or otherwise emphasize the patient's unusually low platelet count. Diagnostic study reports include a comment on the findings by the radiologist. CMAs must promptly report any abnormal results to the healthcare provider.

Pharmacology

Medications

Classes of Drugs

The provider is aware that prescription drugs are classified according to the chemical activity of the active elements or by the target disease. This means that antineoplastic medications are chemically active against cancer cells, while antidepressant medications are used to treat depression.

In addition, certain substances are also included in one of five schedules according to the potential for abuse under the **Controlled Substances Act**. The provider must be aware that Schedule I substances, such as LSD and peyote, do not have any medical application, are not safe for use even under medical supervision, and are noted to have great potential for abuse. Schedule II through Schedule V include substances based on the potential for psychological or physical dependence exerted by the individual substance. The provider is aware that Schedule II substances, such as oxycodone, have greater potential for abuse than Schedule V substances, such as Robitussin with codeine.

Drug Actions/Desired Effects

The provider understands that the efficacy of any medication is determined by how well the medication acts to produce the desired effects. This assessment includes a cost-benefit analysis, which measures the adverse effects of the normal action of the medication against the resulting improvement in the patient's condition or disease status.

Adverse Reactions

The provider must differentiate between the side effects of a medication and an **adverse reaction** to that medication. Side effects, common to all therapeutic agents, are often temporary reactions to a given medication that seldom require intervention or alterations in the medication administration. In contrast, adverse reactions are more serious events that often require the provider's intervention and discontinuation of the therapy. Adverse reactions can result from an allergic reaction to the medication, an exaggerated response to the drug action, or provider error, and the provider must document and report all of these events according to agency policy.

Contraindications

There are two kinds of contraindication for a pharmacotherapeutic intervention: absolute and relative. An **absolute contraindication** means that the administration of the drug or combination of drugs can result in life-threatening adverse effects that must be avoided. A **relative contraindication** means that the potential for adverse effects should be weighed against the expected therapeutic effect. An absolute contraindication can be related to the reaction of one or more drugs with another drug, or with certain patient populations, such as pregnant women, patients with renal failure, and people with other drug allergies. An example of an absolute drug-to-drug contraindication is that warfarin cannot be given with aspirin; one drug potentiates the effect of the other, resulting in an increased risk for bleeding. Absolute contraindication for pharmacotherapeutic interventions in pregnant women is associated with **teratogenicity**, which is the risk for birth defects due to maternal exposure to the drugs. Patients with renal disease are at risk from the drug interactions because most drugs are excreted by the kidneys, and when there is any degree of altered renal function, the plasma concentration of the drugs, and therefore the risk of adverse effects, will be increased. Patients with identified allergies are at greater risk for hypersensitivity reactions to other drug therapies. Many of the recommended contraindications are contained in condition-specific protocols such as oral contraceptive use, smoking cessation, and obesity therapy. For example, absolute contraindications to oral contraceptive therapy include a known or suspected pregnancy or a history of thrombotic disease. Relative contraindications include the presence of hypertension and current smoking history. In children, there is an absolute contraindication for the use of aspirin in patients recovering from a viral infection due to the risk of Reye's syndrome, which is rare but often fatal.

Storage of Drugs

The provider will meet safety and environmental requirements for all medications. All medications, including those that require refrigeration, must be secured in locked devices or medication areas. In addition, the provider will verify that the refrigerator is used exclusively for medication.

Preparing and Administering Oral and Parenteral Medications

Rights of Medication Administration

The "six rights" must be addressed for every medication dose. The provider will:

- Use two means of identification (ID) to verify the right patient, which can include the patient's verbal report and the agency ID band
- Verify the prescription and the medication as provided by the pharmacy
- Compare the route of administration documented in the medication record with the original prescription
- Verify the time schedule as documented in the medication record
- Calculate the correct dose and verify the result with another provider as required by agency policy

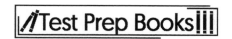

- Document the administration of the medication and the patient's response in the medication record according to agency policy

Dosage of Medications

Metric Conversion

The provider must be able to calculate **metric conversions** as necessary for safe medication administration.

Units of Measurements

The provider will recognize common metric and household measurements, including liter, centimeter, milliliter, kilogram, gram, milligram, pound, ounces, tablespoon, teaspoon, foot, and inch.

Calculations

The licensed provider will calculate all dosage amounts with 100 percent accuracy according to agency protocol. Recent research indicates that the use of dimensional analysis to calculate intravenous (IV) drip rates and other dosage calculations is associated with improved provider accuracy.

Routes of Administration Including Safety Precautions

The provider will utilize the appropriate **administration route** to ensure the optimum efficiency of the medication.

Intramuscular

The provider will use an **intramuscular injection** to ensure rapid absorption of a medication into the bloodstream when the intravenous infusion of the medication is inappropriate or inaccessible. Common sites for intramuscular injection include the deltoid, vastus lateralis, and ventral gluteal muscles.

Z-Tract Injection

When injecting medications capable of causing skin irritation or discoloration in the event of leakage from the injection site, the provider will apply traction to the skin surrounding the injection site with the nondominant hand, insert the needle into the muscle at a 90-degree angle, inject the medication, withdraw the needle, and release the traction on the skin, trapping the injected solution in the muscle.

Subcutaneous

The provider will choose a **subcutaneous site** to inject medications that will absorb more slowly because of the limited blood supply in the fatty subcutaneous space. Using the nondominant hand, the provider will pinch the skin, insert the needle at a 90-degree angle into the fatty layer just under the skin, inject the medication, and withdraw the needle. It should be noted that for small children and individuals with little subcutaneous fat, a 45-degree angle is recommended to ensure the medication enters the subcutaneous tissue rather than muscle.

Oral/Sublingual/Buccal

The provider understands that the oral, sublingual, and buccal administration routes are appropriate for agents that will be rapidly absorbed into the bloodstream through the mucous membrane of the gastrointestinal tract. In addition, the sublingual and buccal routes are appropriate if the patient is unable to swallow a medication, or when the medication would be poorly absorbed or inactivated in the stomach. The provider is aware that sublingual and buccal medications are provided in tablet, film, and spray forms.

The provider will assist the patient to swallow **oral medications** that will be processed in the stomach or small intestine.

The provider will place **sublingual medications** under the tongue to facilitate rapid absorption of the medication into the bloodstream.

The provider will place **buccal medications** between the cheek and the gum where the medication will be absorbed through the capillary bed.

Topical/Transdermal

Topical medications are applied to the skin, mucous membrane, or body tissue, and may be provided as transdermal patches; ointments, lotions, and creams; or powders. The provider will assess the administration site for local reaction, and will rotate the site as appropriate for transdermal patches. In addition, the provider will avoid personal contact with the medications that are commonly absorbed rapidly through the skin.

Inhalation

The provider understands that **inhalant drugs** are used to deliver the medication directly to the target organ, which results in more rapid and efficient local absorption of the medication, in addition to decreased systemic exposure to the effects of the medication.

The provider will use medication-specific metered dose inhalers, dry powder inhalers, or nebulizers to administer inhaled agents that may include antimicrobials and corticosteroids. The licensed provider is also responsible for verifying the patient's understanding of the proper use and administration of these medications.

Instillation (Eye, Ear, and Nose)

The provider understands that medications may be instilled into the eye, ear, or nose to promote absorption or to treat local irritation of the site.

To instill **eye drops**, the provider will clear any accumulated secretions, use the nondominant hand to expose the conjunctival sac, instill the prescribed solution into the inner canthus while avoiding any contact with the eye, and use a sterile cotton ball to dry the eyelid.

To instill **eye ointment**, the provider will clear any accumulated secretions, use the nondominant hand to expose the conjunctival sac, apply the prescribed ointment along the sac from the inner canthus to the outer canthus while avoiding any contact between the eye and the medication container, and use a sterile cotton ball to dry the eyelid.

To instill medications into the ear, the provider will warm the solution to normal body temperature, position the patient with the head turned to the unaffected side, gently pull the ear up and back, instill the medication avoiding contact between the medicine dropper and the ear canal, place a sterile cotton ball loosely in the outer ear and instruct the patient to remain supine for fifteen minutes.

To instill **nasal drops**, the provider will instruct the patient to gently blow their nose, position the patient supine with the head tilted back, and instill the drops while avoiding contact between the inner nares and the medicine dropper.

Intradermal

The provider will use a 1 milliliter tuberculin syringe with a 5/8 inch 25- to 27-gauge needle to inject the prescribed medication into the interior portion of the forearm. The provider must identify the appropriate injection angle for the prescribed treatment; for example, allergy testing requires that the injection is 15-to-20 degrees, while insulin may be injected **intradermally** at 90 degrees.

Transdermal

The provider understands that transdermal medications, which are absorbed through the skin, provide the continuous release of a precise amount of the medication for a specific period of time. When applying a new dose of the medication, the provider will remove remaining residue from the previous dose, verify that the skin is intact and free of irritation, and sign and date the patch. Birth control pills, smoking cessation medications, pain relief agents, and nitroglycerin are some of the medications that are applied **transdermally**.

Vaginal

The provider understands that **vaginal medications**, which are available as suppositories, foams, ointments, and sprays, are used to alter the pH of the vagina, treat local infection, and provide comfort. The provider will insert the suppository form into the vaginal vault where it will liquefy as a result of body temperature. The provider will apply the ointment and spray medications according to the manufacturers' directions.

Rectal

Antiemetics, analgesics, and cathartics are commonly available as suppositories. The provider will insert the rectal suppository above the internal anal sphincter to prevent displacement.

Injections

Site Selection

The provider will select the appropriate injection site with consideration of the age and stature of the patient and the administration requirements of the prescribed medication. The provider is aware that injection sites must be systematically rotated for medications such as insulin that are repeated daily.

Needle Length and Gauge

The provider will select the needle gauge and length that is consistent with the selected injection site and the administration requirements of the prescribed medication.

Medication Documentation

Documenting Administration of Medications

The CMA observes the six rights of the patient with every medication administration. The patient has the right to 1) the right medication, 2) the right route, 3) the right time frame in which the medication is to be delivered, 4) the right client to whom the medication is to be administered, 5) the right dosage, and 6) the right documentation that the drug has been administered. These rights work to ensure patient safety.

In addition to the rights of the patient, the CMA should ensure that the appropriate physician and pharmacist orders have been given. The CMA should assess the patient for any allergies. This information can be found in the patient's medical record or chart if they have been previously admitted.

The allergy information on the patient should include the specific type of reaction they had, whether it was a mild rash or a severe, anaphylactic reaction.

After administration of a drug observing the six rights of the patient, it is important that the CMA correctly evaluate the treatment and observe if the expected outcome was achieved. This information can be obtained through physical assessment, the taking of the patient's vital signs, lab work, and subjective data from the patient.

Reporting Medication Errors

Medication errors can cause significant patient harm if not addressed promptly. CMAs have the responsibility to report medication errors, should they occur. Every healthcare facility should have a protocol for reporting medication errors. Errors can be reported internally within the facility or to a couple of organizations, including the Institute of Safe Medication Practices and the US Food and Drug Administration (FDA) via their MedWatch reporting system. An incident report is used to gather information related to the event, not as a means to discipline an employee. For quality improvement purposes, the information is then used to analyze factors that led to the error.

Medication errors can occur during any stage of administering treatment. Medications administered to the wrong patient occur as a result of failure to verify a patient's identity by using their full name, date of birth, or other specific identifiers. Administering the wrong medication to a patient should also be reported. Three medication checks must occur to ensure the correct medication is administered. These checks occur during preparation, dispensing, and returning of the medication. Other medication errors include administering the drug via the incorrect route, administering the incorrect dose, and administering the medication at the wrong time based on the provider's prescription.

Immunization Resources

Centers for Disease Control and Prevention (CDC)

Childhood/Adult Immunizations

The provider understands that a vaccine for a specific disease will stimulate the patient's immune system to produce antibodies that will protect the patient against the occurrence or severity of that disease.

The provider must be aware of current vaccination recommendations in children from birth to eighteen years of age for the following diseases: diphtheria, tetanus, pertussis (DPT); Haemophilus influenzae type B (HIB); hepatitis B; measles, mumps, rubella (MMR); pneumococcal infections; poliovirus; varicella; human papillomavirus (HPV); and meningococcal conjugate in adolescents.

The provider must be aware of current vaccination recommendations for adults that include initial and additional vaccination for the following diseases: diphtheria, tetanus, pertussis (DPT); pertussis (Tdap); Haemophilus influenza type B (HIB); hepatitis A and B; measles, mumps, rubella (MMR); pneumococcal infections, influenza, and herpes zoster.

Recordkeeping for Immunizations

Vaccine administration records are important for a variety of reasons, including availability for health department audits and work or school requirements. The information on the vaccine record should be accurate, complete, and up to date. The type of information required on a vaccine record includes the type of vaccine administered, the date it was administered, and the route and site of administration.

Each vaccine has an identifying lot number and manufacturer. The record should also include the signature and title of the person who administered the vaccine. Should a recall occur or a problem with the vaccine be identified, recordkeeping enables easy tracking.

Vaccine Information Statement (VIS)

The Centers for Disease Control and Prevention (CDC) issues a Vaccine Information Statement that documents the benefits and risks associated with an individual vaccine.

The provider must supply the Vaccine Information Statement to the patient or the patient's legal representative before the vaccine is administered.

Vaccine Adverse Event Reporting System (VAERS)

Patients may develop an adverse effect when they receive a vaccine. Should injury be caused by the vaccine administration, healthcare providers are required by law to report adverse effects such as anaphylaxis and skin reactions to the toxoid that occur shortly after a vaccine is administered. The **Vaccine Adverse Event Reporting System (VAERS)** is a program analyzed by the Centers for Disease Control and Prevention (CDC) and the FDA. The report should include information on the patient, reporter, facility, vaccine, and accompanying details. All reports filed on the VAERS system are analyzed to determine whether the adverse events were directly caused by the vaccine or resulted from a medical condition or other occurrence.

Vaccine Storage

The provider must meet all of the requirements for vaccine-specific storage as identified by the CDC. Specifications for storage temperature, preparation, inventory control, and transport are included in the CDC Vaccine Toolkit.

Practice Quiz

1. Which of the following is the best way to prevent the spread of infection?
    a. Keeping the mouth covered when coughing or sneezing
    b. Disinfecting shared patient equipment
    c. Practicing proper hand hygiene
    d. Avoiding contact with infectious patients

2. What are the correct steps to follow when using a fire extinguisher?
    a. Pull the pin, Squeeze the handle, Aim the nozzle, Swirl around the fire
    b. Pull the pin, Aim at the base of the fire, Squeeze the handle, Sweep from side to side
    c. Squeeze the handle, Aim at the base of the fire, Pull the pin, Sweep from side to side
    d. Stand back, Pull the pin, Squeeze the handle, Sweep from side to side

3. When preparing to transfer a patient from their bed to a wheelchair, what is the first step to take?
    a. Ensure that the bed is locked.
    b. Inform the patient about what is going to happen.
    c. Get another staff member to help.
    d. Have the patient sit up in bed.

4. When attempting to lift something heavy, which of the following should NOT be done?
    a. Keep the legs straight and bend over to use back muscles.
    b. Spread legs apart and bend at the knees.
    c. Stand close to the object.
    d. Use only feet and legs to turn.

5. An aide is caring for a patient in their home. Which of the following items should the aide recognize as a fire hazard?
    a. Multiple electrical cords plugged into a power strip
    b. A pack of matches on a coffee table
    c. A potholder lying on the stove
    d. A toaster left out on the counter

See answers on the next page.

Answer Explanations

1. C: All of the answer choices are types of standard precautions, but research has shown that handwashing is the best way to prevent the spread of germs.

2. B: Use the acronym PASS to answer this question. The pin should always be pulled first. Choices *A*, *C*, and *D* are not listed in the correct order or with the correct wording. The correct directions and order are: Pull the pin, Aim at the base of the fire, Squeeze the handle, and Sweep from side to side.

3. B: Anytime a task or procedure is about to occur, the patient should be informed first. All of the other options are part of the procedure, but the first step is to explain the task to the patient. Another staff person may not be needed, the patient may not be able to sit up in bed on their own, or they may wonder why they are being asked to sit up.

4. A: When lifting a heavy object, the lower back should not be strained; therefore, bending over and using the back muscles should be avoided. Choices *B*, *C*, and *D* should be done when lifting. Stand close to the object, bend at the knees with legs apart, and use feet and legs to turn if needed.

5. C: Anything flammable that is on top of a stove should be moved off of the stove surface to avoid a fire if the burners are turned on. Keep in mind that this patient is in their own home. All of the other choices are acceptable and pose no immediate fire hazard. Multiple cords should be plugged into a power strip, and a toaster left on the counter is not a hazard. The pack of matches on the table could be a hazard, but the patient is still living independently and may still be capable of using matches correctly. If there are no children in the home, the matches are not of immediate concern.

Legal and Ethical Issues

Health Insurance Portability and Accountability Act (HIPAA)

The patient has the right to have health information kept private, and only shared with those who are given permission to view it. The Health Insurance Portability and Accountability Act (HIPAA) was passed by Congress in 1996 to protect health information. HIPAA is responsible for patient privacy in each of the various means that personal health information can be shared: verbally, digitally, over the phone or fax, or through written messages.

The CMA plays an important role in keeping a patient's health information private. Sharing personal details—such as a patient's name, condition, and medical history—in an inappropriate way violates the person's right to privacy. For example, telling a friend who does not work in the facility that the CMA took care of the friend's aunt, without the aunt's consent or knowledge, is considered a violation of privacy. Another way a CMA could violate a patient's privacy is to access the medical record when they are not actually caring for that particular patient. For example, if a celebrity has been admitted to a different unit, and the CMA—curious to find out the details—accesses the celebrity's electronic health record, then they are in violation of HIPAA. Those who violate HIPAA and are caught could lose their jobs, among other punitive actions.

Protected Health Information

Authorization to Release

A patient is usually asked to sign a **consent to release** PHI before receiving treatment. This allows the healthcare provider to release their information for treatment, payment, and healthcare operations, abbreviated to TPO. Treatment is all care given to the patient by the healthcare provider; payment involves claims, billing, and collection by insurance companies; and healthcare operations involves educational purposes such as training new CMAs. Healthcare operations does not include using patient information for research; a different consent must be signed for that purpose.

Drug and Alcohol Treatment Records

Certain patient health records regarding the treatment of **drug and alcohol addictions** are specifically protected by federal regulations. Violation of the confidentiality of these records could result in a criminal penalty to the offender. There are certain emergency situations in which this information may be shared as well as research purposes in which release of information is allowed.

HIV-Related Information

HIV-related information is protected by law. Reports on diagnoses and treatments are to be kept private and confidential by healthcare providers. The reason this information is kept confidential is that persons with an HIV-AIDS diagnosis may face discrimination because of some people's unfair prejudices.

Mental Health Records

Part of HIPAA provides special protection to **mental health records**. For example, though mental health information is largely grouped together with general health information about a patient, psychotherapy

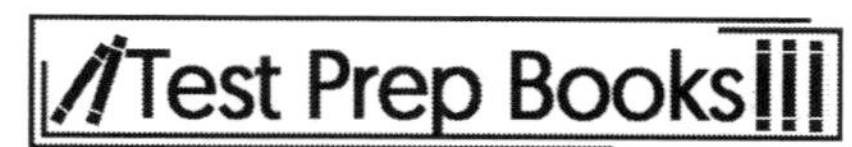

notes have special safeguards that keep them confidential. In the case of minors with mental health issues, there are specific guidelines that dictate who can be talked to about which issues, such as discussing a teen's medication regimen for mental illness with a legal guardian or parent.

Genetic Information Nondiscrimination Act of 2008 (GINA)

In 2008, Congress enacted **GINA** to prevent employers and health insurers from discriminating against people based on their genetic information. **Genetic discrimination** means to discriminate against a person based on defects or perceived defects in their DNA.

Use and Disposal of PHI

- Consent/Authorization to Release: A patient is usually asked to sign a consent to release PHI before receiving treatment. This allows the healthcare provider to release their information for treatment, payment, and healthcare operations, abbreviated to TPO. **Treatment** is all care given to the patient by the healthcare provider; **payment** involves claims, billing, and collection by insurance companies; and **healthcare operations** involves educational purposes such as training new CMAs. Healthcare operations does not include using patient information for research; a different consent must be signed for that purpose.

- Drug and Alcohol Treatment Records: Certain patient health records regarding the treatment of drug and alcohol addictions are specifically protected by federal regulations. Violation of the confidentiality of these records could result in a criminal penalty to the offender. There are certain emergency situations in which this information may be shared as well as research purposes in which release of information is allowed.

- HIV-Related Information: HIV-related information is protected by law. Reports on diagnoses and treatments are to be kept private and confidential by healthcare providers. The reason this information is kept confidential is that persons with an HIV-AIDS diagnosis may face discrimination because of some people's unfair prejudices.

- Mental Health Records: Part of HIPAA provides special protection to mental health records. For example, though mental health information is largely grouped together with general health information about a patient, psychotherapy notes have special safeguards that keep them confidential. In the case of minors with mental health issues, there are specific guidelines that dictate who can be talked to about which issues, such as discussing a teen's medication regimen for mental illness with a legal guardian or parent.

Consent

Informed Consent

An important part of the patient's bill of rights is **informed consent**. This means the patient has been adequately informed about their healthcare plan, whether that involves new medications, vaccinations, procedures, diagnostic screenings, and so on. The patient is granting their permission to go ahead with the care plan. It is up to the healthcare team to obtain this informed consent. This usually takes the form of a patient-signed document that goes in the permanent healthcare record.

Implied Consent

This type of consent does not involve the patient signing a document or even verbally granting permission, but rather it is assumed that any reasonable person would consent to the healthcare interventions being performed. The most common use of **implied consent** is in emergency situations, in which lifesaving interventions are necessary and there is not enough time to perform informed consent with the patient, such as cardiopulmonary resuscitation (CPR) after cardiac arrest.

Expressed Consent

Expressed consent means that the patient consents to a medical intervention either verbally, nonverbally through a gesture such as a nod, or in writing. This type of consent differs from informed consent in that there is not necessarily an education process that precedes it. This type of consent generally requires a witness.

Patient Incompetence

A patient who is unable to make their own informed decisions about their healthcare plan is termed **incompetent**. In the case of an incompetent patient, it may be necessary to use a proxy, such as a power of attorney, to make healthcare decisions for them.

Emancipated Minor

If a minor is legally **emancipated**, it means they are freed from having parental consent to certain things. The legal age for emancipation is generally sixteen. A patient may be medically emancipated if they become pregnant, thus freeing them to give consent with associated medical procedures and maintaining confidentiality of their records at that point.

Mature Minor

The **mature minor** concept applies to unemancipated minors and says that if a patient is deemed mature enough and the medical intervention is not especially serious, they may make their own decisions and give their own consent without parental consent.

Federal and State Regulations

Professional Liability Torts

To be liable means to be responsible for something in a legal sense. As a member of the CMA profession, a CMA has legal obligations called **professional liability** that may arise if they commit a serious error. Usually this takes the form of money owed to a patient filing a lawsuit for some sort of negligent act on the part of the professional. Legal penalties could be as severe as losing one's license to practice.

Negligence

Negligence is a wrongful civil act that results from failure to provide an acceptable standard of care that is comparable to the care that a competent CMA would provide. The most serious form is malpractice, in which a patient is harmed due to a direct patient care action or lack of patient care action. For example, a CMA fails to follow the six rights of medication administration, gives the wrong medication to a patient, and the patient suffers a code arrest.

Slander

Slander is an intentional tort that involves purposeful verbal harm to another person's reputation. A CMA might slander a patient or a co-worker. For example, a CMA is working with a nurse who delegates many tasks to the CMA. To damage the nurse's reputation, the CMA informs the supervisor that the nurse was seen stealing narcotics from the medication room, even though the event did not occur.

Libel

Libel is an intentional tort that involves documenting something false about someone else in order to cause damage to their reputation. For example, a CMA does not get along with a healthcare provider assigned to the unit. The CMA documents in a patient's chart that the healthcare provider failed to perform patient care interventions, even though this is false.

Abandonment

Patient **abandonment** is a negligent tort that occurs when healthcare personnel do not provide adequate treatment to a patient. For example, a CMA is assigned to do a direct observation assignment on a confused patient with high risk for falls. The CMA leaves the patient room at the change of shift before the next CMA arrives.

Assault

Assault is an intentional tort that involves a threat of injury. However, actual injury does not occur. For example, a CMA is providing care to a patient who refuses to bathe. The CMA tells the patient that they will be restrained if they do not agree to bathe. However, the CMA does not physically restrain the patient.

Battery

Battery is a physical, intentional tort that consists of offensive or harmful contact with a person. For example, a CMA is providing care to a patient who is verbally aggressive toward the CMA. The CMA grabs the patient's arm and causes bruising to the skin. This physical contact can lead to the patient filing a civil suit against the CMA.

Current Standard of Care

The CMA must stay within their scope of practice and always meet **current care standards** to avoid the consequences of malpractice. Each state has specific guidelines defining a CMA's scope of practice. In most states, a CMA may administer medications, perform office administrative duties, assist an MD with office procedures, draw blood, and prepare a patient for examination, among other assistive-type duties. A CMA generally cannot independently triage, diagnose, or treat a patient. If a CMA makes an error involving independent diagnosis and treatment of a patient that results in patient harm, the CMA will most certainly be liable and subject to legal penalties.

Legal Terms and Doctrines

The following is a list of common legal terms the CMA should be acquainted with should they come up in their practice.

- **Subpoena duces tecum**: This Latin term translates to "under penalty you shall bring with you." This is a legal document ordering a person to come to court and bring any relevant documents to the case.

- **Subpoena**: This simply entails the person must produce evidence for a case.

- **Respondeat superior**: This Latin term literally means "let the master answer." This legal term refers to an employer being responsible for the actions of their employees, usually used in the case of tort.

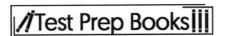

- **Res ipsa loquitur**: In Latin, this term means "the thing speaks for itself." It applies to medical malpractice where negligence is implied when an accident occurs.

- **Locum tenens**: This phrase is Latin for "one holding a place" and in medicine usually refers to one physician filling the place of another.

- **Defendant/plaintiff**: A defendant is the person against whom the plaintiff is filing a complaint or suit. A patient would be the plaintiff, and the physician would be the defendant if the patient filed a lawsuit against the physician.

- **Deposition**: A deposition is a legal statement that is recorded outside of the court, usually an oral testimony that is written down as evidence.

- **Arbitration/mediation**: Both these terms refer to a way of settling legal disputes outside of court. Arbitration is a cheaper, faster alternative to settling disputes. An arbitrator, a third party, is selected to help resolve the dispute. They decide who to award, if anyone. If one decides to go the arbitrary route, the case may not be tried in court, since it is considered legally resolved. Mediation differs from arbitration in that it is more flexible, can occur before arbitration, is more informal, and the mediator simply facilitates communication between opposing parties in search of a resolution.

- **Good Samaritan laws**: These laws protect persons who choose to assist someone in need of emergency medical assistance outside of a healthcare facility. If an unintended consequence results, or the person's life is not saved, the person is protected if they had good intention and offered reasonable assistance.

Contracts (Physician-Patient Relationships)

- **Legal obligations to the patient:** Due to the sensitive nature of information exchanged between a doctor and their patient, confidentiality is an obligation that must be honored, or there will be legal consequences.

- **Consequences for patient noncompliance:** There are some cases in which a patient becomes **noncompliant**, or refuses to follow medical advice regarding their care. In some cases, the physician might feel the need to protect themselves from any potential legal consequences of the patient's noncompliance, telling the patient to seek a new provider. There may be documents that the physician can have the patient sign, indicating that they were advised one way and that they refused to follow medical direction, thus freeing the physician from any liability.

- **Termination of medical care**

  1. Elements/behaviors for **withdrawal of care**: The patient has the right to refuse to follow medical advice; however, they cannot hold the physician liable for any consequences they suffer, such as a medical emergency or worsening of their condition. The CMA and other healthcare staff must respect the patient's right and always treat them with respect despite difference of opinions.

  2. Patient notification and documentation: It is important when terminating care of a patient to properly notify them and thoroughly document the case for legal protection.

- **Ownership of medical records:** Each state in the United States has different rules as to who owns medical records. In some states, the hospital and/or the physician has ownership; in other states, the patient owns the information; and in some states, there is no legal specification as to who owns medical records. Under HIPAA, all patients have a right to access their own medical record and may argue this legally.

Pharmaceutical Laws

Prescriptions

In ambulatory care centers or acute care facilities, a CMA assists the healthcare provider in organizing the patient's medical record, including prescriptions. Before a prescription is given to the patient, several requirements must be met. The CMA should ensure the prescription has the patient's first and last name, address, the medication name, strength, quantity, frequency, dose, and directions for use. The practitioner's full name and signature should also be included, along with the Drug Enforcement Agency (DEA) number if the prescription is for a controlled substance. The prescription should also include the number of medication refills.

E-Prescribing

The licensed provider can use a secure computer network to send medication prescription orders to participating pharmacies as allowed by federal and state laws.

Drug Schedules

The Controlled Substances Act (CSA) is a federal drug policy regulated by the DEA. Certain medications such as stimulants, narcotics, depressants, hallucinogens, and anabolic steroids have the potential for abuse and a likelihood of causing dependence. There are five schedules under the CSA. Schedule I drugs have a high potential for abuse with no medical necessity. Schedule V drugs have a low risk of dependence if managed appropriately. All prescriptions that include medications within the CSA should include the prescribing provider's DEA number for tracking and recordkeeping purposes.

Controlled Substances (Use and Abuse)

The provider will understand that:

- Pharmacies require either a handwritten and signed prescription, a faxed copy of a handwritten and signed prescription, or a prescription transmitted on a secure computer network in order to dispense controlled substances.
- Individual state laws may impose limits on the number of times that a prescription for a controlled substance can be written for an individual patient.
- Prescription authority is granted to licensed providers in accordance with federal and state laws and professional practice acts in the individual states.

Mandatory Reporting/Public Health Statutes

Communicable Diseases

Entities must disclose information about **communicable diseases** to public health authorities to prevent the spread of disease in a community or nation. The information is usually reduced to the minimum of what is needed to protect the privacy of patients.

Vital Statistics

Birth records, birth rates, and death records are examples of **vital statistics** that must be disclosed to public health authorities for tracking and monitoring the population.

Abuse/Neglect/Exploitation of Child, Elder, Partner

Entities that discover **abuse** or **neglect** in a child or elderly person must report this mandatorily in the interest of the abused. This may be done without the authorization of the victim.

If **domestic abuse** is likewise suspected, it also must be reported to the proper authorities. In some cases, this is the local police department. The police department is authorized to receive and respond to such reports.

Wounds of Violence

Domestic, child, and elder abuse leave damaging and long-lasting psychological wounds on their victims that remain long after any physical wounds have healed. These internal wounds have an effect not only on the victim but also children and other relationships in the victim's life. Recognizing that abuse may be occurring and reporting it appropriately is part of the CMA's role as a patient advocate. These wounds cannot heal until the problem is acknowledged.

Ethical Standards (Behaviors, Decisions, and Reporting)

The CMA adheres to a **code of ethics** like others in the medical profession, but especially to the physician who employs them. There will always be gray areas in patient care that raise ethical questions about how to proceed with the patient's care. When there is an ethical question, the CMA must respect human dignity first and foremost, maintain confidentiality, and seek to provide the greatest service to the patients they serve. These principles are part of the creed set forth by the American Association of Medical Assistants (AAMA).

Medical Directives

Advance Directives

An **advance directive** is a legal document that a patient draws up to ensure their wishes are honored even if they are unable to make their own decisions due to an incapacitating healthcare condition.

Living Will (Do Not Resuscitate [DNR] and Do Not Intubate [DNI])

A **living will** is a legal document that allows a patient to make clear their wishes regarding different end-of-life medical decisions should they become incapacitated in some way and unable to make these decisions. Part of a living will can name a person to make medical decisions for the patient, though a living will is not the same as a medical durable power of attorney.

Medical Durable Power of Attorney

A **power of attorney** document names a patient-appointed representative to make healthcare decisions on their behalf should they become incapacitated. The difference between this document and the living will is that the living will is more focused on **end-of-life care**, while the power of attorney can span a longer period and can end when the patient regains the ability to make their own decisions.

Patient Self Determination Act (PSDA)

The **patient self-determination act**, passed in 1990, mandates that healthcare facilities inform and protect a patient's right to make decisions about their care. This right extends even if they become incapacitated through advance directives such as the living will and power of attorney.

Communication

Interpersonal Relationship Skills/Customer Service

Understanding Human Behavior and Mental Health

Behavior describes the actions an individual takes in their day-to-day lives toward others. Interpreting patient behavior, and what it means for their care, is a judgment skill a CMA must possess.

The two main theories that are often used to categorize and interpret human behavior are those of psychologists Abraham Maslow (developed in 1935) and Erik Erikson (1959).

Maslow

Maslow's hierarchy of human needs is a diagram in the shape of a pyramid. Each level of the pyramid represents a human need in order from the most basic on the bottom to the most complicated on the top. These needs are at the heart of human behavior and what motivates people. At the bottom are physiological needs such as food, water, warmth, and rest. A person must meet these basic needs before moving on to the next level, which is the need to feel secure and safe. The next set of needs are psychological in nature—first the need to belong and feel loved, followed by the need to be esteemed. Being esteemed entails feeling accomplished and respected. The final need at the top of the pyramid is that of self-actualization, in which a person feels they have achieved their full potential in life. This final step can include creative activities. The CMA must keep this hierarchy of needs in mind when managing a patient's care. Maslow's pyramid will assist in understanding what motivates a patient's actions and behavior.

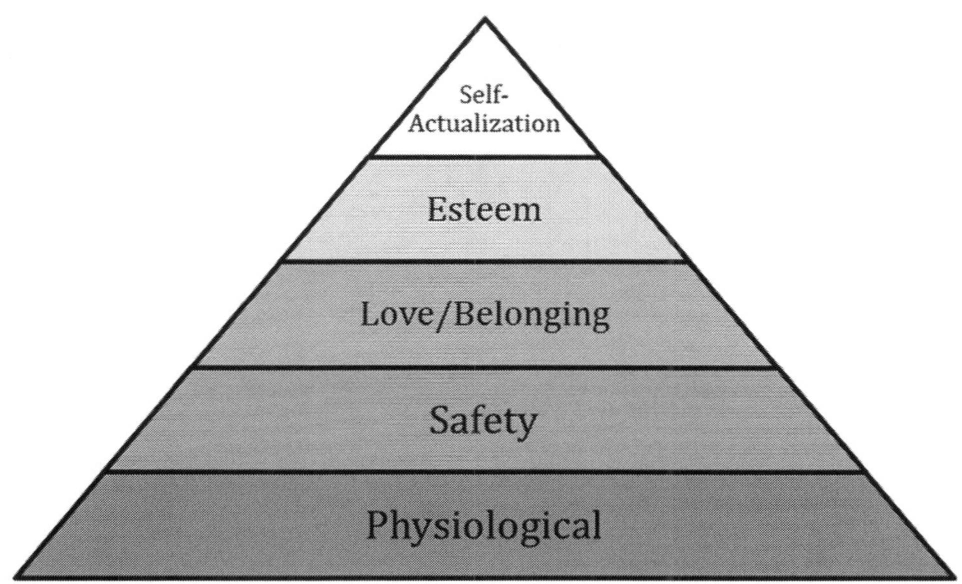

Erikson

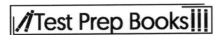

Erikson developed eight stages a person must pass through, from birth to death, that encompass their growth and development as an individual. Each stage names a virtue that is developed if the crisis of ego is overcome successfully.

- **Birth–18 months:** In the first year and a half of a child's life, they will develop **trust vs. mistrust**, based off the nurture they receive from their parents. **Hope** is the product of proper nurture and trust. If they do not receive proper care, mistrust, along with insecurity and a feeling of worthlessness, may develop.

- **Ages 2–3:** Between the ages of two and three, the child will work through **autonomy vs. shame**. The parents must guide the child through their attempts at being independent so that **autonomy** can develop. When this happens, the child develops will. Without proper guidance, whether too permissive or too strict, the child cannot find a sense of autonomy, and shame develops.

- **Ages 4–5:** A child aged four to five will go through the **initiative vs. guilt** stage of development. This involves a modeling behavior of adults. Parents must be supportive of this initiative stage to help the child develop **purpose**. Without this encouragement of initiative, the child will feel guilt, leading to inhibition.

- **Ages 6–12:** Ages six to twelve are defined by **industry vs. inferiority**. Industry involves the capability to learn, create, and build skills and knowledge. Imagination and impulsive behavior must be tamed to develop **competence**. If the child does not move through this stage properly, inferiority develops.

- **Ages 13–19:** The thirteen- to nineteen-year-old must grapple with the crisis of **identity vs. role confusion**. A teen may experiment with different identities, most likely going through identity crises. If the crises are navigated successfully, the person develops **fidelity**, an ability to have relationships with many different people of different value systems. Failure to resolve an identity crisis results in identity diffusion and role confusion, or failure to "fit in" in a satisfactory way with the society around them. This sometimes may manifest itself in fanaticism.

- **Ages 20–24:** From age twenty to twenty-four, the young adult will work though the crisis of **intimacy vs. isolation**, in which they can have close relationships and develop **love**. Failure to do so results in isolation, in which a person is either promiscuous or exclusive. With promiscuity, the person becomes too intimate, too quickly, with many different people, but no loving relationships develop. The opposite may occur, termed **exclusivity**, in which the person rejects all relationships and those in them.

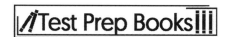

- **Ages 25–64:** This is the stage in which a person goes through the crisis of **generativity vs. stagnation**. With generativity, the person feels satisfied with the work they have completed in their lifetime. They may feel successful, having developed a legacy of which they can be proud. This develops the virtue of **caring**, manifested by caring for future generations and free giving. If this generativity has not occurred, the person will feel stagnant. This stagnation is marked by little contribution to society, meaninglessness, and potentially a midlife crisis.

- **Age 65–death:** From age sixty-five to death, the developmental stage is **integrity vs. despair**. Integrity involves an acceptance of one's accomplishments and the development of **wisdom**. If integrity does not develop, despair results, entailing a dread of death. If the person develops too much wisdom, they may display presumption. On the opposite hand, too little wisdom results in disdain, or contempt toward others and life.

Defense Mechanisms

Defense mechanisms in human beings can refer to either a physical response, such as the immune system's response to infections, or a mental response involving a behavioral pattern when one's emotional balance is threatened. The latter will be the defense mechanisms discussed here.

Common Types

There are many well-known, well-studied defense mechanisms, ranging from primitive to mature, that human beings exhibit. Primitive reactions can be effective in the moment but damaging in the long run, while more mature reactions are healthier and better for relationships.

- **Denial:** One of the common primitive defense mechanisms, denial is when a person rejects a reality to protect themselves from having to process it emotionally. For example, a patient may have received a diagnosis of a terminal, untreatable cancer but refuse to acknowledge the reality of their condition to avoid the painful emotions that might accompany it.

- **Undoing:** A less primitive defense mechanism, undoing involves a person trying to right a wrong they have done to someone they care about. For example, after saying something hurtful to a child, a father might heap praise upon the child and take him out to get ice cream to undo the pain of the earlier statement.

- **Sublimation:** Sublimation is an example of a mature defense mechanism. A person is sublimating when they redirect the energy they once might have put into a negative activity or impulse into something more positive and productive. Someone who might have the impulse to cheat on their significant other but does not actually want to may instead focus that energy into exercise and meditation.

Recognition and Management

It is part of the CMA's responsibility to be aware of these psychological aspects of the patient's care. Knowledge of Maslow's hierarchy of needs is important in categorizing human needs. Erikson's stages of psychological development are helpful in pointing out what ego conflict a person is going through as well as what virtues have developed. Being able to recognize common defense mechanisms and how to work through them is vital, especially in heavily emotional situations that may arise during a patient's care.

Approach to Communication Barriers with Empathy and Compassion

Death and Dying

Not only will each individual respond differently to grief based on personality and relationship with the deceased, but also the response will differ based on their own spiritual beliefs and cultural influences. These beliefs and influences affect how a person thinks they should act during the mourning period, what to wear, what rituals need to be performed, and what happens after a person dies.

Each individual culture will not be discussed since there are many variations of how different people handle this process. It is not necessary for the CMA to know each and every one, but rather have a general knowledge of differences and be respectful towards them.

Some cultures believe an outward show of emotion is appropriate and necessary. Sometimes, this entails an outward expression of weeping and wailing. Other cultures may be more conservative and think it is appropriate to be stoic, serious, and somber, without crying and losing one's composure. Some have specific rituals before and after the death, involving holy men, priests, or other clergy who prepare the person and/or the body for an afterlife. Some may not have any religious affiliation and may not believe in a life after this one.

Regardless of what cultural and spiritual beliefs are present, the role of the healthcare team is to respect those wishes as much as possible. It is imperative that the team explore the resident and family's wishes in this respect, rather than overlooking or refusing to allow them. It is always appropriate to politely ask how best to respect the resident and family's wishes when performing tasks for the dying or deceased resident. For example, some family members may prefer to clean the body themselves after death, an important ritual to express grief and ensure proper care in their view.

Each member of the healthcare team, including the CMA, needs to assess their own beliefs about death and dying. Self-knowledge on the subject is valuable as it may not be something one has consciously acknowledged. This self-assessment also helps reveal any unfair biases and prejudices towards cultures and people whose worldview is different than one's own. Discovering what one's own beliefs and others' beliefs are leads to a better understanding between groups. These groups can then begin to find ways to work together during the difficult end-of-life period.

Terminal Illness

Navigating the tricky area of communicating with a patient who is diagnosed with a **terminal illness** can present a real challenge to the CMA. It is important to be honest with the patient. The CMA should be an active listener, looking for opportunities to connect the patient with valuable resources and support. The CMA should offer compassion but not false hope. The CMA may want to say something meaningful or helpful, but this is not always the best option. Sometimes simply being present, offering a hug, or holding a patient's hand is better than any words. The CMA should also look for opportunities to communicate with and support the family of the terminally ill patient. After the patient passes, they will need guidance to bereavement, loss, and grief resources.

Visually Impaired

A patient with a **visual impairment** will require adaptations to the CMA's communications techniques to ensure a clear message is sent and received. The CMA should identify themselves clearly when beginning their assessment. The CMA should never treat the patient who has a **visual impairment** as if they have a deficit in intellect or as if they are deaf. The CMA should check the environment to make

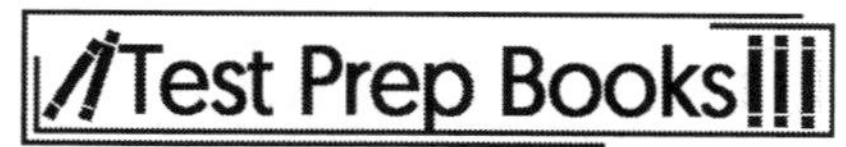

sure there are no distractions, such as a loud TV, that may make it difficult to be heard. The CMA should ask questions to ensure the message has been received and understood by the patient. Assessing the level of visual impairment will assist in knowing how much assistance the patient will need. Someone who is legally blind versus someone with complete vision loss from birth will have different needs for assistance.

Deaf and Hard of Hearing

When communicating with persons who are **deaf** or **hard of hearing**, an important first step is to assess the level of hearing loss. This will guide further communication. Depending on the amount of hearing loss, lip reading, visual tools, hearing aids, an increased volume of the CMA's voice, or the hiring of a sign language interpreter may or may not be useful. The CMA should directly face the person with a hearing impairment when addressing them so that understanding can be better assessed. The CMA should not be in another room, have their back to the patient, or compete with a loud TV or other distraction while trying to communicate. The CMA may ask the patient questions to ensure understanding of the message.

Non-English Speaking/English as a Second Language/Interpreter

In the case of a **non-English-speaking** patient, the CMA should seek out translation services. This can come from a family member who accompanies the patient or possibly be provided by the facility where the CMA works. Seeking educational materials in the patient's native tongue will be helpful in clearly communicating with the patient after they leave the facility.

Americans with Disabilities Act Amendments Act (ADAAA) Compliance

Passed in 2008, the **ADAAA** amends a previous act, the ADA, to better define what "disability" means for certain Americans as well as protecting and upholding the rights of those with **disabilities** in the United States. The ADAAA was a response to several Supreme Court decisions that were thought to have limited the rights of those with disabilities.

Illiterate

A person who is **illiterate** cannot read and/or write. It is not always apparent to a CMA which patients may have this problem. There is a type of illiteracy called **health illiteracy** in which a patient is highly unfamiliar with medical information and is, therefore, unable to apply it to their own health and healthcare management. In illiteracy and health illiteracy, asking questions and listening for comprehension are both tools the CMA can use to determine how well the patient understands their individual healthcare plan. If a patient cannot read or write, the CMA can offer their health information to them in a different format. The CMA can read through instructions for home care and ensure that a literate caregiver is accessible to the patient to assist them with written materials. Patients with low healthcare literacy tend to make their healthcare decisions based on emotions and practical considerations such as if they will be able to get a ride to the doctor. An example of emotional decision-making would be a patient who doesn't go to the doctor because he "doesn't like needles"; this is irrational, since not every doctor visit implies needles, yet it creates a barrier to successful healthcare. Identifying these barriers is the first step to overcoming illiteracy.

Intellectually Challenged

A patient who is **intellectually challenged** may need additional help communicating with the healthcare team. The CMA will need to practice patience and allow extra time for communicating messages with and receiving messages from a person with an intellectual disability. The CMA should work with caregivers to get helpful tips for working with a patient. Every patient is different, and a full-time caregiver or loved one will know what works best when trying to communicate with the patient. The CMA should try to explain care in the simplest terms possible, avoiding complicated medical jargon. The CMA should focus on the patient's strengths rather than pointing out and focusing on weaknesses. As with all communication, the CMA should concentrate on being an active listener, open to receiving the patient's concerns and giving them time to voice them.

Age-Specific Therapeutic/Adaptive Responses

There are considerations to be made regarding the age of the person the CMA is communicating with.

Geriatric

Geriatric refers to an older adult, a population of patients the CMA may work with quite frequently. The CMA should remember that active listening is as important as, if not more important than, speaking as far as communication goes. The CMA should ask questions but listen intently to the answers to ascertain if the patient understands. The CMA needs to remember that interrupting is rude and can compromise trust and good communication. The CMA should take their time when giving instructions, ensuring understanding. It is not wise to use jargon, slang, or other language that the geriatric patient may not understand. If the patient needs to use new technology such as an online patient account, an assessment of Internet usage and proficiency would be useful.

Pediatric

There are a few tricks a CMA should have up their sleeve when addressing a **pediatric** patient to make them feel comfortable and safe in a medical environment. The CMA should address the child by name to create a tone of familiarity. Getting down to the child's level physically—in other words, squatting down to eye level—will help the child feel they are on the same level as their caregiver, rather than the CMA towering over them. Smiling and exuding a positive attitude will create the right environment for the CMA to care for the child. Making medical tools and equipment into toys when appropriate, such as gloves or tongue depressors, can help the child feel at ease. The CMA should enlist the parents as team members in the child's care.

Adolescent

Communicating with teenagers can present its own unique challenges for the CMA. No longer a child and not quite an adult, the **adolescent** must feel they are part of the care team and that they have a say in decision-making. It may be useful to conduct interviews with adolescents without their parents being present, if possible. This will help when trying to conduct a frank discussion on the patient's sexual activity as well as potential drug/alcohol usage. The assessment of an adolescent should include questions about mental health issues, such as depression and anxiety. The teen may feel more comfortable discussing these issues without their parent present, though the parent should be made a member of the team when addressing any issues that are discovered. Another important topic to approach with teens is stress, its causes, and coping mechanisms. In some cases, it is important to inform the adolescent which topics will remain confidential. This may encourage them to share more with the CMA.

Nonverbal Communication

The CMA not only communicates with their words but also with their body language. Knowing what one is **communicating nonverbally** and taking care to send the right message is vital to quality patient care.

Body Language

- **Posture:** Slouching indicates disinterest, fatigue, and disengagement. The CMA should have erect posture, not only for the health benefit, but to show the patient they are engaged in their care.

- **Position:** The CMA should be facing the patient, both their face and body. Not facing the patient indicates the CMA does not care about sending a good message and that they do not care about their situation.

- **Facial expression:** It is not necessary for the CMA to have a big, bright smile on their face at all times, but a pleasant expression that is responsive to the patient's own facial expression gives off a positive energy that the patient may find encouraging.

- **Territoriality/physical boundaries:** Different cultures have different boundaries that are considered acceptable. The CMA should maintain a respectful distance from the patient, never too far away or too close for comfort. The patient's reaction is a good measure of whether the CMA is at an appropriate distance.

- **Gestures:** Most people use hand gestures to help communicate a message. The CMA may use hand gestures but must be aware of how much they are doing this. The CMA should avoid overgesturing, as this will take away from their overall message.

- **Touch:** Therapeutic touch is appropriate in certain instances with certain patients. This could involve touching their hand, putting one hand on their shoulder, or even a hug. Caution should be used when employing therapeutic touch, as some patients might find this uncomfortable. The CMA should use their best judgment on when this type of intervention is most appropriate and helpful.

- **Mannerisms:** Everyone has certain unique mannerisms, or a way they speak or gesture. The CMA should be aware of their own quirks and idiosyncrasies if possible and make certain they do not interfere with the patient's care or cause offense.

- **Eye contact:** Good eye contact is crucial to good patient care. Not enough eye contact shows lack of interest and boredom; too much eye contact can be construed as weird and scary. The CMA should be aware of their eye contact and use it as a listening tool to properly tune in to the patient's message they are trying to send.

Personal Boundaries (Sexual Harassment, Bullying, Unwanted Attention)

Boundaries in the workplace are an important part of maintaining professionalism. As a CMA, maintaining a professional attitude, demeanor, behavior, and appearance ensures a good working relationship with other colleagues. Healthy teamwork provides the best outcomes for patients. **Personal boundaries** are rules and limits that are set when forming relationships and interacting with others. Relationships at work should be kept professional. It is not uncommon for people to be unaware that personal boundaries are being crossed in the workplace, especially when there is an imbalance of power.

For example, a CMA is approached by a charge nurse assigning a new admission. The charge nurse touches the CMA's shoulder and states, "Hey, sweetie, I know you're busy, but I have to give you an admission." The charge nurse has crossed personal boundaries by touching the CMA and using endearments. It is often difficult to voice discomfort when another person crosses personal boundaries. Expressing discomfort should be done clearly, respectfully, and confidently. For example, the CMA might respond, "I will gladly take the admission. However, I am uncomfortable with you touching me or calling me sweetie. Please call me by my name." Setting these boundaries helps to prevent future occurrences. Should retaliation occur, the CMA should refer the concerns to a supervisor or manager.

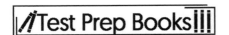

Every workplace should establish a culture of safety. A culture of safety ensures that anyone can report misconduct, bullying, sexual harassment, or unwanted attention without experiencing retaliation. Sexual harassment in the workplace is defined as any unwelcome sexual behavior or remark by another colleague. Bullying in the workplace is characterized by a persistent pattern of mistreatment by other colleagues that can cause emotional, mental, or physical harm to an individual.

All facility employees should receive training on how to identify dangerous and unwanted behaviors, how to address them, and how to report them so they don't occur in the future. Safe reporting should be free of barriers. Employees should have a clear understanding of how and whom to report their concerns to. Employees should also feel safe and confident that their concerns will be investigated. Furthermore, they should be free of retaliation. Reporting unwanted behaviors can leave the employee feeling vulnerable and insecure. The main goal of reporting is to improve accountability and create positive change in work culture.

De-Escalation Techniques

CMAs often encounter patients who are upset, agitated, or aggressive. Patients undergo a great amount of stress when hospitalized, sick, or feeling helpless. Therapeutic communication and maintaining safety are vital when managing a patient who becomes agitated, aggressive, or violent. Verbal aggression involves statements that are demeaning, hurtful, or threatening. Patients may be under the influence of medications or substances, or they may be cognitively impaired. CMAs should be prepared to de-escalate situations without causing harm to patients. During a heated situation, it is imperative to make the patient feel safe. The CMA's tone of voice should be kept soft, low, and calm when speaking to the patient. Statements should be clear and concise. Body language should be relaxed, with the hands in full view. It is important to maintain a safe distance. Close contact may appear threatening to the patient. Additionally, verbal aggression may turn physical, so it is important to stand at a safe distance.

For example, a CMA walks into a patient's room to perform hourly rounding. The patient is visibly agitated, pacing in the room, and starts to raise their voice at the CMA, demanding pain medication. A visibly agitated patient may turn violent, so it is important for the CMA to stand at a safe distance. The CMA would have to explain to the patient that only the nurse can administer pain medication. To de-escalate the situation, the CMA might tell the patient, "I understand you are in pain, and I will make sure your nurse is informed. How about we call your nurse while I'm here, and I'll check on you after you receive your pain medication?" This strategy may help the patient realize the CMA values their concern and their needs will be taken care of. It is important for the CMA to keep their word to establish trust with the patient.

Listening Skills

Active/Therapeutic

One of the best communication skills the CMA can employ is active or **therapeutic listening**. This involves being especially engaged when the patient is sending their message back to the CMA. Listening

carefully allows the CMA to better sync care with the patient's unique needs. Failure to listen properly will result in conflicts with the patient's care.

Service Recovery/Patient Satisfaction

Patient satisfaction is a highly valued benchmark of healthcare quality. Data relating to patient satisfaction can be collected internally by a healthcare organization or through external institutions that focus on healthcare quality. In the business of healthcare, patient satisfaction often serves as the "demand" in a supply and demand economy. Higher patient satisfaction scores are associated with better patient health outcomes, and consequently associated with happier patients, patients who are more likely to return to and recommend a particular healthcare organization, higher quality of medical staff that the healthcare organization retains, increased level of outside funding that the healthcare organization receives, and fewer medical malpractice suits. Patients report higher satisfaction when they receive care that they find to be tailored to their needs, care that is safe yet efficient, and care that is accessible. In this regard, healthcare delivery requires a nuanced level of customer service; however, rather than delivering a tangible manufactured product, medical staff deliver a product that affects the patient's ability to live well and their long-term physical, mental, and emotional state.

All medical staff are able to provide exceptional patient service by being welcoming and concerned about the patient, allowing space for the patient to voice their concerns and fears, treating the patient like a person rather than a medical case, respecting the patient and showing concern for the patient's family, and being reliable and punctual in their interactions with the patient. Many burdensome aspects of care that could be looked at negatively, such as patient wait times, can be alleviated by simple communication that explains the reasoning behind the issue. Communication and transparency are simple tools that often serve as the key players in managing patient expectations. Medical staff can also maintain communication with the patient after discharge, such as through an online patient portal, to ensure adequate care continues through the patient's full recovery and make the patient feel valued.

Therapeutic/Adaptive Responses

Cultural Diversity and Beliefs

The CMA must be competent in **culturally sensitive care** toward people of many different backgrounds. The CMA must first check their own feelings and biases about people who are different from themselves to treat these people fairly. Everyone has the right to fair and quality healthcare. The best thing a CMA can do when presented with someone of a different background is to offer respect, give dignified care, and ask questions before proceeding to avoid any unnecessary offense.

Recognizing Stereotypes and Biases and Displaying Impartial Conduct

Self-awareness is an important tool that a CMA must employ to assess their own feelings about people who are different from themselves. Armed with this self-knowledge, the CMA may then be more aware of any partialities they may be displaying toward people of the same background vs. impartiality toward people who are different from them. All patients coming to the CMA seeking quality healthcare have a right to impartial treatment, without bias, judgment, or prejudice.

Along with providing **culturally competent care**, the CMA must be able to treat people of all different backgrounds and lifestyle choices. Awareness of one's own biases and prejudices is the first step, followed by a conscious effort to provide dignified and respectful care to all.

Learning Styles

Assessing and Adapting to Level of Understanding (Sender-Receiver-Feedback)

An understanding of the basics of communication, involving the **communication cycle**, is important for the CMA to know to communicate effectively with their patients.

The communication cycle starts with a **sender**. The sender sends the message to the receiver and looks for feedback. This goes on and on through a circular cycle until transmission is ended, such as the end of a conversation.

Barriers to Communication

Internal Distractions

- **Pain:** If a patient is in pain, their ability to communicate will break down. Treating the pain first will facilitate communication between the patient and the healthcare team.

- **Hunger:** A patient who is hungry will have difficulty concentrating on sending and receiving messages effectively. In some instances, it is impossible to avoid a hungry patient, as many must fast for tests and procedures. Alleviating hunger, where possible, will ensure better communication.

- **Anger:** If there is something angering a patient, this could pose a potential blockade to effective communication. Identifying the inflammatory stimulus and working toward a resolution will improve future communications with the patient.

External/Environmental Distractions

- **Temperature:** A patient who is distracted by feeling too hot or too cold will have difficulty maintaining a normal conversation with the CMA. Warm blankets for a cold patient and fans/open windows/air conditioning for a hot patient are helpful for fixing this problem.

- **Noise:** The CMA would be wise to eliminate unnecessary noise when communicating with a patient. This may entail closing the door of the patient's room to block hallway chatter and/or turning a TV's volume down.

Healthcare Team Roles

Plan of Care and Referral Coordination

The plan of care begins with assessment of the patient, followed by recommended interventions. These interventions are then evaluated for their effectiveness and modified based on patient response, starting the whole care planning process over again.

An example of care performed according to a care plan is when a patient is assessed to be at risk for skin breakdown. Recommended interventions would include turning and repositioning the patient every two hours, providing regular perineal care and incontinence care, and ensuring that an adequate amount of the meal tray is consumed by the patient.

The CMA schedules all patients referred to the agency as soon as possible, communicates directly with the new patient, confirms all insurance information, and verifies that all patient data is appropriately

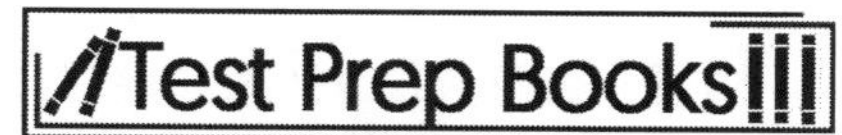

prepared for the provider's use prior to the patient's appointment. The CMA also forwards all resulting patient data to the referring physician as appropriate.

When it is established that the patient is a **physician referral**, the CMA gathers all relevant documentation, confers with the responsible person in the provider's agency, and schedules the patient's appointment. When possible, the patient's preference for date and time for the appointment is accommodated. If necessary, the CMA provides a written referral for the patient's appointment. The CMA provides the patient with the details for the appointment in person or in written form as appropriate. The details should include location, directions, contact numbers, and any additional pre-visit requirements.

Serving As Patient Navigator, Advocate, Case Manager, or Health Coach

Many patients who enter a healthcare facility are unable to coordinate their own care or voice their healthcare preferences. CMAs may take on the role of patient advocate to ensure a patient's needs are well represented. To guarantee that outcomes are in the best interest of the patient, CMAs should be aware of any conflicts between their own value systems and those of the patient. As a patient navigator, a CMA can help coordinate community resources, provide important contact information, assist with insurance and billing, and help patients make independent choices about their medical care.

Utilizing a Team Approach to Patient Care Management

Positive patient outcomes result from a team-based healthcare approach. A CMA is part of the healthcare team responsible for ensuring patients understand how to manage their care. A CMA may assist a patient with initiating referrals, contacting specialty services, or following up with their healthcare provider. For example, a patient who is homeless is discharged from the emergency room with an infected wound. The patient will require outpatient services, pain management, and wound care. The CMA can help navigate the patient's experience by collaborating with nurses for pain management, social workers for medication assistance, physical therapists for wound care, and case managers for housing placement.

Identifying Medical Specialties

Once certified, medical assistants can work in various settings supporting physicians, nurses, and advanced healthcare providers. A CMA's training provides general guidelines for patient care and ensures the CMA is competent providing safe and effective patient care in all areas of healthcare. Further training allows the CMA to work in specialty areas such as cardiology, dermatology, obstetrics, oncology, orthopedics, and neurology. Each specialty area provides services to a unique population of patients. CMAs are trained to assist in diagnostic procedures, claim processing, and specialized patient examinations. For example, a CMA working in obstetrics may assist a provider with gynecological examinations, colposcopies, and diagnostic ultrasounds.

Professional Telephone Etiquette/Techniques

At times, the CMA may be called upon to handle phone calls in a practice setting, using triage techniques as well as providing information to the callers.

Message Protocols

Taking Messages

When **taking a message**, the CMA must be able to gather the appropriate information about the caller, why they called, and who needs to receive their information. Too much or too little data will result in mishandled situations and conflicts that will require more work to resolve in the future.

Leaving Messages

The CMA will need to **leave messages** at times for both patients and healthcare providers. Providing succinct information in the message is appropriate. Again, too much or too little information will result in further conflicts to be handled in the future.

Screening/Gathering Data

The CMA must be able to collect data from the caller to **screen** them and direct them to the proper outlet. This ensures an office is run smoothly.

Practice Quiz

1. What is one example of nonverbal communication that assists therapeutic communication?
   a. Making good eye contact
   b. Scrolling through one's phone
   c. Giving a look of boredom or disinterest
   d. Looking at the door constantly

2. Which of the following is the proper abbreviation for "weight"?
   a. lb
   b. kg
   c. wa
   d. wt

3. Delirium differs from dementia in what way?
   a. Delirium is slow, progressive, and untreatable.
   b. Delirium has an acute onset and is treatable.
   c. Delirium includes increased alertness.
   d. The cause of delirium is unidentifiable.

4. What resident right allows a resident to make their own healthcare decisions?
   a. Self-expression
   b. Confidentiality
   c. Privacy
   d. Self-determination

5. A fax containing resident information and prescriptions is sent from a doctor's office. This is what type of communication?
   a. Verbal
   b. Written
   c. Nonverbal
   d. Non-sequential

See answers on the next page.

Answer Explanations

1. A: Making good eye contact shows the person that the CMA is interested in the resident's message. The other options are all nonverbal barriers to therapeutic communication.

2. D: The most commonly used abbreviation for weight is "wt," not "wa." Kilograms (kg) and pounds (lb) are both measurements of weight.

3. B: Delirium has an acute (sudden) onset and is usually treatable. Dementia has a slow onset and is irreversible. Delirium and dementia are both characterized by decreased alertness, and the cause is usually identifiable.

4. D: The right of the resident to make their own, informed healthcare decisions is the right to self-determination. The other terms refer to other resident rights.

5. B: This type of communication is called written. Verbal communication is spoken, nonverbal communication does not use words (either spoken or written), and the other term does not refer to communication types.

Administrative

Billing, Coding, and Insurance

Coding Applications

Procedural Coding (Current Procedural Terminology [CPT])

CPT is a standardized coding scheme that facilitates the reporting of medical, surgical, and diagnostic procedures for payment.

Modifiers

The CMA understands that a CPT modifier refines the original CPT definition of the procedure to reflect some addition or alteration in the original category. Modifiers add details to the original CPT that more closely reflect the patient encounter, which increases revenue and decreases the potential for denial of services.

Upcoding

The CMA recognizes that **upcoding** refers to the fraudulent practice of reporting a CPT that represents a higher level of care or more complex diagnosis than is supported by the patient's diagnosis or EHR and provider documentation. The level of service for evaluation and management of a single patient encounter is coded according to the complexity of the care. The CMA understands that an example of upcoding could be using a level 5 code to report the care of a patient with a minor complaint for a brief encounter.

Downcoding

CMAs that are responsible for billing and handling patient records need to be aware of how to properly use codes to submit claims to a patient's insurance or create bills for service. **Downcoding** refers to the process of assigning a low-level code to a medical service, lower than is accurate for the service that was provided. Insurance companies reimburse a healthcare facility at a lower rate when downcoding occurs. For example, a patient visits their healthcare provider for an annual physical. During the examination, multiple medical concerns are addressed, and the patient requires more services and tests than were originally intended. The patient's insurance denies the claims for additional services and only reimburses the care associated with a standard annual physical.

Bundling of Charges

Bundling of charges or episode-based payments is a reimbursement plan that reimburses providers for all episodes of care for an individual disease, diagnosis, or condition. For instance, the provider receives one payment for all outpatient and inpatient care for the patient with a total knee replacement, which contrasts with the traditional fee-for-service plan that includes charges and reimbursement for each care encounter or procedure. Proponents of the episode-based payment model view it as a cost savings measure that can contribute to improved patient outcomes, and positive provider and patient satisfaction. The potential cost savings are based on three assumptions: the contracted cost for episode-based care is less than fee-for-service cost for the same care; the savings that are generated are divided between the provider and the payer; and complications associated with the compensated illness or condition are not reimbursed. In addition, when hospitals participate in the episode-based payment model, providers who do not contract for bundled payment options that care for patients during a hospital stay receive fees for that care from the hospital, not the third-party payer.

Unbundling of Charges

When a claim is submitted to the patient's insurance, current procedural terminology (CPT) codes need to be entered for the services provided. When multiple CPT billing codes are used for one visit, this is termed "unbundling." Unbundling charges for each individual service leads to higher costs and larger reimbursements for the facility. Various CPT codes are inclusive, bundling services that properly account for the care provided. For example, a patient has a pelvic exam with a Pap smear and collection of tissue samples. Submitting a claim for all three individual services as opposed to an inclusive procedure would be considered **unbundling of charges**.

Diagnostic Coding (International Classification of Diseases, Clinical Modification [ICD-CM])

The **International Classification of Diseases (ICD)** is a system of codes that classifies diseases and medical diagnoses. ICD codes are regulated by the World Health Organization and are used to communicate and file patient insurance claims for reimbursement. Each ICD code is unique and defines a specific disease process or medical illness. The most current ICD version is 10, with a newer version (ICD-11), replacing it in January of 2022. When submitting a claim, a procedural code must be included defining the services provided. Modification of codes is often necessary when multiple, complex procedures are performed for a particular disease process. Modifiers require supplemental information explaining why additional procedures, tests, or exams were medically necessary.

Healthcare Common Procedure Coding System (HCPCS Level II)

The **Healthcare Common Procedure Coding System (HCPCS)** is a code system used by medical providers to submit service claims to health insurers and Medicare. Level II HCPCS is a national procedure code set for healthcare providers, practitioners, and medical equipment suppliers to use when they file health plan claims for any patient supplies, medications, devices, transportation services, and other needed items or supplies. Unlike CPT codes that define which medical services were performed, HCPCS codes define which supplies, medications, or items were used.

Linkage of Procedure and Diagnostic Coding to Meet Medical Necessity Guidelines

Every service claim that is submitted to a patient's health insurance or Medicare must include a CPT code. Additionally, the CPT code must be linked to an ICD code, which defines the medical condition that necessitates the service. For example, a healthcare provider determines a patient has symptoms of a third-degree heart block and orders an electrocardiogram to confirm the diagnosis. The CPT code for the electrocardiogram may be 93000 but requires an ICD code to justify its need. The accompanying ICD code for this medical condition would be I44.2.

Insurance Fraud and/or Abuse

The health insurance system is unfortunately prone to fraud, waste, and abuse by its users. **Insurance fraud** means an individual knowingly deceives a health benefit program to obtain said benefits. **Waste** entails an overuse of services that results in unnecessary costs to the system. **Abuse** occurs when a patient misrepresents the facts of their case to obtain payment for services for which they were not legally entitled. The CMA is to be aware of fraud, waste, and abuse as it applies to their patient population and report any suspected cases to the proper authorities.

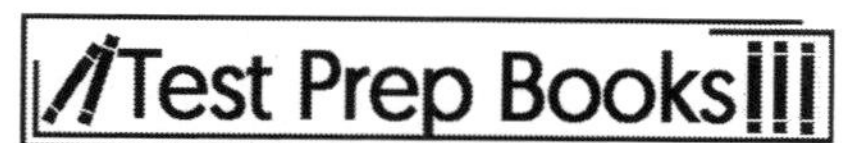

Coverage for Patient Services and Waivers

Insurance Eligibility Verification

To verify insurance coverage, the CMA retrieves the patient's demographic and insurance data from the EHR, and then contacts the insurance provider to verify coverage for the intended date of service, identifies the amount of any co-pay or costs not covered by the policy, and verifies any deductible. If there are costs not covered by the policy, the CMA should notify the patient prior the agency appointment.

Insurance Claims

Submission

The CMA understands that the submission of a claim to a third-party payer is an intricate process that relies on comprehensive documentation in the EHR, identification of all applicable ICD-10 and CPT codes, accurate preparation of all accompanying documentation required by the individual insurer, and timely electronic submission of the completed claim. Errors or omissions in any step of the process can result in denial of the claim, which interrupts the agency revenue cycle.

Explanation of Benefits (EOB)

The CMA understands that MCOs issue periodic statements to patients that include claims and reimbursement details for care provided for a specific time period. Insurers view this document as protection against fraud and abuse because the patient can identify procedures or services that were provided. Many MCOs provide forms that include all billing codes; however, the CMS distributes a Medicare Summary Notice every three months to all Medicare recipients that uses simple language to identify the claims.

Remittance Advice (For Providers)

After patient care services have been provided and charged to the patient's insurance, Medicare, or Medicaid, the provider will receive a **remittance advice (RA)**. An RA is a summary explaining the reimbursement, adjustment, or denial of payment to the provider. If applicable, the document will include denial codes with explanations of why services were adjusted or not reimbursed. For example, if a patient had surgery and the claim was submitted to the insurance without an operative report, the RA document may include a denial code pending submission of progress notes and operative documentation.

Claim Rejection and Follow-Up

Claims that are denied or rejected by the insurance companies require follow-up. Some of the denied claims require supplemental documentation in order to obtain reimbursement. Denial codes found on the remittance advice document explain the missing or incomplete criteria for reimbursement. For example, a patient has a chest x-ray performed to rule out pneumonia. When submitting the claim, the CMA misses entering an ICD code. The insurance company may deny the claim based on insufficient documentation supporting the necessity of the procedure.

Tracking Unpaid Claims

Tracking unpaid claims is a vital task for healthcare facilities. Service claims should be filed as quickly as possible to the insurance companies to prevent payment delays. Unpaid claims that appear on aging reports should be followed up on promptly. Follow-up includes submitting inquiries to the insurance, Medicare, or Medicaid. A re-submission of the claim may be required along with supplemental documentation. Unpaid claims may result in a loss of revenue for the provider and the healthcare facility.

Advance Beneficiary Notice (ABN)

Advanced beneficiary notices (**ABNs**) of non-coverage of rendered care by Medicare apply only to individuals with original Medicare coverage. All patients enrolled in the Medicare Advantage plans receive a notice of Medicare non-coverage in the event that the provider does not believe that Medicare will allow the claim. The CMA must generate an ABN whenever the medical necessity requirements for the care or procedure are not met. That means that every procedure or service must be supported by documentation of the required clinical manifestation or patient complaint to meet the necessary and reasonable standard for that care. ABNs are not generated for procedures that are never covered by Medicare. The CMA must provide the patient with an ABN when the standard is not met, and the CMA documents the notification process in the EHR.

Providers may voluntarily issue an ABN, and the CMA is aware that patients' preferences often result in denied claims at one of three points in the care relationship. The three points are initiation, reduction, and termination. For example, at the beginning of a care relationship a patient may request a prescription for physical therapy that is not supported by the provider's documentation, or once a therapy is ordered and the frequency of treatments is eventually decreased or the therapy is terminated, the patient may request that the that the therapy be continued even though the request no longer meets the necessary and reasonable standard.

Insurance Types/Third-Party Players

Commercial Plans

The CMA is aware that there are multiple variations and coverage criteria for third-party payer plans; however, most plans take the form of a **health maintenance organization** (**HMO**) or a **preferred provider organization** (**PPO**). An HMO assumes all financial risk and provides all care for its members in return for a fixed, pre-paid fee. An individual HMO is most often located in a specific geographic location. Variations of the HMO structure and function include group, staff, or network models. The **group model** includes salaried physicians from a single specialty group that provides patient care at per capita negotiated rates. In the staff model, the patient has access to a limited number of physicians who are employees of the HMO, and all care is provided in HMO-owned facilities. In the **network model** the HMO contracts with several physician groups to provide care for its members. The physicians in the contracted groups may provide care for HMO members as well as non-members.

In the PPO model, patients receive care from a network of selected physicians who contract for that care with the third-party payer. Patients may access care from providers outside of the network, but most often there are increased deductibles and co-payments, and additional non-discounted charges for that care.

Medicare/Medicare Advantage Plans

Medicare covers all individuals over the age of sixty-five and all patients with end-stage renal disease. It also provides hospital insurance coverage and additional medical insurance coverage. Most patients who are eligible for Part A and Part B Medicare opt to enroll in Medicare Advantage plans that offer all covered Medicare services in addition to optional coverage for medications and other services. The organizational structure and financial stability of third-party payers that offer these supplementary plans

must be initially reviewed and approved by Medicare. The Medicare Advantage plans are often hybrid models of the HMO and PPO care models.

Medicaid

Medicaid is a federally mandated plan that is administered by individual states, which means that the CMA must be familiar with applicable state laws for these programs. Medicaid plans cover low-income individuals and certain protected populations. Depending on the details of the negotiated contracts with an individual state, the plan may resemble a fee-for-service plan or an HMO. Many more individuals became eligible for Medicaid as a result of the Affordable Care Act (ACA); however, the temporary provider reimbursement increases have expired and fewer providers are willing to care for patients covered by Medicaid.

State Children's Health Insurance Program (SCHIP)

State Children's Health Insurance Program (SCHIP) provides insurance coverage for children whose caregiver's income is above the cutoff for Medicaid assistance but not enough to purchase private health insurance. SCHIP provides coverage for hospitalizations, emergency room visits, immunizations, and doctor visits. The extent of covered services and monthly premiums are determined by each state-run program and household income levels. For example, in California, the income cutoff to qualify for SCHIP in a two-person household is $3,629/month. In Texas, the same household size has a qualifying income cutoff of $2,918/month.

TRICARE

Tricare is a federally administered insurance program for service members, reservists, dependents, and some retirees. The options for coverage are similar to other commercial plans with respect to networks, deductibles, and co-pays. There are also optional plans for dental coverage for active and reservist members.

CHAMPVA

Civil Health and Medical Program of the Department of Veterans Affairs (CHAMPVA) covers dependents of veterans who are 100% permanently disabled as a result of their active duty, or dependents of veterans who have died as a result of a disability that resulted from active duty.

Managed Care Organizations (MCOs)

MCOs are medical insurers that negotiate contracts with providers and healthcare agencies to provide cost-effective care for plan members. All members understand that the MCO sets deductibles, co-payments, referral procedures, and access to the network of providers. In addition, members when members receive care outside of the MCO network, they incur additional expense. In general, the more flexible plans are associated with increased premiums. MCOs exist in three forms: HMOs, PPOs, and point of service plans (POS plans) that allow members to choose either the HMO or PPO option each time they access care. Most HMO plans reimburse in-network care only, while PPO plans reimburse in-network care at a higher rate than out-of-network care.

Managed Care Requirements

The CMA recognizes that the individual MCOs have varied requirements for the plan members and the providers. Although the patients are ultimately responsible for understanding the terms of their contract with the MCO, the CMA can minimize the incidence of denied claims by maintaining current with the MCO requirements for the payers that contract with the agency.

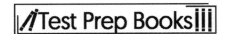

The contract between the MCO and the provider defines covered expenses, the definition of medical necessity, the grievance or appeals process for denied claims, requirements for preauthorization or pre-certification for treatment, and the definition of the standard of care. Providers require explicit information for each of these issues. As a first step in the contract negotiation process, providers must identify the financial status, ownership, community and patient reputation, and accreditation status of the MCO. The provider also must review all enrollment procedures for the MCO including printed media that explains plan options. The MCO should provide clear instructions for appeals of denied claims and the process of de-enrolling patients from the plan. The standard of care and the concept of medical necessity as it relates to covered expenses are critical issues that providers must consider in the process of contract negotiation. If a provider determines that a procedure or test is medically necessary even though it is not a covered expense under the contract, the provider's agency then assumes all the financial risks to meet that standard of care. Providers must also contract to provide only the care that can be reasonably provided with existing resources, including provider expertise, staffing quotas, and facilities.

Care Referrals

All HMOs and many other MCOs require providers to consult with the MCO before ordering outpatient procedures such as physical therapy or referring the patient to a specialty provider. After the MCO has been notified, the patient may obtain a referral for the treatment or visit. The CMA understands that while most MCOs allow phone messaging for the referral process, the process is specific to the individual MCO contract, and the CMA verifies that all patient referrals comply with the individual MCO.

Workers' Compensation

Workers' compensation insurance reimburses providers for the care of individuals with injuries related to their employment. A claims adjuster who represents the workers' compensation commercial carrier is assigned to the patient when a claim is made. The adjuster will initially determine whether the patient is cared for by their primary care physician or by a provider representing the workers' compensation carrier. The adjuster then is responsible for authorizing all care requests from the provider. The CMA understands that the procedure for filing workers' compensation claims is state mandated and that the claims are completed as pen and paper documents that are mailed to the carrier rather than submitted electronically. Timely agency reimbursement for care of an individual whose care is covered by workers' compensation requires accurate and comprehensive documentation of all care and proper submission of complete, accurate, and legible handwritten forms. Only the carrier of the workers' compensation insurance is billed for care that is provided for the work-related injury. The patient's private insurer is billed for services not associated with that injury that are provided while the patient is receiving the pre-authorized care.

Authorizations and Resources

Precertification

Pre-certification is the process of demonstrating the medical necessity of a patient's admission to an acute care facility. The provider is responsible for documentation that supports the need for admission, and for contacting the MCO to verify the details of the patient's condition. The CMA is responsible for verifying that all required documentation is complete, accurate, and forwarded to the appropriate hospital representative and to the MCO as necessary. The CMA also communicates the details of the admission and any additional information to the patient and the patient's family.

Pre-certification is also required for various diagnostic tests such as CT scans, MRIs, or PET scans, and outpatient surgical procedures such as cataract surgery and cochlear implants. The CMA recognizes and satisfies the pre-certification requirements for the individual MCOs.

Prior Authorization

To contain costs, prevent drug interactions, and provide patients with the best therapy, MCOs also require prior authorization for prescription medications under certain conditions. The provider must obtain prior authorization for any medication that can be replaced by a generic drug with the same efficacy, for medications prescribed at higher than usual dosages, for medications that treat non-life threatening conditions, or for very expensive medications. The CMA makes every effort to process the preauthorization requests and any subsequent appeals for coverage in a timely manner to ensure that patients receive the prescribed medications.

Denials/Appeals

The first time that MCOs deny a claim, the decision is based on whether the claim is within the plan guidelines. Providers should recognize that the most common reason for denial is improper documentation. Providers are encouraged to communicate directly with the reviewer to explain extenuating circumstances and to include a summary letter that clearly defines the details of the claim. If the appeal is rejected, the provider understands that a second appeal is reviewed independently of the details of the insurance plan. This means that the provider who references peer-reviewed evidence in the summary letter to support the original treatment or service is more likely to achieve a favorable decision. Patient participation in the appeals process is discouraged because, in the first appeal, reviewers are only comparing the provider's documentation to the details of the plan, and the patient is not able to contribute any substantive information to that inquiry. The CMA understands that the most important part of the claims process is the accuracy of the documentation that supports the coding.

Financial Terminology

Accounts Receivable

Accounts receivable is money owed to the agency by its debtors, e.g., insurance companies and patients.

Accounts Payable

Accounts payable are monies owed to vendors and may be designated as current liabilities. Accounts payable do not include contractual liabilities such as salaries.

Debits

As an accounting procedure, a debit either increases an asset or decreases a liability.

Credits/Credit Balance

As an accounting procedure, a credit either decreases an asset or increases a liability.

Deductible

While on an insurance plan, a patient has a deductible, which is the amount the patient must pay before their insurance company begins to pay.

Patient Account Financial Procedures

Post Charges

The CMA understands that accurate posting of patient charges requires knowledge of the terms of the patient's insurance coverage, complete documentation of all care rendered by the agency providers, correct medical coding of all procedures, and knowledge of the agency fees for service. All these elements must be accurate and complete to prevent denial of the insurance claim for the visit.

Post Payments

The CMA examines all payment statements to confirm that all procedures that were initially billed were reimbursed at the correct rate. In addition, the CMA identifies any denied claims and reviews the explanatory information. Once the charges and the payment data have been reconciled, the CMA identifies any outstanding patient charges and processes those invoices, which must contain details of all procedures provided, incurred charges, and insurance adjustments.

Post Adjustments/Write-Offs

The CMA understands that the adjusted collection rate is equal to the total reimbursement received from an insurer based on the agency's contractual agreement as compared to the total amount that should have been collected if there were no lost revenue issues inherent in the agency billing cycle.

End-of-Day Reconciliation

Keeping track of daily financial transactions in a healthcare facility is known as an **end-of-day reconciliation**. All cash payments, credit card transactions, and insurance reimbursements for the working day are totaled. This amount is then compared to all claims submitted to insurance companies or bills sent to patients. Ideally, incoming and outgoing transactions should match to avoid long-term loss of revenue.

Financial Calculations

The CMA may be responsible for calculating agency **financial statements** if they are educationally prepared to do so.

Billing/Collections

Itemized Statements

The CMA verifies that all billing statements issued in the name of the agency contain documentation of all procedures and costs, any insurance adjustments, and instructions for addressing any questions or concerns related to the charges.

Aging of Accounts

The CMA uses the accounts receivable aging report to identify the outstanding balances owed to the agency by insurance companies, patients, or other entities. The report lists the balances based on elapsed time since the billing date or due date, and the CMA understands that there is a correlation between the number of entries on the aging report and the financial vitality of the agency.

Collecting Payments (Co-Pay, Pre-Pay, Co-Insurance, and Self-Pay)

Payments for patient care services are obtained through several methods. **Co-pays** are determined by the patient's insurance plan and are generally paid in full by the patient at the time of service. Co-pays are established by the insurance companies for services offered, and they vary depending on the level of service. For example, a health insurance plan may require the patient to pay a $30 co-pay for a visit to a specialist. If the patient requires outpatient diagnostic radiology, the co-pay for that service may be an additional $45. **Pre-payments** are collected from patients before services are offered. This strategy helps to prevent loss of revenue. However, if the patient overpays, the money has to be refunded by the healthcare facility. For example, a female patient who is pregnant may pay $2,000 as pre-payment to a hospital before the actual delivery date. This helps facilities ensure the majority of expenses are paid prior to delivering services. Other methods include **self-pay**, in which the patient is fully responsible for the cost of services, and **co-insurance**, in which the patient's insurance pays a percentage of the cost while the patient covers the rest of the bill.

Preplanned Payment Options

The CMA recognizes that the average patient with insurance coverage still may incur large out-of-pocket expenses because deductibles, co-payments, and costs not covered by the policy have increased dramatically. Agencies that do not collect the monies owed by the patient "up front" risk the development of bad debt that requires the use of a collection agency, which potentially harms the reputation of the provider and the agency. Providers must communicate effectively with all patients to identify actual costs and establish an equitable payment plan. The CMA understands that some of these options include; no-interest financing, payment discounts for up-front payments, and on-line payment options. The CMA provides information and empathetic financial counseling to identify the best solution for every patient.

Use of Collection Agencies

The CMA understands that while the services of a collection agency may be necessary at times, satisfying the debt by offering the patient alternative payment options often leads to a more favorable outcome.

Account Collection Rules

Service bills that have not been paid by the patient require a collection process. There are various techniques that can be used to attempt to collect payment such as mailed letters, telephone calls, or electronic mail or messaging. Notifications should be sent when the outstanding balance is 30 days past due. If not paid, an additional notification is sent at the 60-, 90-day, and 120-day mark. Many patients may be going through financial hardships, so it important to offer preplanned payment options or credit arrangements whenever possible. If all collection techniques are exhausted, the patient account is sent to a collection agency for further follow-up.

Scheduling Appointments and Health Information Management

Scheduling Appointments

New Patient

The **new patient appointment** should be scheduled for 30-45 minutes, per protocol. The CMA verifies that the patient understands the scheduling details, and the CMA informs the patient of any pre-appointment paperwork to be completed. In addition, the agency provides the patient with a welcoming package that includes the details of the agency policies, providers, and staff.

To schedule an appointment for a new patient, the CMA identifies the patient's **demographic data**, the reason for the requested visit, and, if applicable, the name of the referring physician. If the patient has been referred for treatment by another physician, the CMA consults with the provider for proper patient scheduling. The CMA also must be aware of insurance referral requirements for agency providers.

Established Patient

The CMA understands that per insurance regulations, an established patient is an individual who has been seen by an agency provider in the previous three years and has a current medical record.

Routine Versus Urgent

The provider identifies the time period for follow-up visits on the patient encounter form, such as six weeks, one month, or annually. The CMA schedules the follow-up visit within the requested time frame for the appropriate amount of time required for the visit. Whenever possible, the CMA accommodates the patient's request for specific appointment dates and times. The appointment entry in the database requires verification of the patient's name, date of birth, and name of the provider. The CMA also gives the patient a written reminder card for the appointment that includes the date and time of the appointment, the provider's name, and instructions for canceling the appointment.

The providers establish the agency protocol for scheduling urgent or emergent patient care needs which includes specific instructions for the CMA when communicating with patients who are reporting emergency conditions. The CMA recognizes that common urgent or emergent conditions that may be accommodated with same-day appointments include: muscle strains and sprains; wounds that are not accompanied by bone fracture or dislocation; episodes of nausea, vomiting, and diarrhea that persist for more than 3-4 days; sore throat, especially if associated with elevated temperature; urinary symptoms with fever or bleeding; fever greater than 101° F. in adults and 102°F.-103°F. in children, and any other illness or severe pain without bleeding, fainting, or loss of consciousness.

Coordinate Facility/Equipment/Personnel Requirements

All aspects of the patient experience, from the availability of adequate parking to the numbers of available support staff, affect patient flow in the primary care practice. Patient flow procedures must be designed to minimize congestion in the reception area by providing separate areas for patients who are checking in and out, and to minimize patient wait time in the reception area and in the examining rooms. The CMA may be responsible for maintaining and documenting time checks to measure patient

flow times from one point of the patient encounter to the completion of the patient visit. Providers can use this data to measure agency efficiency and to revise and improve patient flow practices.

Ancillary Services

In most instances, the CMA schedules laboratory and imaging studies, and outpatient diagnostic procedures for the patient. Surgical procedures and hospital admissions are scheduled by the CMA. Large surgical practices often employ a CMA to function as a dedicated admission coordinator.

To schedule outpatient laboratory, imaging, and diagnostic procedures, the CMA collects the necessary information that includes: the patient's name, contact information, the procedure to be performed, the reason for the order, the requested time frame for completion of the test or procedure, informed consent documents, and insurance details related to any necessary written referrals or preauthorization. Once the appointment details are established the CMA must contact the patient to review and confirm the date, time, location, and directions for the testing. The CMA also reviews the instructions for any patient preparations that are required prior to the examination. The patient also should be provided with written instructions by mail or in person well in advance of the testing date. The CMA documents the details of this pre-procedure notification process in the EHR, as well as the details of the patient's notification of the testing results. The CMA recognizes that this documentation is an important protection against claims of malpractice or patient abandonment.

The CMA understands that the patient's medical record must contain all required data to validate the reason for hospital admission. This data includes all provider documentation, laboratory testing and imaging results, informed consent documents, prescription history, and any additional data that relates to the patient's admitting diagnosis. The CMA is also responsible for obtaining preauthorization from the insurer, and the CMA is aware that failure to verify insurance details prior to admission can result in the patient being responsible for all costs of care. Once the appropriate information has been collected, the CMA verifies all admission details with the hospital's admissions department. When the admission is for an elective procedure, the CMA attempts to honor the patient's requests for specific days; however, the hospital is ultimately responsible for the final schedule. Depending on the circumstances, the CMA faxes the admitting orders to the admissions department at the hospital or to the appropriate unit.

Once the admission schedule is confirmed, the CMA provides the patient with an information packet that includes the details for the patient's admission, including directions to the hospital, parking and patient registration instructions, requirements for pre-operative testing if ordered, visiting hours and regulations, and the date and time for a post-operative check-up visit with the provider. The CMA documents a list of the instructions and the method used to inform the patient of these instructions in the EHR.

Cancelations and No-Shows

The CMA keeps a daily record of the patients that cancel and reschedule an appointment, patients that cancel an appointment without rescheduling the appointment, and patients that are "**no-shows**." The provider establishes an agency protocol to address the contact methods for patients that do not comply with recommended follow-up appointments, or patients who are consistent no-shows for scheduled appointments. The CMA understands that all attempts to contact these patients must be documented in the EHR to avoid possible charges of patient abandonment or malpractice. If the provider decides to dismiss the patient from the agency, the CMA sends the provider letter by certified mail and includes the signed receipt in the patient's EHR.

Physician Delay or Unavailability

If the physician becomes unavailable, the CMA reschedules all patients as soon as possible. If a provider is delayed, the CMA confers with patients present in the reception area to advise them of the delay and to reschedule the appointments per the patients' preferences. The CMA anticipates the patients' concerns related to the inconvenience and makes every effort to accommodate their requests.

Medical Reception/Patient Registration

Patient Identification/Obtain Patient Demographics

The CMA understands that the required **demographic data** associated with the medical record includes the patient's preferred language, gender, race, ethnicity, and date of birth. If a patient declines to provide any of this data, or if the recording of any of this data is prohibited by state law, the CMA is required to include that circumstance in the health record per agency policy.

Identity Theft Protection

Providers are required to make all reasonable efforts to protect privileged health information (**PHI**) from cyber-security breaches by outside sources. In addition, the CMA must comply with all agency protocols that are designed to minimize the risk of **identity theft** in the form of insurance fraud whereby an individual misuses the identity of another person to access care. The CMA may be responsible for adding a patient's photograph to the EHR, verifying the patient's picture ID upon arrival at the agency, or participating in routine audits of financial data.

Accurate Billing Information

The CMA understands that the key elements of the billing cycle include the processes related to patient check-in, verification of insurance coverage, accurate coding of the patient's diagnosis and procedures, calculation and entry of charges, claims submission, and posting of the payment. The CMA also understands that a documentation error or omission at any point in the cycle adversely affects the entire process.

Electronic Health Records

Patient Portal

The meaningful use criteria mandate the use of the patient portal to facilitate patient access to PHI. Providers are responsible for purchasing the computer platform, educating agency staff in its use, and ensuring timely posting of relevant PHI. Although many providers are looking forward to second generation software to eliminate the initial implementation difficulties, the use of the portal as a communication tool has improved patient satisfaction, and its use as a scheduling tool has decreased the number of missed appointments. Many providers contend that patients are more likely to become more involved in their own care and report feeling less isolated from their providers.

Recognize/Identify/Organize Medical Reports

The CMA recognizes the purpose and appropriate format for each element of the EHR, and collates all data per agency protocol.

History and Physical

The provider performs a physical examination and collects a **medical history** from every patient during the initial contact. This data is documented as the history and physical, and is most often the initial clinical element of the EHR.

Discharge Summary

The provider completes a **discharge summary** when a patient is moved from one facility to another, discharged to home, or to the care of an alternate provider. The discharge summary should include the initial presenting complaint and all subsequent PHI. The CMA verifies that the transcription is accurate and appropriately signed and dated.

Operative Note

The provider completes the **operative note**, which includes the details of any surgical procedure with notation of all events from the pre-anesthesia unit to the post-anesthesia unit. Depending on the agency format, the operative note should also contain the operative data from the anesthesia and nursing services.

Diagnostic Test/Laboratory Report

The CMA verifies that all **diagnostic testing data**, including imaging studies, laboratory tests, and pathology reports, is added to the EHR.

Clinic Progress Note

The CMA understands that the format of the clinical progress notes is dictated by the documentation format of the providers. As noted below, the record may be a **problem-oriented medical record** (**POMR**) which means that all providers address the patient problems in chronological order in a single document. A **source-oriented medical record** (**SOMR**) contains chronological notes from each individual provider: physician's notes, nurse's notes, physical therapist's notes, and so on. The CMA understands the requirements for each format and verifies that the clinical notes are complete.

Consultation Report

The **consultation report** documents the patient care from an alternate provider at the request of the **primary care provider** (**PCP**). The CMA verifies that the EHR includes data from all consulting providers.

Growth Charts, Graphs, Tables

As previously mentioned, the analysis and documentation of patient outcomes are essential elements of the primary care practice. The CMA verifies that any patient data generated in the form of **charts, graphs, and tables** is included in the EHR.

Medical Record Preparation/Previsit Planning

The certified medical assistant (CMA) understands that the **medical record** is a legal document that is unique to the individual patient. The medical record is prepared and maintained by all providers who render care to the patient. Depending on contracted responsibilities, the CMA may assemble the necessary components of a blank record, or they may provide and document patient care in the medical record.

Although there are government incentives for primary care agencies to implement electronic health records (**EHRs**), those programs are temporary, and approximately 20% of providers have not yet implemented EHRs. The CMA must be aware that all software interfaces for the EHR require training and continuing education to ensure the accuracy of the documents. In addition, all providers are required to be prepared to transfer an electronic copy of the EHR to another provider or agency upon receipt of a written request from a patient or the patient's representative. Individual requests for copies of EHRs must be satisfied within thirty days, unless there is satisfactory evidence of a reason for a one-time 30-day extension. The CMA understands and complies with all agency policies related to the confidential transfer of documents.

If the CMA is responsible for paper documents, the CMA recognizes that, as a legal document, the medical record must be accurate, complete, legible, and arranged in a logical order per agency policy. The CMA verifies that any corrections to the document are noted in the accepted manner: the entire original entry must be legible, struck with a single line, and signed with the provider's name and the date of the correction.

Practice Quiz

1. Which of the following interventions is most consistent with the competencies of caring practices, advocacy, and moral agency?
    a. Developing cultural awareness of care team members
    b. Mentoring novice medical professionals in the use of research findings
    c. Facilitating the patient's transition from one level of care to another on the health continuum
    d. Refining educational programs for patients and families

2. CMAs are responsible for which of the following elements of informed consent?
    a. Identification of alternatives to the planned procedure
    b. Description of associated risks and benefits
    c. Explanation of the planned procedure or diagnostic test
    d. Assessment of the patient's understanding of the information that is provided

3. Which of the following correctly identifies a critical distinction between the two concepts of advocacy and moral agency?
    a. Advocacy is legally binding.
    b. Moral agency requires accountability for right and wrong decisions.
    c. Advocacy is implied in the paternalistic view of patient care.
    d. Moral agency only refers to support for at-risk populations.

4. Which of the following ethical principles is MOST closely related to advocacy?
    a. Distributive justice
    b. Beneficence
    c. Nonmaleficence
    d. Fidelity

5. Which of the following choices is most consistent with the CMA's responsibilities for advocacy?
    a. Notify the supervisor of any conflict to assure resolution of the patient issue.
    b. Consider the patient's point of view and support and explain the point of view as needed.
    c. Provide comprehensive documentation of the patient's care in the EHR.
    d. Understand all relevant laws associated with the care of the patient.

See answers on the next page.

Answer Explanations

1. C: Facilitating a patient's transition from one point on the health continuum to another requires caring practices in addition to advocacy and moral agency. Moral agency may be employed to ensure that the patient's wishes are considered, especially those wishes associated with end-of-life concerns. Developing cultural awareness is an example of a response to diversity, and the remaining two choices refer to the facilitation of learning.

2. D: While the physician is legally responsible for satisfying all elements of informed consent, CMAs are ethically responsible for assessing the patient's ability to process and understand the implications of informed consent. CMAs protect the patient's autonomy by raising these questions and concerns. The remaining elements of informed consent are required of the physician.

3. B: Moral agency refers to decision-making that includes accountability for right and wrong decisions by the moral agent. Advocacy is an ethical principle that is not legally enforced. However, many argue that paternalism is contrary to advocacy because of the assumption that the "system" knows what is best for the patient without concern for the patient's wishes. Moral agency is not restricted to a specific population; however, the CMA will assess the ability of all patients to make informed decisions.

4. A: Distributive justice refers to the allocation of scarce resources, and advocacy is support for policies that protect at-risk populations. The CMA understands that scarce resource allocation may be sub-standard in certain populations. Nonmaleficence means non-harming or inflicting the least harm possible to reach a beneficial outcome. Fidelity refers to faithfulness but does not specifically address resources or the patient population.

5. B: Sharing, supporting, and explaining the patient's point of view are activities that are consistent with advocacy. The remaining choices contribute to good professional practice but are not specifically related to the concept of advocacy.

Practice Test #1

1. Which drug often requires concurrent use of docusate?
   a. Pantoprazole
   b. Verapamil
   c. Metformin
   d. Naproxen

2. Which of the following is a humanistic outcome?
   a. BP 120/80
   b. EKG: normal sinus rhythm
   c. Pain increases with exercise
   d. Plasma Na^+ 142 mg/dL

3. Which drug increases Parkinsonian manifestations?
   a. Metoclopramide
   b. Cyclosporin
   c. Rapid-acting insulin
   d. Nicotine

4. Human anatomy is divided into geographical planes for the purpose of identifying structures. Which of the following definitions is correct?
   a. The sagittal plane is a horizontal line that divides the core of the body into the right and left sides.
   b. The caudal plane is a vertical line that divides the body into the right and left sides.
   c. The transverse plane is a horizontal line that divides the body into upper and lower sections.
   d. The coronal plane is a horizontal line that divides the body into upper/superior and lower/inferior sections.

5. A patient asks the CMA to explain the Jaeger chart. Which of the following statements correctly describes this chart?
   a. A series of paragraphs of increasingly smaller text that tests near vision
   b. A panel of letters of different sizes that tests visual acuity
   c. Circles containing colored letters embedded in a background of another color to test for color blindness
   d. A grid square of straight lines to test for macular degeneration

6. CMAs should understand that the lipid-soluble drugs dissolve across the capillary membrane. Which of the following is an additional advantage of lipid solubility?
   a. Lipid-soluble drugs are the only substances that can passively diffuse across the blood-brain barrier.
   b. Lipid solubility is associated with 100 percent absorption rates.
   c. Lipid-soluble drugs cross the cellular membrane by passive diffusion.
   d. The first-pass effect decreases lipid solubility.

7. A patient has a history of chest pain and was recently hospitalized for a myocardial infarction, or heart attack. The patient is now an outpatient seeing his cardiologist for a follow-up evaluation. The CMA is asked to perform a procedure to assess the electrical rhythm of the patient's heart known as which of the following?
    a. ECG
    b. ECHO
    c. EFG
    d. EEG

8. The CMA works in a college health center. Providers in this setting must be alert for students exhibiting manifestations of meningitis. Which of the following symptoms are associated with this condition?
    a. Nuchal rigidity with headache
    b. Numbness and tingling in the hands and feet
    c. Right lower quadrant pain
    d. Hyperactivity

9. A new anti-Parkinson's drug at the usual adult dosage has been prescribed for a 68-year-old patient newly diagnosed with Parkinson's. Which of the following will have the most significant effect on the patient's reaction to this new drug?
    a. The patient's age
    b. The medication dose
    c. The amount of medication that crosses the blood-brain barrier
    d. The patient's individual genetic and environmental influences

10. As a healthcare provider, the CMA must understand the limits of the Good Samaritan Law. Which of the following statements is consistent with this law?
    a. All individuals that provide emergency care are protected by the law.
    b. The Good Samaritan Law is a federal law that has been ratified by all states.
    c. Providers are protected from legal action.
    d. Trained healthcare providers are covered for emergency care delivered in their place of employment.

11. Which of the following criteria is included in the MELD classification of liver disease to estimate the expected three-month survival?
    a. Creatinine level
    b. Ascites
    c. Encephalopathy
    d. Nutritional status

12. The provider is conducting a physical urinalysis. Which of the following characteristics will be assessed?
    a. Turbidity
    b. Glucose
    c. Specific gravity
    d. pH

13. What is dimensional analysis?
    a. A mathematical equation used to identify Body Mass Index (BMI)
    b. A process that uses three-dimensional positron emission technology (PET) scans to identify tumors in the body
    c. The automated cell counting process used to determine the WBC
    d. The process used to calculate medication doses

14. The CMA is preparing to take the vital signs of a patient with an electronic blood pressure machine. The CMA notices that the wires are frayed on the electrical cord of the machine. What is an appropriate action that the CMA should take when seeing this?
    a. Proceed with taking the blood pressure.
    b. Try using a different electrical outlet to plug the cord into.
    c. Attempt to repair the cord by wrapping some medical tape around it.
    d. Report the issue to maintenance or whoever maintains equipment in the CMA's facility; look for a different blood pressure machine to take the reading with or check the blood pressure manually.

15. What is the most common reason for failure to report elder abuse?
    a. The patient asks the provider not to report the abuse.
    b. Psychological abuse is too hard to prove.
    c. The provider is afraid of malpractice lawsuits.
    d. Adult abusers rarely leave visible marks.

16. The CMA is preparing to assist with a sterile procedure. After the outer packaging containing the sterile gloves is removed, what is the next step?
    a. Position the thumb against the palm of the hand and slip the hand into the glove.
    b. Position the fingers under the cuff of the glove and insert the hand.
    c. Pick up the inside cuff of the glove with the non-dominant hand.
    d. Open the inside sterile wrapper using the paper tabs.

17. The CMA is taking care of a patient who has recently been diagnosed with a terminal cancer. It is looking like the disease will take a long time to take its course, and the patient has talked about euthanasia as an option. The CMA knows that which of the following is false regarding euthanasia?
    a. Euthanasia is an ethical gray area with which the CMA may not agree.
    b. Euthanasia is sometimes called "physician-assisted suicide" or "death with dignity."
    c. Euthanasia allows a patient to die on their own terms rather than having a lot of potential pain and suffering with a drawn-out disease.
    d. Euthanasia is illegal in all 50 states of the United States.

18. CMAs should understand that pharmacogenetic alterations that affect cellular metabolism can result in which of the following circumstances?
    a. Altered plasma concentration of the drug
    b. Reduced binding of the drug at the receptor site
    c. Idiosyncratic changes that alter excretion of the drug
    d. Increased drug potency

19. How are diseases designated as reportable?
    a. By the average death rate from a disease in four states
    b. Surveillance case definitions
    c. Consensus as to personal risk for the disease in the community
    d. Published data from the CDC

20. Which alteration can result in abnormal increases in the plasma concentration of a drug?
    a. Induction
    b. Inhibition
    c. Desensitization
    d. Absorption

21. With what variables are high patient satisfaction scores associated?
    a. Rural locations
    b. Female patients between the ages of 15 and 30 who are in relatively good health
    c. Better patient outcomes and higher patient retention
    d. Lower patient weight over time

22. Which of the following contexts would likely require advanced triage processes?
    a. A pediatric clinic early in the morning
    b. A makeshift clinic set up to assist victims of a major avalanche
    c. A free flu shot clinic
    d. An emergency department clinic that is fully staffed, has empty beds, and a slow morning

23. Which of the following techniques will aid in communicating with a patient who is blind?
    a. Speaking loudly to ensure the patient can hear the message
    b. Using hand gestures to aid in conveying the message
    c. Turning off the TV to decrease distractions
    d. Speaking slowly so the patient can keep up with the message

24. Which of the following lab reports is consistent with acute renal failure?
    a. BUN 12 mg per dL
    b. Serum creatinine 5.4 mg per dL
    c. Glomerular filtration rate (GFR) 92 L/minute X 1.73^2
    d. Hemoglobin 14.5 mg per dL

25. CMAs should understand that hs-CRP can be used to assess cardiac risk, and that risk can be lowered. Which of the following is NOT associated with improving the hs-CRP result?
    a. NSAID administration
    b. Omega 3 fatty acids
    c. Aspirin
    d. Lifestyle changes

26. The CMA is caring for a patient with relapsing-remitting MS which has not responded to treatment. Which of the following must be included in the teaching plan for the patient who is beginning therapy with the newly available drug Mavenclad® (cladribine)?
    a. Anemia is common with cladribine due to bone marrow suppression of red blood cell production.
    b. A negative pregnancy test is required before each cycle of therapy with cladribine.
    c. Cladribine has proven effective in patients infected with HIV.
    d. Cladribine therapy results in photosensitization.

27. Aminoglycosides such as gentamicin are absolutely contraindicated for the treatment of which condition?
    a. Multiple sclerosis
    b. Parkinson's disease
    c. Myasthenia gravis
    d. Amyloidosis

28. The CMA is attempting to gather some information from the patient for a health history, but the patient appears to be grimacing, uncomfortable, and distracted. What type of distraction is the patient likely experiencing?
    a. Pain
    b. Noise
    c. Disinterest
    d. Temperature

29. Which of the following medications should not be taken in combination with nitroglycerin and what would be the result if they were taken together?
    a. Warfarin, excessive blood thinning
    b. Sildenafil, irreversible hypotension
    c. Allegra®, increased heart rate
    d. Sertraline, increased depression

30. The CMA has taken the patient's vital signs and notes her to be "bradycardic." What does this mean?
    a. Her blood pressure is less than 90 systolic and 60 diastolic.
    b. Her rate of breathing is less than 12 breaths per minute.
    c. Her heart rate is less than 60 beats per minute.
    d. Her bowel sounds are occurring less than 5 times per minute.

31. Which of the following drugs is on the STOPP list of the current START/STOPP list?
    a. NSAIDs with moderate HTN
    b. Beta-blocker with stable angina
    c. ACE inhibitor with heart failure
    d. PPI therapy for GERD

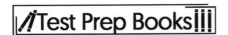

32. Which of the following Latin phrases means "let the master answer" and means that the employer is legally responsible for the actions of their employees?
    a. Subpoena duces tecum
    b. Res ipsa loquitur
    c. Locum tenens
    d. Respondeat superior

33. A patient had an IV infusing at 50 ml/hour, a heparin drip infusing at 8 ml/ hour, an enteral infusion at 30 ml/ hour, and 50 ml of D5W with Clindomycin IV every six hours. The Foley catheter was emptied three times—450 ml, 375 ml, and 525 ml—and the total wound drainage was 46 ml. Which of these would be correct documentation of the 24-hour intake and output?
    a. Intake = 2,312 mL, output = 1,396 mL
    b. Intake = 1,920 mL, output = 1,350 mL
    c. Intake = 1,520 mL, output = 1,296 mL
    d. Intake = 2,200 mL, output = 1,446 mL

34. An OB/GYN clinic requires patients to fill out their name, address, phone number, and insurance type on a clipboard upon check-in. The clipboard stays at the front reception until the front desk staff are able to remove the sign-in sheets and check the patients in electronically. What is a legal issue in this procedure?
    a. All patients should check themselves in electronically, rather than using pen and paper, according to the Affordable Care Act of 2010.
    b. OB/GYN patients are more likely to have small children with them, so requiring them to fill out paperwork in the office could be a liability.
    c. Patient privacy is compromised during the time that the clipboard remains on the front desk.
    d. Some patients may not be able to write, so this is a violation of the American Disabilities Act.

35. The medical identifies the agency responsibilities for blood-borne pathogen management. Which of the following statements is NOT correct?
    a. "The Occupational Safety and Health Administration (OSHA) requires agencies to maintain employee training records."
    b. "All employees must be provided with appropriate personal protective equipment."
    c. "The agency must enforce universal precautions."
    d. "To facilitate a prompt response to any occupational exposure to a blood-borne pathogen, the agency will annually review and maintain all employees' medical records."

36. The CMA is caring for a patient who is being treated for chronic pain. The patient says, "My pain medicine doesn't work anymore. I woke up twice during the night in such pain." The patient is most likely describing which event associated with pain therapy?
    a. Addiction
    b. Habituation
    c. Addiction
    d. Tolerance

37. When healthcare providers see patients who are unconscious or not of a sound state of mind, what principle is utilized in order to provide treatment?

a. Assumption
b. Risky consent
c. Informed consent
d. Implied consent

38. A CMA is taking care of a patient who has been incapacitated by a severe stroke two years ago. The patient's daughter makes her healthcare decisions for her legally through which specific legal document?

a. Medical durable power of attorney
b. Living will
c. Advance directives
d. Patient Self-Determination Act

39. Which condition is an inherited cause of insulin resistance?

a. Abdominal obesity
b. Insulin receptor mutations
c. HIV antiretrovirals
d. Anti-insulin antigens

40. The CMA understands that the Clinical Laboratory Improvement Amendments (CLIA), established by Centers for Disease Control (CDC), the Food and Drug Administration (FDA), and the Center for Medicare and Medicaid Services (CMS), provide for the use of at-home laboratory tests. Which of the following criteria is NOT consistent with these amendments as they relate to waived test kits for at-home use?

a. Waived lab tests will not cause harm if used incorrectly.
b. The testing kits for at-home use must be approved by the FDA.
c. The tests must not produce false-positive or false-negative results.
d. Providers who recommend the use of the kits will provide appropriate instruction for their use.

41. The CMA is admitting a 35-year-old male patient with a leg injury. The x-ray indicates that the tibia is fractured, and there is an open wound at the site of the fracture. Which of the following correctly identifies this injury?

a. Compound
b. Comminuted
c. Stable
d. Greenstick

42. Which of the following is NOT consistent with Ranson's criteria for the prediction of mortality associated with acute pancreatitis?

a. Age: 38
b. Serum calcium 7.2 mg/dL
c. Plasma glucose: 280 mg/dL
d. WBC 19,000/mm^3

43. The CMA observes the following rhythm on the patient's cardiac monitor. Which of the following is the CMA's best response?

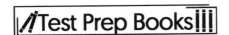

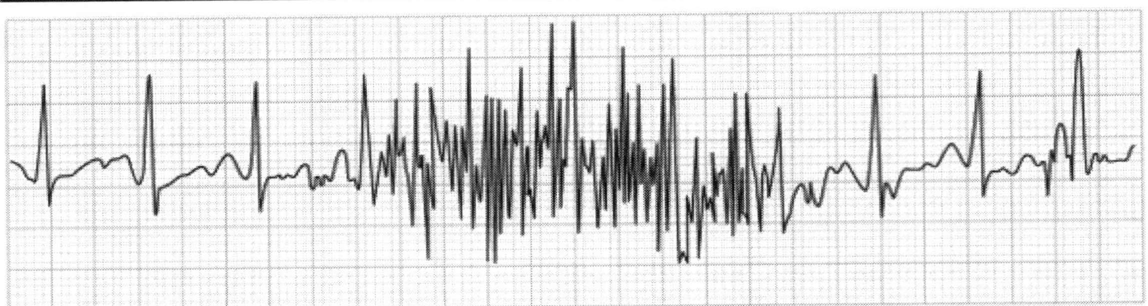

a. Check the patient's electrodes to reduce the artifact.
b. No action is necessary because the tracing has returned to normal sinus rhythm.
c. Adjust the gain on the cardiac monitor to improve the quality of the tracing.
d. Notify the charge nurse and check the patient's vital signs.

44. What is the rationale for the "brown bag" approach to increasing the patient's adherence to the therapeutic drug regimen?

a. The plan requires the patient to construct a written drug plan.
b. The plan allows the provider to identify all prescription drugs, OTC preparations, and all other supplements at each appointment and to assess the patient's knowledge of the drug plan.
c. The patient can identify ways to coordinate the drug administration schedule with the activities of daily living (ADLs).
d. The patient can use the brown bag contents to learn about the individual drugs.

45. The CMA is caring for an elderly patient who often asks that words be repeated but is able to watch TV with the sound set at a normal volume. Which of the following interventions is most appropriate to the care of this patient?

a. The CMA should speak more loudly when addressing the patient.
b. The CMA should arrange for an interpreter who is fluent in sign language.
c. The CMA should refer the patient to an audiologist to be fitted for a hearing aid.
d. The CMA should maintain a normal volume, speak slowly, and allow the patient time to process the conversation.

46. The differential diagnosis for sudden loss of vision includes which of the following conditions?

a. Uveitis
b. Amblyopia
c. Hyphema
d. Pituitary tumor

47. Which of the following is a change associated with the integumentary system in the elderly?

a. Acne
b. Psoriasis
c. Vernix caseosa
d. Collagen alterations

48. Which of the following activities is associated with the "A" of the SHARE approach?
   a. Explore the patient's values
   b. Engage the patient in shared decision-making
   c. Review all treatment options
   d. Reassess patient priorities

49. The CMA has concerns with which element of guardianship?
   a. Potential restrictions on patient autonomy
   b. Identification of patient's inability to care for self
   c. Variable guardian oversight by the individual states
   d. Financial decisions that might not reflect the patient's wishes

50. A small fire has developed in the employee's break room of the facility. The CMA grabs the fire extinguisher and follows which of the following instructions to operate the extinguisher properly?
   a. CMAs are not authorized to use fire extinguishers. The CMA should find an authorized member of the team to use the extinguisher.
   b. Aim at the middle of the fire, pull the pin, and sweep from side to side while squeezing the trigger.
   c. Squeeze the trigger, aim at the top of the flames, and sweep up and down until the flames are extinguished.
   d. Pull the pin, aim at the base of the fire, squeeze the trigger, and sweep from side to side until the fire is extinguished.

51. Which kind of wound is NOT commonly associated with the development of tetanus?
   a. A wound that occurred four hours ago
   b. A stellate wound
   c. A puncture wound
   d. A wound with compromised tissue

52. A fire alarm has been pulled in the office building where the CMA works. Which of the following steps of the RACE acronym will help contain a fire?
   a. Close all facility doors, including patient room doors.
   b. Remove clutter from the hallway to ensure emergency exits are easily accessed.
   c. Activate the emergency response system.
   d. Rescue anyone directly threatened by the fire.

53. The CMA understands that the vacuum tubes used to collect blood samples are color coded in order to identify the additive that is required for specific laboratory tests. Which of the following tubes contains a coagulant that facilitates the clotting of the blood in preparation for plasma tests?
   a. Tiger top (red/black)
   b. Red top
   c. Purple top
   d. Light blue top

54. Which of the following refers to a doctor who specializes in treating blood disorders such as sickle cell anemia?
   a. Hepatologist
   b. Hematologist
   c. Cardiologist
   d. Immunology

55. Which of the following is the most critical element of the documentation that is required to arrange a hospital admission?
   a. The patient's preference for the admission date
   b. The referring physician's specialty
   c. The patient's age
   d. EHR data that supports the need for admission

56. Which field of public health can healthcare professionals support by establishing symptom surveillance systems?
   a. Health policy
   b. Nutrition services
   c. Epidemiology
   d. Health promotion

57. The CMA is providing home care for a patient recently diagnosed with hypertension. Which of the following menu items is appropriate for this patient?
   a. Green salad with Ranch dressing
   b. Grilled cheese sandwich
   c. Grilled chicken and pasta
   d. Tomato soup and crackers

58. The problem list generated in a POMR is most often displayed as a database. Which of the categories is an essential element of that database?
   a. The patient's age
   b. The date of onset of the problem
   c. The list of the patient's previous medications
   d. The patient's weight

59. Which of the following is NOT one of the categories for notifiable diseases?
   a. Outbreak
   b. Infectious
   c. Noninfectious
   d. Reproducible

60. Which of the following correctly identifies individuals that are eligible for CHAMPVA insurance coverage?
   a. Dependents of active-duty service members
   b. Adult children of active-duty service members
   c. All retired veterans
   d. Dependents of veterans who are 100% disabled due to their active duty

61. Which of the following may be necessary to treat the Hawthorne effect?
   a. Random selection
   b. Random assignment
   c. Blinding of the researcher
   d. Placebo control group

62. Reye's syndrome is associated with liver failure and noninflammatory encephalopathy. Which of the following correctly identifies the pathogenesis of increased intracranial pressure?
   a. Aspirin-induced hypervolemia
   b. Hyperammonemia that damages astrocytes
   c. Plasma protein leakage to the interstitial space
   d. Hypertension related to hepatocyte damage

63. According to the nursing theories of culturally congruent practice, which of the following is the FIRST step?
   a. Cultural self-awareness
   b. Cultural skill development
   c. Cultural knowledge acquisition
   d. Cultural implementation training

64. Which of the following statements best identifies the meaningful use initiative?
   a. The meaningful use initiative provides financial rewards to providers for better patient outcomes.
   b. The meaningful use initiative is focused on decreasing medication errors.
   c. The meaningful use initiative requires the use of the SOMR for compliance.
   d. The development and use of the electronic health record is the focus of the meaningful use initiative.

65. Which of the following is NOT an element of informed consent for a surgical procedure?
   a. A detailed explanation of the planned procedure
   b. Identification of all reasonable alternative options
   c. Waiver of injury compensation
   d. Discussion of possible complications that may occur if the procedure is not performed

66. The CMA will provide information for the treatment of diarrhea for patients traveling to high-risk areas. Which of the following is considered a high risk for the development of GI effects?
   a. Central America
   b. Eastern Europe
   c. Caribbean islands
   d. South Africa

67. Which of the following measurements is one of the mensuration assessment parameters?
   a. Range of motion of the shoulders and arms
   b. Fundal height in a pregnant woman
   c. Bowel sounds
   d. Body symmetry

68. A patient asks the CMA to explain the use of Fluticasone with Salmeterol, the new medication that the provider just ordered. Which of the following responses is most appropriate?
   a. "Open the container, click the dose into position, take a deep breath, exhale, inhale the medication through the mouth, and hold your breath for 10 seconds."
   b. "It is best if you swallow the medication with a full glass of water."
   c. "Press the inhaler as you breathe in slowly, and then hold your breath for 10 seconds."
   d. "Be sure to take this medication with food to avoid nausea."

69. The CMA is aware that peripheral venous stasis ulcers differ from arterial ulcers. Which of the following findings is associated with venous stasis ulcers?
   a. Regular margins
   b. Often extending to the depth of the tendon
   c. Most often located on the foot
   d. Copious secretions are common

70. Which of the following is consistent with developmental anticipatory guidance?
   a. Identification of family coping strategies
   b. Assessment of delayed grief resolution
   c. Identification of patient expectations for treatment success
   d. Assessment of physical and cognitive benchmarks

71. The CMA receives a call from a patient stating that a child may have ingested an unknown cleaning agent. Which of the following is the CMA's best response?
   a. "Take the child to the hospital immediately."
   b. "Call the poison control center and follow their directions."
   c. "Try to induce vomiting with Ipecac."
   d. " The doctor can see you right away."

72. Which of the following statements related to workers' compensation claims is correct?
   a. The CMA bills all the patient's care to the patient's private insurer first.
   b. The patient receives all care from their primary care provider.
   c. The CMA verifies that preauthorization for all care and procedures is obtained.
   d. All documentation will be electronically transmitted to the insurance carrier for the workers' compensation plan in the individual state.

73. Providers widely debate the importance of which characteristic of analog insulin?
   a. Hyperglycemic control
   b. Alterations in body weight
   c. Effect on long-term complications
   d. Cost

74. The CMA is caring for a patient with hypertension who takes digoxin. Which of the following patient remarks should be reported to the charge nurse?
   a. "I don't buy processed foods."
   b. "I take St. John's Wort for my depression."
   c. "I cook my vegetables without salt."
   d. "I will tell my doctor if I feel lightheaded."

75. Which of the following statements correctly defines the criteria for an established patient for insurance purposes?
    a. The patient saw the provider one time, five years ago.
    b. The provider consulted on the patient's care in the hospital last month.
    c. The patient was seen by one provider two years ago and has a current EHR.
    d. The patient is being scheduled for a visit by a referring provider.

76. A patient tells the CMA that he is doing well with his recovery from an MI three weeks ago. Which of the following statements by this patient indicates the need for additional instruction?
    a. "I'm walking 20 minutes every day."
    b. "My blood pressure is well controlled by my new medication."
    c. "I think the ginseng that I am taking is helping me to exercise easier."
    d. "I've stopped using salt at the dinner table."

77. Which of the following statements about HMO models is correct?
    a. The staff model and the group model have the same provider reimbursement structure.
    b. In the network model, patients receive care in HMO-owned medical facilities.
    c. Physicians in the network model provide care exclusively for HMO members.
    d. HMOs commonly exist in a single geographic area.

78. At what time during a patient's stay are medical errors most likely to be made?
    a. During bloodwork
    b. During labor for pregnant patients
    c. When extra tests are ordered
    d. During any transition of care

79. Which of the following statements correctly defines the difference between sanitization and disinfection?
    a. Sanitization is the removal of all pathogens on inanimate objects.
    b. Disinfection is more effective than sterilization for cleaning surgical instruments.
    c. Sanitization inhibits the action of microorganisms.
    d. Disinfectants can remove all pathogens from a surface.

80. What is the main purpose of the Z-tract intramuscular injection technique?
    a. Identify patient-specific allergens
    b. Avoid possible local skin reaction
    c. Maximize the absorption of the medication
    d. Minimize the pain associated with the injection

81. Which of the following is true regarding behavioral anticipatory guidance and developmental anticipatory guidance?
    a. Developmental level is the basis for assessing expected and unexpected patient behavior.
    b. Behavioral anticipatory guidance is only used to assist parents with abnormal child behavior.
    c. Developmental anticipatory guidance is only appropriate when a child is not reaching expected benchmarks.
    d. Behavioral anticipatory guidance is less useful in elderly populations than developmental anticipatory guidance.

82. Which of the following is the best example of indirect contact?
    a. Shaking hands with a friend
    b. Children playing with blocks
    c. Sitting next to someone who is sneezing
    d. Caring for a patient with HIV

83. Which of the following manifestations would the CMA expect to observe in a patient with a serum potassium level of 2.5 mEq/L?
    a. Palpitations
    b. Paresthesias
    c. Decreased deep tendon reflexes (DTRs)
    d. Prolonged P-R interval

84. Which of the following correctly defines reduced practice?
    a. Physician oversight is required for all aspects of APRN practice.
    b. APRN practice is unrestricted except for physician oversight of documentation.
    c. Physician oversight is required only for prescriptive practice.
    d. There are no restrictions on APRN practice.

85. What is the difference between quantal and graded drug responses?
    a. A graded response is an objective measurement of a biological drug effect such as BP changes.
    b. A quantal response is the patient's subjective report of the drug's biological effect.
    c. The graded response for a given dose of a drug is the same from one patient to the next.
    d. A quantal response is considered to be a negative outcome.

86. A patient is to receive Valsartan 0.16 g by mouth one time. There are 80 mg tablets available. Which of the following is the correct dose?
    a. 0.5 tabs
    b. 1.5 tabs
    c. 1 tab
    d. 2 tabs

87. Recent evidence-based practice guidelines have recommended limiting the conditions that are treated with proton pump inhibitors (PPIs). Therapy with PPIs is recommended for the continued management of which condition?
    a. Peptic ulcer disease that has been treated
    b. H. pylori infection that is asymptomatic
    c. Barrett esophagus that has been treated
    d. GERD that is asymptomatic

88. Which racial or ethnic group demonstrates a higher than normal incidence of lactose intolerance?
    a. Arab Americans
    b. Asian Americans
    c. Native Americans
    d. African Americans

89. Elias has been a registered nurse since he received his Bachelor of Science in Nursing in 2005. He loves his job and has decided he would like to return to school to receive his Master's degree. What is this an example of?
   a. A promotion
   b. Continuing education
   c. Specializing
   d. Work-life balance

90. Which of the following defines pure-tone audiometry?
   a. Subjective measure of the hearing threshold
   b. Speech discrimination measure
   c. Otoacoustic emission test
   d. Auditory brainstem response

91. A TB skin test is considered positive at 15 mm in which of the following patient populations?
   a. Patients with no risk factors for the development of the disease
   b. HIV+ patients
   c. Immunocompromised patients
   d. Recent immigrants

92. Which of the following statements best describes upcoding?
   a. Upcoding is a method that is used to upgrade the EHR to reflect the patient's current status.
   b. Upcoding is a coding modifier that indicates that more than one test was completed during the patient encounter.
   c. Upcoding is a coding method that reports a level of care that is not documented in the EHR.
   d. Upcoding is the process of updating CPT modifiers.

93. Which statement about either community- or hospital-acquired pneumonia is correct?
   a. Hospital-acquired pneumonia is responsible for signs and symptoms of pneumonia for seven days after discharge.
   b. The incidence of hospital-acquired pneumonia is associated with changes in reimbursement schedules.
   c. Community-acquired pneumonia is responsible for signs and symptoms of pneumonia for 72 hours after admission to the hospital.
   d. Patients with community-acquired pneumonia should be hospitalized for at least 48 hours to ensure adequate anti-infective agent coverage.

94. Which of the following is an example of a healthcare provider showing cultural consideration to a patient?
   a. A healthcare provider does not allow a patient's same-sex spouse to visit in the recovery room due to the healthcare provider's religious beliefs.
   b. A healthcare provider allows a patient of the Islamic faith to keep her headscarf on during a physical exam.
   c. A healthcare provider tells a person who identifies as Asian on his intake form that she does not like Chinese food.
   d. A healthcare provider tells an older patient that unless he or she enrolls in the online patient portal, the provider will not provide treatment.

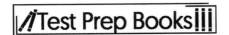

95. Which of the following is NOT included in the Post-Exposure care of a healthcare worker following occupational exposure to the HIV virus?
   a. Post-exposure anti-viral therapy is contraindicated if the exposed person is pregnant.
   b. HIV testing will be repeated at 6 weeks, 12 weeks, and 6 months at a minimum.
   c. The exposed person should avoid blood or tissue donation, breastfeeding, or pregnancy for 6 to 12 weeks after exposure.
   d. Renal and hepatic studies and a CBC will be done at baseline and repeated frequently.

96. Which assessment is required for a patient who is taking sumatriptan for the first time?
   a. Blood glucose
   b. Platelet count
   c. Glaucoma testing
   d. ECG

97. Which of the following is a characteristic of high-quality research evidence?
   a. Results obtained from observational studies
   b. Variable estimates of effect size
   c. RCT study design
   d. Case controlled analytics

98. What is the difference between the hemoglobin A1c lab test and the blood glucose test?
   a. The hemoglobin A1c lab test is a fasting test.
   b. The blood glucose test must be drawn before breakfast.
   c. The hemoglobin A1c lab test provides a three-month average glucose level.
   d. The blood glucose test requires a venipuncture.

99. As a community healthcare provider, the CMA must be aware of the manifestations of possible substance/alcohol abuse in the agency population. While many of the manifestations are common to both forms of abuse, which of the following manifestations most likely indicates substance abuse as opposed to alcohol abuse?
   a. Depression
   b. Violent behavior
   c. Lack of interest in the family or activities
   d. Abrupt weight changes

100. What is the highest level of Maslow's hierarchy of needs?
   a. Prestige
   b. Accomplishment
   c. Self-esteem
   d. Self-actualization

101. Which of the following elements is NOT required to schedule an appointment for an established patient?
   a. The patient's height and weight
   b. The patient's current complaint
   c. The provider's vacation schedule
   d. The dates of national holidays

102. Which statement about U-500 Humulin® R Insulin is correct?
   a. It can be administered intravenously.
   b. It can be mixed with other insulins in the same syringe.
   c. Hypoglycemia may occur 15 to 18 hours after injection.
   d. The vial must be discarded after 14 days of use.

103. Which statement about chlamydia is correct?
   a. Men are more often asymptomatic than women.
   b. Antibody testing is the most reliable indicator of the presence of the condition.
   c. Testing is not currently recommended for men.
   d. The degree of risk for complications in women is similar to a UTI.

104. The patient asks the CMA to explain how glaucoma affects the eye. Which of the following statements is the CMA's best response?
   a. "Excess fluid collects in the front of the eye, potentially causing pressure on the optic nerve in the back of the eye, which can result in vision loss."
   b. "Nerve damage causes the loss of central vision."
   c. "Cellular debris eventually causes the lens to become cloudy, which decreases visual acuity."
   d. "Changes in the blood vessels due to hypertension and hyperglycemia can increase pressure on the retina, resulting in blindness."

105. What are the manifestations associated with a serum potassium level of 7.5 mEq/L?
   a. This value is within normal limits.
   b. Anorexia and shortened Q-T interval on the ECG
   c. Paresthesias, elevated T waves and QRS widening on the ECG
   d. Prolonged P-R interval and U waves on the ECG

106. Which category of adverse drug reactions (ADRs) is commonly considered to be due to incorrect administration of the drug?
   a. Rapid reactions
   b. First dose reactions
   c. Early reactions
   d. Intermediate reactions

107. Which of the following should be reported to the FDA as an ADR?
   a. Intractable vomiting following oral chemotherapy
   b. Acute cirrhosis secondary to self-induced acetaminophen overdose
   c. Intervention is required to prevent permanent damage following the reported ADR.
   d. Alteration of the pharmacotherapeutic plan is required due to the reported ADR.

108. The CMA is caring for a patient with right-sided heart failure. Which of the following manifestations is associated with this condition?
   a. Increased respiratory rate
   b. CVP 21 cm water
   c. Serum sodium 145 mg/dL
   d. Dyspnea on exertion

109. The CMA is assessing the fluid intake of an assigned patient. The patient states that she drank an 8-ounce container of milk for breakfast. Which of the following is the correct documentation of this intake?

a. 8 ounces
b. 0.3 L
c. 1 cup
d. 240 ml

110. The CMA has recently completed an in-service presentation about patient safety measures. Which of the following statements by the CMA indicates the need for additional instruction related to patient safety?

a. "I will leave the beds in the lowest position."
b. "If a patient is having a seizure, I will insert a tongue depressor to maintain the airway."
c. "I will check the patient's documentation for fall precautions."
d. "I will notify environmental services of any fluid spills."

111. Which of the following statements is one of the assumptions of the savings potential of the bundled payment model of reimbursement?

a. Patient outcomes will not be affected by the bundled payment plan.
b. The providers and payers will share the savings that result from the model.
c. Patients will consume less healthcare.
d. The providers will be reimbursed for complications of care.

112. Which of the following is an age-related change in the GI system?

a. Dry mouth or xerostomia
b. Increased contractions of the upper esophageal sphincter
c. Increased risk of peptic ulcer disease
d. Malnutrition

113. The CMA is assisting with the care of a patient with suspected myocardial infarction. The CMA correctly places the patient in which of the following anatomical positions?

a. Lithotomy
b. Trendelenburg
c. Supine
d. Semi-fowler's

114. A CMA suspects that a physician he works for has been abusing painkillers. The physician has been coming to work seemingly under the influence, slurring his speech and more clumsy than usual. The CMA knows that he is going through a divorce, and it has been causing him extra stress. Normally, the physician is completely competent and has a good rapport with his patients. What should the CMA do since the physician is his supervisor?

a. Tell his fellow CMAs what he thinks but not take it any further.
b. Wait until there is more solid evidence, such as a medication or prescription error.
c. Report his suspicions to the appropriate supervising body, such as human resources.
d. Keep an eye on the physician for the next couple months; maybe after the divorce is completed, he will quit taking the painkillers.

115. Which of the following differentiates a legend drug from an OTC drug?
   a. Legend drugs are not approved by the FDA.
   b. OTC drugs require black box labels.
   c. OTC drugs have labels that provide adequate drug instruction for adults.
   d. Opioid drugs are not included as legend drugs.

116. Which of the following conditions requires that all who have contact with the patient use a particulate respirator capable of filtering particles smaller than five microns?
   a. Diphtheria
   b. Tuberculosis
   c. Adenovirus
   d. Clostridium difficile infection

117. What is the rationale for glucose testing of the CSF obtained from the lumbar puncture of a patient with meningitis?
   a. Verification of the ICP
   b. Assessment of protein levels
   c. Differentiation of bacterial and viral disease
   d. Identification of ketoacidosis in diabetic patients

118. The Health Insurance Portability Accountability Act (HIPAA) was enacted for all but which of the following reasons?
   a. Decrease inefficiencies and reduce paperwork within the health insurance system
   b. Ensure that the testing of human laboratory specimens meets federal standards
   c. Prevent duplication of services through coordination of care
   d. Protect patient health information privacy and confidentiality

119. Which of the following drugs is contraindicated for the treatment of otitis externa in a seven-year-old child with otitis externa?
   a. Polymyxin B sulfate
   b. Tobramycin dexamethasone
   c. Neomycin
   d. Hydrocortisone

120. Which statement correctly identifies the distinction between equitable healthcare and equality of healthcare?
   a. Equitable healthcare means that everyone in a population receives all the care that they require.
   b. Equality of healthcare means that scarce resources are managed appropriately.
   c. There is no distinction between the two kinds of healthcare.
   d. Equality of healthcare means that all people are treated equally.

121. What is the difference between the DNP and the PhD degrees?
   a. The DNP is not an appropriate terminal degree for nursing faculty.
   b. The PhD does not require clinical expertise.
   c. The DNP degree is considered to be a clinical practice degree.
   d. The PhD is required for all nurses in leadership roles.

122. Which of the following statements about Medicaid is correct?
   a. The federal government funds and sets the policies for the plan.
   b. The purpose of the plan is to provide healthcare services for low-income individuals and families.
   c. All primary care providers are required to accept Medicaid patients.
   d. The Affordable Care Act resulted in fewer people seeking Medicaid coverage.

123. What is one of the main differences between the POMR and the SOMR?
   a. Only nurses can add data to the SOMR.
   b. The POMR facilitates the assessment of patient outcomes.
   c. The SOMR generates less paper.
   d. The POMR separates the notes from each discipline.

124. Which of the following menu choices is the best source of fiber?
   a. One cup of fresh strawberries
   b. Two pieces of whole wheat bread
   c. One ounce dry roasted almonds
   d. One cup of split pea soup

125. The differential diagnosis for conductive hearing loss includes which of the following disorders?
   a. Ménière's disease
   b. Arnold-Chiari malformations
   c. Multiple sclerosis
   d. Glomus tumor

126. The CMA is discussing the purpose of buccal and sublingual routes of medication administration with a patient. Which of the following patient statements indicates a need for additional information?
   a. Buccal medications have an additional component that allows for the decreased permeability of the gums and palate.
   b. Sublingual medications provide immediate release of the medication to the systemic circulation.
   c. Buccal medications are formulated to withstand the acid environment of the stomach.
   d. Sublingual medications may exert a local or a systemic effect.

127. The CMA is caring for a patient with serotonin syndrome. Which drug decreases the reuptake of serotonin?
   a. Procarbazine
   b. Fenfluramine
   c. Ondansetron
   d. Lithium

128. What is the difference between nociceptive pain and neuropathic pain?
   a. Nociceptive pain only affects hollow organs.
   b. Neuropathic pain is caused by damage within the peripheral or central nervous system.
   c. Nociceptive pain should be treated by NSAIDs first.
   d. Neuropathic pain requires opioid analgesics for acceptable pain relief.

129. A patient is taking 50 mg of spironolactone daily. Which of the following drugs is contraindicated for the patient at this time?
   a. Simvastatin 40 mg PO daily
   b. KCl 20 mEq/L PO BID
   c. Clorazepate 3.75 mg PO
   d. Metronidazole 500 mg in 100mL D_5W IV over 60 minutes

130. The CMA is taking care of a patient who has been advised to have a carotid endarterectomy. The CMA knows that this procedure is done to prevent which life-threatening condition?
   a. Myocardial infarction
   b. Pulmonary embolism
   c. Stroke
   d. Hyperthyroidism

131. The CMA is conducting a patient interview to gather a health history. The CMA asks the patient if she has taken her blood pressure medicine today. This is an example of which type of information-gathering question?
   a. Exploratory
   b. Rhetorical
   c. Open-ended
   d. Closed

132. Which of the following medications can contribute to or worsen hypertension?
   a. Acetaminophen
   b. Dextromethorphan
   c. Dapagliflozin
   d. Bupropion

133. Which of the following is an example of objective data?
   a. EKG tracings
   b. Chief complaint
   c. Family history
   d. Present illness

134. Wasting of muscle, bone deformities and tenderness, and joint pain or swelling are commonly due to which of the following nutritional deficiencies?
   a. Zinc and B12
   b. Folic acid and Vitamin C
   c. Vitamin C and Vitamin D
   d. Ferritin and niacin

135. Which of the OARS communication tools can potentially enhance the patient's self-efficacy?
   a. "Tell me more about that experience."
   b. "Are you saying that ...?"
   c. "I understand your concerns."
   d. "Is there anything else that you would like to say?"

136. A CMA is assisting a patient from the bed to his wheelchair. When using proper lifting technique, which of the following is incorrect?
   a. Bend at the knees, and lift with the legs.
   b. Maintain a wide base of support for maximum strength.
   c. Keep the patient load an arm's length away from the body for infection prevention.
   d. Maintain proper and erect posture.

137. What is the purpose of the Wells score?
   a. Assess the risk potential for venous stasis ulcers
   b. Confirm the presence of a DVT
   c. Assess the probability of a PE
   d. Stratify ankle-brachial index scores

138. What is a "sick day" plan?
   a. Hydration regulations for a patient with cardiac disease who is experiencing flu symptoms
   b. Insulin administration protocol for Type 1 diabetics with decreased intake due to illness
   c. Antihypertensive medication plan for dialysis patients with fluid volume alterations
   d. Fluid rescue plan for infants with severe gastrointestinal losses

139. Diabetic ketoacidosis and insulin shock are life-threatening emergencies. Which of the following manifestations is an indication of insulin shock?
   a. Diffuse abdominal pain
   b. Anorexia
   c. Nausea and vomiting
   d. Sweating and anxiety

140. The CMA is providing home care for a patient with heart disease and diabetes mellitus. Which of the following manifestations is associated with diabetic ketoacidosis?
   a. Shaking and tremors
   b. Sweating
   c. Fruity breath odor
   d. Anxiety and irritability

141. Which of the following culturally and linguistically appropriate services (CLAS) criteria requires mandatory compliance and reporting for all federally assisted healthcare institutions?
   a. Provide effective, equitable, understandable, and respectful quality care and services.
   b. Recruit, promote, and support a culturally and linguistically diverse governance, leadership, and workforce.
   c. Conduct ongoing assessments of the organization's CLAS-related activities.
   d. Ensure the competence of the individuals who provide language assistance.

142. Which of the following is a characteristic of the black box warnings issued by the FDA?
   a. All drug labels contain a black box label.
   b. Mandatory restrictions for the administration of the drug are listed.
   c. The black box information is intended for consumers.
   d. Black box warnings refer to the most common reactions associated with the drug.

143. The CMA is aware that an elevated C-reactive protein level is associated with which of the following conditions?
   a. Coronary artery disease
   b. Gastrointestinal bleeding
   c. Antibiotic sensitivity
   d. Pregnancy

144. Which of the following statements regarding preauthorization is correct?
   a. The requirement is waived for outpatient surgery.
   b. The provider assumes all financial risk if a service is provided without preauthorization.
   c. The provider must obtain preauthorization for all hospital admissions.
   d. Preauthorization is only required for Medicare patients.

145. In what way does the skeletal system support the immune system?
   a. Bones support and protect the spleen.
   b. Calcium is stored in the bones.
   c. The bone marrow is the site of white blood cell production.
   d. The osteoclasts make new bone cells when necessary.

146. A client is admitted to the emergency room with a respiratory rate of 9/min. Arterial blood gases (ABG) reveal the following values; pH 7.32, pCO_2 50 mmHg, HCO_3 25 mEq/L, PO_2 90 mmHg, O_2 sat 88%. Which of the following correctly identifies this condition?
   a. Fully respiratory alkalosis
   b. Partially compensated metabolic acidosis
   c. Fully compensated metabolic alkalosis
   d. Uncompensated respiratory acidosis

147. At the end of one's life, what virtue does Erikson's stages of development say develops when one has positively overcome the ego conflict of integrity vs. despair?
   a. Fidelity
   b. Wisdom
   c. Caring
   d. Love

148. The CMA understands that a Safety Data Sheet (SDS) is required for every individual hazardous material present in an agency. Which of the following items are noted on the SDS?
   a. Storage location of the substance in the agency
   b. Identification of personnel allowed to use the substance
   c. First-aid instructions for the home user
   d. Identification of potential hazards related to the use of the substance

149. What is the most common cause of off-label drug use in pediatric populations?
   a. Many prescription drugs do not contain labeling information for small children.
   b. The Pediatric Research Equity Act forbids off-label use of all prescription drugs.
   c. Most drugs can be used for pediatric patients with altered doses.
   d. Pediatric drug therapies do not require FDA review.

150. The CMA is providing home care for a patient who recently had a TB skin test. Which remark by the patient should be reported to the CMA's supervisor?

a. "I will let the clinic nurse know when the spot turns red."
b. "If the test is positive, I will need to take medication to treat the infection."
c. "I should avoid people that have the flu."
d. "If I have TB, my family will need to be tested as well."

151. The doctor has just finished explaining a procedure to a patient and answering their questions. The patient seems to understand and has signed a document stating they are permitting the procedure to be done and that they understand the side effects and potential complications. What type of consent was obtained?

a. Expressed consent
b. Informed consent
c. Implied consent
d. Verbal consent

152. Which of the following exam/position pairs is stated incorrectly?

a. Vaginal examination: lithotomy position
b. Sigmoidoscopy: prone position
c. Fleet's enema: lateral position
d. EKG/ECG: Fowler's position

153. Which of the following characteristics is consistent with a diagnosis of bulimia?

a. The disorder is common in men and women
b. Refusal to consume any amount of food
c. Damage to the oral cavity
d. Long-term health effects are rare

154. The patient tells the CMA, "I don't understand how to take this new pill, the nitroglycerin, that my doctor just ordered." Which of the following is the CMA's best response?

a. "Be sure to take the pill with food."
b. "Grapefruit juice will interfere with the absorption of the pill."
c. "The pill should be placed under your tongue and allowed to dissolve."
d. "You should drink eight ounces of water with this pill to be sure it reaches the stomach."

155. Which condition can alter the pharmacodynamic reaction of a drug at the cellular receptor site?

a. Type 2 diabetes
b. Cushing's disease
c. Addison's disease
d. Thyrotoxicosis

156. A CMA should try and present a professional image through all but which of the following?

a. Come to work wearing the appropriate uniform and grooming appropriately.
b. Speak to patients with care and courtesy.
c. Take part in volunteer events to help the poor and needy in the community.
d. Post pictures to social media of the workplace, and post status updates talking about work gossip.

157. Which of the following statements regarding the advanced beneficiary notice (ABN) is correct?

   a. The CMA sends the ABN to all Medicare recipients when preauthorization for a procedure is denied.
   b. ABNs are only sent to patients enrolled in original Medicare programs, not Medicare Advantage programs.
   c. A patient's request for therapy that does not meet the necessary and reasonable standard always requires an ABN.
   d. ABNs are only sent to patients for denied hospital claims.

158. The medical assistant must report which of the following findings to the primary nurse immediately?

   a. Five-year-old boy, T=100.2 rectally, Heart Rate = 90, Respiratory Rate = 28, BP = 90/50
   b. 12-year-old girl, T=99.6 orally, Heart Rate = 110, Respiratory Rate = 30, BP = 150/92
   c. Newborn, T= 98.3 axillary, Heart Rate = 146, Respiratory Rate = 42, BP = 64/40
   d. 38-year-old woman, T= 99.0 orally, Heart Rate = 72, Respiratory Rate = 18, BP = 120/78

159. Which of the following diseases is a vector-borne disease?

   a. Lyme disease
   b. Legionnaire's disease
   c. Varicella
   d. Impetigo

160. The CMA is assessing the patient's level of understanding preceding a complicated procedure. The patient explains their impression of what will happen, and the CMA paraphrases what the patient says back to them. What type of technique did the CMA employ here?

   a. Restatement
   b. Reflection
   c. Clarification
   d. Feedback

161. Which of the following manifestations is associated with hyperosmolar hyperglycemic states?

   a. Fruity-smelling breath
   b. High levels of ketones in the urine
   c. Flushing of the skin
   d. Cerebral edema in younger patients

162. Which set of laws comprised the biggest healthcare reform in the last 50 years?

   a. The Patient Protection and Affordable Care Act
   b. The Privacy Act
   c. The HiTech PHI Act
   d. The Emergency Medical Treatment and Labor Act

163. Which of the following activities is within the scope of practice of the CMA?

   a. Collecting blood and urine specimens for analysis
   b. Creating a teaching plan for a newly prescribed medication
   c. Explaining the results of the A1C to a patient
   d. Evaluating the patient's compliance with the plan of care

164. Which of the following conditions is considered as an obstructive disorder of the respiratory system?

   a. Pneumonia
   b. Small cell cancer
   c. Emphysema
   d. Asthma

165. Which statement regarding "no-shows" is correct?

   a. People who consistently miss appointments may be dismissed from the primary care practice.
   b. The provider is legally required to report "no-shows" to the patient's insurance company.
   c. "No-shows" are not contacted about rescheduling.
   d. The provider may report the "no-show" to the insurance company, but only at the provider's discretion.

166. What is the most common initial assessment finding used to diagnose child abuse?

   a. Patient report
   b. Bruising
   c. Onset of bed wetting
   d. "Acting out" behavior

167. Knowing the geographical risks to a healthcare facility and resources available to the community is a component of which aspect of medical assistants?

   a. Disaster management
   b. Epidemiology
   c. Community service
   d. Continuing education

168. Which of the following correctly pairs the medication name with its description?

   a. Diclofenac, opioid analgesic
   b. Paroxetine, serotonin reuptake inhibitor (SSRI)
   c. Hydroxyzine, potassium-sparing diuretic
   d. Ondansetron, proton pump inhibitor

169. What is the rationale for including individual patient identifiers for reportable diseases?

   a. To identify patients with multiple illnesses
   b. To measure the effectiveness of the prescribed medications
   c. To enroll the patient in a mandatory treatment program
   d. To provide immediate disease control and prevention

170. Which of the following is an appropriate order of events for a CMA to do with a patient whose provider has decided to dismiss the patient from the agency?
   a. The CMA should send the patient a letter by certified mail and include the patient's "no-show" schedule with the provider's list of specific complaints.
   b. The CMA should find the patient in person and tell them face-to-face that the provider no longer wishes to see them.
   c. The CMA should send the patient a letter by certified mail and include the signed receipt of the patient's EHR.
   d. The CMA should email the patient their medical history and the detailed reason why they are being dismissed from the agency.

171. A patient is verbally abusive toward the CMA. On a follow-up visit, the same patient is overly nice to the same CMA, flattering them and complimenting them nonstop. The CMA recognizes this as which defense mechanism?
   a. Undoing
   b. Denial
   c. Sublimation
   d. Repression

172. The CMA is reviewing the details of the DEXA or bone density screening test with a patient who is menopausal. Which of the following statements is consistent with this screening test?
   a. The scan can also identify arthritic changes in the hip joint.
   b. Medications containing magnesium should not be taken for 24 hours prior to the exam.
   c. The scan does not provide a reliable assessment of bone density in men.
   d. Fasting for six to eight hours prior to the exam is recommended.

173. What type of law is based on previously decided court cases, or precedents?
   a. Common
   b. Civil
   c. Criminal
   d. Statutory

174. Which of the following is a form of tertiary prevention for a newborn infant?
   a. MMR vaccination
   b. Pavlik harness application for developmental dysphagia of the hip (DDH)
   c. Phenylketonuria (PKU) screening
   d. Blood transfusion for sickle cell disease

175. Which of the following identifies the correct procedure for collecting a 24-hour urine specimen?
   a. For 24 hours, collect each individual urine sample, label the specimen, and transport it to the lab.
   b. Discard the first voided sample, and collect all urine voided for the subsequent 24-hour period.
   c. Collect and refrigerate all voided urine for 24 hours.
   d. Insert an indwelling catheter to collect a sterile urine sample for the 24-hour test.

176. Which element of the "Right to Try" initiative has received the greatest amount of criticism?
   a. Patients must live in a state with "Right to Try" laws to be eligible for care.
   b. Drug companies cannot make a profit from "Right to Try" protocols.
   c. Eligible drug therapies must have completed an FDA-approved Phase 1 clinical trial.
   d. Physicians are required to submit patient requests for treatment.

177. The CMA knows that marijuana, though legalized and used medically in many states, is still listed by the Drug Enforcement Agency (DEA) as a Schedule I drug, meaning which of the following?
   a. No potential for abuse
   b. Low potential for abuse
   c. Moderate potential for abuse
   d. High potential for abuse

178. The CMA protects patient privacy and confidentiality according to which law?
   a. Genetic Information Nondiscrimination Act of 2008
   b. Health Information Technology for Economic and Clinical Act
   c. Health Insurance Portability and Accountability Act
   d. Public Health and Welfare Disclosure

179. What is the final step of a health research project?
   a. Analyzing and interpreting data
   b. Receiving funds to pay incentives to study participants
   c. Publication of a manuscript detailing the study in scholarly literature
   d. Destroying personal information of participants in the data collection system

180. The CMA will immediately report which of the following lab results?
   a. Hemoglobin A1c 6.2%
   b. BUN 19 mg/dl
   c. Potassium 2.8 mEq/L
   d. WBC 9,000 K/μL

181. A patient's blood pressure is measured as 140/90. Which statement about this measurement is true?
   a. It represents low blood pressure.
   b. It represents normal blood pressure.
   c. It represents high blood pressure.
   d. It represents dangerously high blood pressure.

182. A CMA would probably NOT be in violation of the Health Insurance Portability and Accountability Act (HIPAA) if performing which act?
   a. Telling a friend, without the grandfather's consent, that he is taking care of the friend's grandfather at work
   b. Accessing the medical records of a patient at his workplace that he is not actually caring for
   c. Sharing a patient's medical information with students at the facility who are training to become CMAs
   d. Discussing a patient's problems involving drug or alcohol addiction with other CMAs at the facility

183. An adult man has a body mass index (BMI) of 27. According to the Centers for Disease Control and Prevention, which statement about this person is correct?

a. He is obese.
b. He is overweight.
c. He is a healthy weight.
d. He is underweight.

184. What is the main purpose of using Current Procedural Terminology (CPT) modifiers?

a. To correct certain mistakes that were made in the original terminology
b. To modify terminology so that the institution's revenue is increased
c. To record a higher level of care and increase the patient's reimbursement
d. To add certain details that more closely reflect the patient encounter

185. Which example of commonly used medical prefixes and suffixes and their meanings is incorrect?

a. *Bucc-* means breathing; *-plegia* means softening.
b. *Andr-* means male; *-emia* means blood condition.
c. *Lyso-* means breaking down; *-blast* means budding.
d. *Cutane-* means skin; *-penia* means a deficiency.

186. Which choice shows the correct sequence of elements in the chain of infection?

a. Mode of transmission–portal of entry–reservoir–susceptible host–portal of exit
b. Reservoir–portal of exit–mode of transmission–portal of entry–susceptible host
c. Susceptible host–mode of transmission–portal of exit–portal of entry–reservoir
d. Infectious agent–mode of transmission–reservoir–susceptible host–portal of entry

187. If a health insurance company refuses coverage for a woman because she has a mutated BRCA1 gene, increasing her risks for breast and ovarian cancer, what is the name of the federal law that is being violated?

a. Genetic Data Protection Act of 2014
b. Genetic Privacy Protection Act of 2012
c. Genetic Awareness Nondiscrimination Act of 2010
d. Genetic Information Nondiscrimination Act of 2008

188. Medical providers use the Level II Healthcare Common Procedure Coding System (HCPCS) for what purpose?

a. To file claims for any common medical services that were given to the patient
b. To file claims for any patient supplies, medications, devices, or transportation
c. To classify all medical services received in a patient's electronic medical records
d. To classify diseases and diagnoses as regulated by the World Health Organization

189. What is the main federal government agency that is responsible for ensuring the health of Americans in their places of employment through the enforcement of regulations and laws?

a. Department of Labor
b. Department of Health and Human Services
c. Centers for Disease Control and Prevention
d. Occupational Safety and Health Administration

190. What is the standard length of time for a new patient appointment?

a. 15–20 minutes
b. 20–30 minutes
c. 30–45 minutes
d. About one hour

191. A CMA at a hospital has accidentally cut herself with a scalpel on which there was blood from a patient with hepatitis B. What is the main action that the hospital must immediately take to properly address this situation?

a. The hospital must implement its post-exposure plan to take care of the CMA.
b. The hospital must isolate the CMA to prevent the further spread of infection.
c. The hospital must contact the Occupational Safety and Health Administration (OSHA).
d. The hospital must contact OSHA and then give the CMA an anti-hepatitis vaccination.

192. In the images of the draping body positions below, identify the correct numbers for the lithotomy position, Fowler's position, supine position, and Sim's position.

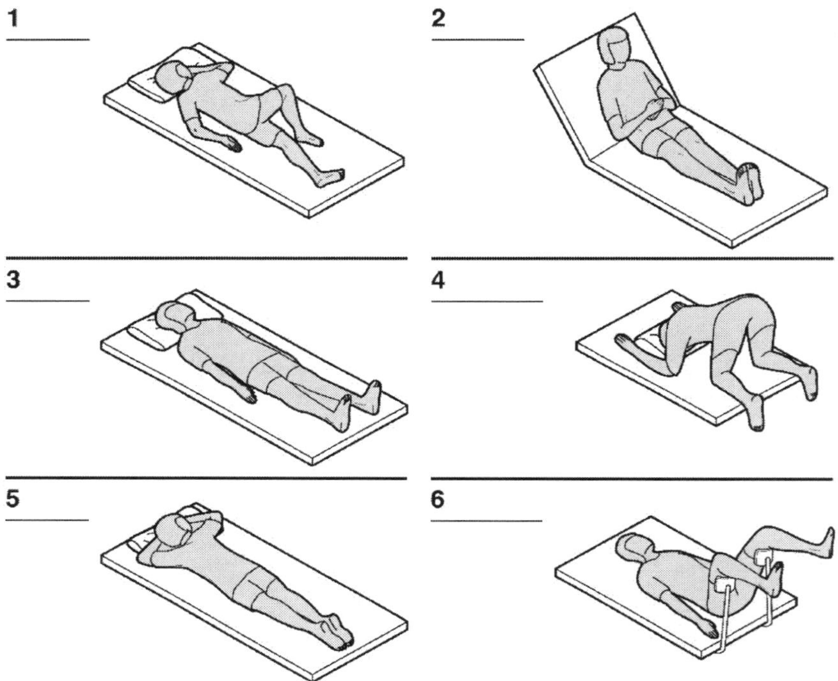

a. Lithotomy=1, Fowler's=6, supine=5, Sim's=4
b. Lithotomy=6, Fowler's=2, supine=3, Sim's=1
c. Lithotomy=4, Fowler's=1, supine=6, Sim's=2
d. Lithotomy=2, Fowler's=4, supine=3, Sim's=6

193. According to Maslow's hierarchy of human needs, usually represented as a pyramid, what is the top, most complicated human need?

a. Being esteemed
b. Self-actualization
c. Love and belonging
d. Physiological needs

194. A pregnant woman receives a prenatal pelvic exam early in her pregnancy. During the course of a normal pregnancy, when is the second pelvic exam typically performed?

a. Late first trimester
b. Second trimester
c. Third trimester
d. Postpartum

195. Which statement best describes a surgical scrub?

a. Thorough disinfection of hands and forearms with sanitizer solution
b. Thorough sterilization of hands and forearms with sanitizer solution
c. Three-minute washing of hands and forearms with soap and water
d. Five-minute washing of hands and forearms with antimicrobial soap

196. For an individual to be considered an "established" patient, he or she must have been seen by an agency provider within what period of time?

a. The previous year
b. The previous two years
c. The previous three years
d. The previous five years

197. The analgesic drugs oxycodone and fentanyl are considered to have a high potential for abuse, though they may have medical applications in certain cases. According to the drug scheduling under the Controlled Substances Act, which schedule would these drugs be classified as?

a. Schedule I
b. Schedule II
c. Schedule III
d. Schedule IV

198. When a person redirects the energy that they use to put in a negative activity, such as getting drunk or high, into a positive activity, such as exercising or meditating, this is an example of what kind of defense mechanism?

a. Denial
b. Undoing
c. Sublimation
d. Transference

199. Children recovering from viral infections should never be given aspirin because of the risk of Reye syndrome, a potentially fatal condition characterized by brain swelling and liver damage. What is the medical term used to describe such circumstances in which drugs should NOT be administered?

a. Side effect
b. Adverse effect
c. Absolute contraindication
d. Relative contraindication

200. When administering a drug to a patient, it is important to verify that certain things about the patient and drug are correct. The list of these things is referred to as what?

a. The six rights of medication administration
b. The 10 rights of medication administration
c. The provider checklist for medication administration
d. The patient checklist for medication administration

Answer Explanations

1. B: Verapamil is commonly associated with constipation that requires intervention beyond dietary measures. The stool softener is sufficient for most patients; however, this common adverse effect should be evaluated at every provider appointment. The remaining choices are associated with common complaints of diarrhea, which would not be treated with docusate. Therefore, Choices *A*, *C*, and *D* are incorrect.

2. C: A humanistic outcome is defined as the patient's perception of the outcome, which is subjective and not directly measurable. The patient's perception of pain is a subjective assessment of the intervention, and it cannot be directly measured. Choices *A*, *B*, and *D* are clinical outcomes that can be measured; therefore, these choices are incorrect.

3. A: The antiemetic drug metoclopramide is a dopamine receptor antagonist that can increase the manifestations associated with Parkinson's disease by antagonizing the metabolism of dopamine and its derivatives. According to the 2019 BEERS report, the antiemetic should be avoided in all patients with Parkinson's disease. The remaining choices, Choices *B*, *C*, and *D*, have no known effect on dopamine function.

4. C: The transverse plane, also called an axial plane, is a horizontal line that divides the body into upper and lower sections. The sagittal plane is a vertical line, not a horizontal line, that divides the body into right and left sections; therefore, Choice *A* is incorrect. Choice *B* is the definition of the sagittal plane, not the caudal plane (which does not exist), so Choice *B* is incorrect. Choice *D* is the definition of the transverse plane, which is a horizontal line, not a vertical one; therefore, Choice *D* is incorrect.

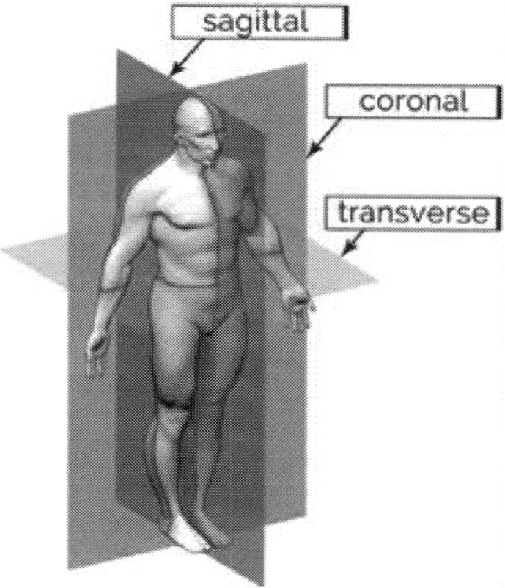

5. A: The Jaeger chart, used to assess near vision, is a card or sheet that contains a series of paragraphs that contain progressively smaller text. The Snellen chart is a panel with a series of letters of different sizes that tests visual acuity; therefore, Choice *B* is incorrect. The Ishihara plates are used to identify color blindness by the identification of the colored number embedded in the circle; therefore, Choice *C* is incorrect. The Amsler grid is a square with a grid of straight lines that is used to diagnose macular degeneration in the eye. If macular degeneration is present, the patient's view of the grid will be distorted; therefore, Choice *D* is incorrect.

6. C: Lipid-soluble drugs move across the cellular membrane by passive diffusion, which means that the absorption rate is increased without the cellular expenditure of energy in the form of ATP. Drugs that are bound to plasma proteins are also capable of passive diffusion across the cellular membrane; therefore, Choice *A* is incorrect. Lipid solubility is one determinant of the absorption rate; however, the rate can also be affected by the remaining factors that are associated with the absorption rate; therefore, Choice *B* is incorrect. Choice *D* is incorrect because the first-pass effect is related to the route of administration rather than the solubility of the drug. All drugs administered orally are subjected to the first-pass effect because the drugs are absorbed in the stomach, and then they enter the GI vasculature and progress to the liver.

7. A: An ECG or EKG, short for electrocardiogram, is a test using electrodes attached to the patient's chest to assess electrical activity of the heart. An echocardiogram, or ECHO, is a test using ultrasound waves to visualize the heart and its chambers to assess heart function. EFG is not a medical test. An EEG, or electroencephalogram, is used to measure and assess the electrical activity of the brain.

8. A: The classic manifestation of meningitis is the nuchal rigidity (stiffness of the neck) that is associated with severe head pain. The head pain is due to the inflammation and irritation of the meninges by the causative organism. Skin rashes, fever, chills, nausea and vomiting, lethargy, and confusion are also associated with this infection. However, peripheral sensory changes, abdominal pain, and hyperactivity are not associated with meningitis; therefore, Choices *B*, *C*, and *D* are incorrect.

9. D: The CMA will have information for the new drug that predicts the average patient response based on the patient's age and the specific characteristics of the drug such as blood-brain barrier absorption. However, the patient's individual differences that result from genetic and environmental factors over time are less predictable and therefore will have the most significant impact on the patient's response to the new medication.

10. C: In many states, trained healthcare providers are not protected from legal action if they render care. The CMA must be aware of all applicable state laws. In some states, healthcare workers are the only class of individuals covered by the law; therefore, Choice *A* is incorrect. The law is a state law rather than a federal law, and while the general intent of the law is common among states, healthcare providers must understand the details of the law in their practice location; therefore, Choice *B* is incorrect. Trained providers are not covered for emergency care in their place of employment; therefore, Choice *D* is incorrect.

11. A: The MELD score uses the serum bilirubin, creatinine level, INR, and sodium levels to predict the severity of end-stage liver disease in patients over the age of 12. Encephalopathy and ascites are clinical manifestations of liver failure; however, their presence or absence is not associated with the calculation of the MELD score. Therefore, Choices *B* and *C* are incorrect. Nutritional status is compromised and restricted in patients with liver failure, but there is no relationship between diet and MELD score, so Choice *D* is incorrect.

12. A: The physical urinalysis includes the assessment of the color and turbidity of the sample. Turbid urine is cloudy and, since freshly voided urine is normally clear, turbidity is an abnormal finding that may indicate the presence of other cells such as proteins or white blood cells in the urine. The provider uses reagent strips to conduct a chemical urinalysis that measures the glucose level, specific gravity, and pH of the urine sample; therefore, Choices *B, C,* and *D* are incorrect.

13. D: Dimensional analysis is a mathematical process that is used to calculate intravenous and medication dosages. The research indicates that dimensional analysis results in fewer provider errors than the ratio and proportion calculation that is also commonly used in clinical practice. Dimensional analysis is not used in the calculation of the BMI. The equation for calculating BMI is indicated below; therefore, Choice *A* is incorrect.

$$BMI = \frac{Weight\ in\ Pounds}{(Height\ in\ inches\ x\ 2)}\ x\ 703$$

14. D: Reporting the issue and obtaining the blood pressure reading via a different machine or manually would be the most appropriate action for the CMA to take. Not doing anything about it could lead to patient or CMA harm. Using a different outlet would not fix the problem. The fraying of the wires presents an electrocution and/or a fire hazard that needs to be addressed.

15. C: The most common reason for providers to not report elder abuse is concern about malpractice claims by the patient's family. The remaining choices are not identified as reasons for non-reporting of abuse. Therefore, Choices *A, B*, and *D* are incorrect.

16. D: The correct sequence of steps for sterile gloving is:

1. Once the outer wrap is discarded, the sterile inner wrap is opened with the paper tabs.
2. The inner cuff of the glove is picked up by the non-dominant hand.
3. The thumb of the dominant hand is held flat against the palm.
4. The hand is slid into the glove.
5. The gloved hand slips under the cuff of the remaining glove.
6. The thumb is held against the palm and the hand is slid into the glove.

The question asks about the first step, what to do after removing the outer packaging. Choice *D* answers the question correctly; therefore, Choices *A, B*, and *C* are incorrect.

17. D: Euthanasia is now legal in a few states in the United States. The other three statements are true. It is an ethical gray area and an issue that may become more prevalent in the coming years as it potentially becomes legalized. It is called "death with dignity" and "physician-assisted suicide" and is a way to bypass potential pain and suffering. The CMA needs to be aware of this ethical issue in their practice.

18. A: Genetic metabolic alterations are associated with changes in the plasma concentration of the drug. Reduced binding of the drug at the receptor site is related to a change in the pharmacodynamics, rather a metabolic process alteration; therefore, Choice *B* is incorrect. Idiosyncratic changes are associated with an increased possibility of hypersensitivity reactions, rather than alterations in the excretion of drugs; therefore, Choice *C* is incorrect. There is no evidence to suggest that alterations in the metabolic processes are associated with an increased potency of the drug; therefore, Choice *D* is incorrect.

19. B: Surveillance case definitions serve as the framework for the designation of reportable diseases. The remaining choices are not associated with this process; therefore, Choices *A, C,* and *D* are incorrect.

20. B: Inhibition of excretion of the medication results in increased plasma concentration of it, which may result in an overdose or ADR. Inhibition of excretion is more common than induction, which is an increase in the excretion rate of the drug. Induction can result in an inadequate systemic response to the drug that may also represent an ADR; therefore, Choice *A* is incorrect. Desensitization is the diminished body response to a drug that is administered over a long period of time. This predictable reaction is also the basis for reversing drug sensitivities in patients with allergies; therefore, Choice *C* is incorrect. Absorption is the first phase of pharmacodynamics and is defined as the presence of the drug in the bloodstream following administration; therefore, Choice *D* is incorrect.

21. C: In addition to these two factors, patient satisfaction is also associated with more resources for the organization and retention of high-quality staff. The other options do not apply.

22. B: Advanced triage processes are normally used in catastrophic events, such as an avalanche. The other options listed probably would not require fast-paced triage processes of any kind.

23. C: Turning off the TV in a patient's room always helps with clear communication. If a patient is blind, the CMA should not treat them as if they are hard of hearing or have an intellectual deficit by speaking loudly or slowly. Using hand gestures is useless if the patient is blind.

24. B: When the kidneys are damaged by disease or injury, waste products such as creatinine accumulate in the bloodstream, which means that a serum creatinine level of 5.4 (normal = .6 – 1.2 mg per dL) is a sensitive indicator of kidney function. The BUN level of 12 mg per dL is normal, and the nurse understands that the BUN is also affected by the patient's fluid volume status, which means that alterations in the BUN are not specific to kidney function. Therefore, Choice *A* is incorrect. The identified glomerular filtration rate in Choice *C* is also normal. Each of the stages of renal failure is defined by the GFR and the serum creatinine levels; therefore, Choice *C* is incorrect. Hemoglobin levels are decreased in acute renal failure due to faulty erythropoietin regulation; however, the hemoglobin level in Choice *D* is normal; therefore, Choice *D* is incorrect.

25. A: CMAs should understand that, although the hs-CRP is an assessment of the inflammatory state of blood vessels, NSAID administration is not recommended as an agent that can improve C-reactive protein (CRP) levels because the research indicates that aspirin administration is more effective. Note that chronic elevated CRP levels (even slightly elevated) can be indicative of atherosclerosis, and thus can increase the risk of CVD. Lifestyle changes such as exercise, weight management, smoking cessation, and omega-3 fatty acid administration are all included in the care plan to lower the potential risk of developing high CRP levels (and subsequent atherosclerosis or CVD). Therefore, Choices *B, C,* and *D* are incorrect.

26. B: The patient must be informed of the risk for teratogenicity. A negative pregnancy test is required for all female patients of childbearing age prior to the start of each cycle of the therapy, and this caution applies to both men and women who do not plan to use contraception for the duration of the therapy. The drug is associated with decreased lymphocytes, not red cells; therefore, Choice *A* is incorrect. The patient is at risk for hepatitis, tuberculosis, herpes, and progressive multifocal leukoencephalopathy as well. The drug is contraindicated for patients with HIV infection; therefore, Choice *C* is incorrect. The adverse effects for the drug include teratogenicity, risk for multiple infections, and high-risk for the

development of malignancy; however, there are no reports of photosensitization; therefore, Choice *D* is incorrect.

27. C: Aminoglycosides such as gentamicin alter neuromuscular transmission, which can cause muscle weakness. In patients with myasthenia gravis, muscle weakness results in respiratory depression. While there is a general caution for the use of aminoglycosides in the elderly, there is no contraindication for their use in the remaining diseases; therefore, Choices *A, B*, and *D* are incorrect.

28. A: The patient appears to be experiencing the internal distraction of pain. Noise and temperature are examples of external distractions that create a barrier to communication and information gathering. Disinterest is a barrier to communication that would present itself differently from pain, in ways such as yawning, lack of eye contact, and slouching.

29. B: Sildenafil and nitroglycerin should not be taken together, as both cause blood vessel dilatation, leading to the potential of irreversible hypotension. The other listed combinations do not have documented direct effects when taken in combination with nitroglycerin.

30. C: The patient is bradycardic when their heart rate is less than 60 beats per minute. Hypotension is a reading of less than 90 systolic and 60 diastolic. Bradypnea is a rate of breaths less than 12 breaths per minute. When a patient's bowel sounds do not occur more than 5 times per minute, it is referred to as having decreased bowel sounds.

31. A: The STOPP list recommends stopping the use of NSAIDs with HTN, even moderate HTN. This is a significant concern in the elderly, who routinely use NSAIDs to treat osteoarthritis. Beta-blockers to decrease the heart rate and contractility are on the START list and are recommended for the treatment of angina, so Choice *B* is incorrect. The use of ACE inhibitors with chronic heart failure to decrease the effect of angiotensin and Aldactone® on target organs, such as the heart and kidney, is also on the START list, so Choice *C* is incorrect. Proton pump inhibitors (PPIs) to treat severe GERD are on the START list, so Choice *D* is incorrect.

32. D: *Respondeat superior* comes from the Latin words that mean "let the master answer" and means that an employer is legally responsible for the actions of their employee. *Subpoena duces tecum* means "under penalty you shall bring with you" and means that a person must come to court with any pertinent evidence. *Res ipsa loquitur* translates from Latin as "the thing speaks for itself" and indicates that negligence can be blamed when an accident happens. *Locum tenens* is Latin for "one holding a place" and is used when a physician is filling in for another.

33. A:

	Intake	**Output**
D5W 50 x 24 =	1,200	Urine = 1,350
Heparin 8 x 24 =	192	Wound = 46
D5W 50 x 4 =	200	
Tube Feeding 30 x 24=	720	
Total Intake	2,312 mL	Total Output = 1,396 mL

34. C: Patient information that is left on the clipboard is visible to other patients who are using the clipboard to check in. This is a direct violation of HIPAA laws, which has a privacy clause stating that identifiable patient information should remain private and safeguarded. The other options do not apply.

35. D: The agency does not review or maintain the medical records of the employees. In the event of an occupational exposure to HCV or HIV, and depending on applicable laws, the agency will test the blood of the source of the exposure and the exposed employee. The exposed worker will be offered appropriate prophylaxis for the causative agent, counseling, and ongoing assessment of any illnesses. The worker's healthcare provider will issue an opinion to the agency, and the worker's medical record will be kept in strict confidence. The remaining choices are OSHA requirements for all agencies; therefore, Choices *A*, *B*, and *C* are incorrect.

36. D: The patient is describing tolerance, which means that changes made by the drug decrease some of the effects of the drug when given over an extended period of time. Addiction is a complex disease that may be due to genetic, environmental, or psychosocial factors. It is manifested by compulsive use of the drug without the control exhibited by individuals who are not addicted, so Choice *A* is incorrect. Habituation is not associated with the use of controlled substances and is defined as adjusting or adapting to something, so Choice *B* is incorrect. Addiction is physical dependence manifested by withdrawal syndrome if the substance is withdrawn abruptly or neutralized by an antagonist, so Choice *C* is incorrect.

37. D: When patients are physically or psychologically unable to provide verbal or written consent to treatment, healthcare providers rely on implied consent, acting on the belief that the patient would like the best treatment to benefit their life.

38. A: The specific document that appoints a person (usually a family member) to make medical decisions for a patient when they become incapacitated is the medical durable power of attorney. The power of attorney can be part of both the living will and advance directives in general. The difference is that a living will, Choice *B*, is a broader document that covers many topics regarding a patient's care, such as if they would ever want a feeding tube should they become unable to feed themselves and/or eat. Advance directives, Choice *C*, is an even broader category covering both living wills and powers of attorney. All patients should be encouraged to draw up advance directive documents. Choice *D*, Patient Self-Determination Act, is the act that requires facilities to give patients certain documents upon arrival and states that facilities cannot discriminate against patients who have or do not have an advanced directive.

39. B: Insulin resistance results from alterations in the INSR gene that change the insulin receptor proteins, decreasing the amount of insulin that is removed from the plasma. Abdominal obesity is associated with insulin resistance; however, it is a modifiable risk factor, not an inherited risk factor, so Choice *A* is incorrect. HIV antiretrovirals have no effect on insulin resistance, so Choice *C* is incorrect. Anti-insulin antigens are not associated with insulin resistance and are not genetically determined, so Choice *D* is incorrect.

40. C: The test kits must provide consistent results within a reasonable margin of error set by the FDA, which means that the potential for both false-positives and false-negatives does exist. Lab tests for home use are judged to be safe for consumers even if test is not used correctly; therefore, Choice *A* is incorrect. All testing kits marketed for at-home use are approved by the FDA. Therefore, Choice *B* is incorrect. In order to optimize the validity of the results, providers who recommend the use of the at-home testing kits must provide the patient with appropriate testing instructions; therefore, Choice *D* is incorrect.

41. A: A compound fracture is defined as a fractured bone that is associated with an open wound. The bone may or may not be visible in the wound. A comminuted fracture occurs when the bone is broken into three or more pieces; therefore, based on the information in the question, Choice *B* is incorrect. A stable fracture occurs when the proximal and distal ends of the fractured bone are not displaced, and there is no breakage in the skin; therefore, Choice *C* is incorrect. Greenstick fractures are long bone fractures that are common in children less than 10 years of age. This fracture may be considered as an incomplete fracture because the soft bones bend; therefore, Choice *D* is incorrect.

42. A: Ranson's criteria is a prediction tool for identifying the risk of mortality associated with acute pancreatitis. CMAs should understand that the criteria calculate the mortality risk for acute pancreatitis caused by gallstones in patients over 70 and for alcohol-induced acute pancreatitis in patients over 55. However, the model does not predict mortality in patients under the age of 55 years old. Decreased serum calcium level, elevated serum glucose and elevated white blood cell count are associated with both forms of the disease in the Ranson model; therefore, Choices *B*, *C*, and *D* are incorrect.

43. D: The middle section of this tracing is an artifact; however, the underlying rhythm is atrial tachycardia at a rate of 150 beats per minute. Therefore, the supervisor should be notified, and the patient's vital signs should be recorded. The artifact in this tracing is caused by the patient's movement, not faulty electrodes; therefore, Choices *A* is incorrect. The underlying rhythm in this tracing is not normal sinus rhythm because the rate is greater than 100 beats per minute; therefore, Choice *B* is incorrect. Adjusting the gain on the monitor will increase the amplitude of the complexes; however, it will not eliminate the artifact. Therefore, Choice *C* is incorrect.

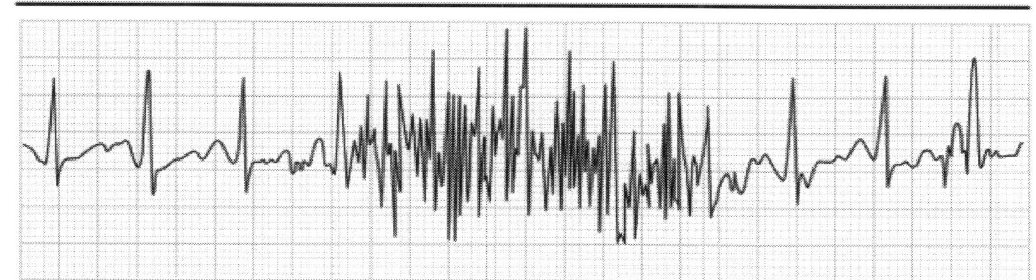

44. B: The "brown bag" approach serves two important functions. The nurse can verify that the patient's drug supply is correct and current, and the nurse can also assess the patient's understanding of the drug plan. Choice *B* is correct because it is the most complete answer. Choice *D* is incorrect because it only identifies one purpose of the approach. Construction of a drug plan and coordination of the drug administration schedule with ADLs may improve patient adherence to the drug plan; however, those activities are not specifically included in the brown bag approach; therefore, Choices *A* and *C* are incorrect.

45. D: Current research indicates that many elderly individuals with normal hearing acuity may still have difficulty with conversation, especially in a noisy environment. The deficit is a delay in the processing or understanding the spoken word, not in "hearing" the words. The most useful strategy is to maintain a normal volume and allow extra time for the patient to process the words; therefore, Choice *A* is incorrect. Sign language interpreters could only be helpful for a limited group of patients who might understand sign language; therefore, Choice *B* is incorrect. Considering that the patient is able to watch TV set at a normal volume indicates that a hearing aid would not improve the patient's ability to process information; therefore, Choice *C* is incorrect.

46. C: Hyphema is the collection of blood in the front of the eye between the cornea and the iris. The most common cause is trauma; however, immediate attention is required in all cases to prevent permanent blindness. Uveitis is an inflammation of the uvea, the middle layer of the wall of the eye, which is associated with blurred vision, eye pain, and redness, but not blindness. Therefore, Choice *A* is incorrect. Amblyopia, more commonly called "lazy eye," is a genetic defect that has several forms and is usually diagnosed in infancy. The vision deficits most often are related to reports of double vision and alterations in peripheral vision, so Choice *B* is incorrect. A pituitary tumor may result in visual alterations; however, the changes are gradual and related to the growth of the tumor, so Choice *D* is incorrect.

47. D: The collagen loses elasticity over time, which results in wrinkling of the skin in old age. The development of acne is most often associated with adolescence, but it may also accompany hormonal alterations in adult women. Psoriasis is an autoimmune disease that first occurs between 15 and 35 years of age but may appear in children. Vernix caseosa is the protective substance that protects the skin of the fetus during the last trimester of pregnancy. After birth, it provides the newborn with antioxidant and heat-regulation benefits. Therefore, Choices *A, B,* and *C* are incorrect.

48. A: Once a rapport has been established with a patient, it is necessary to understand the patient's views about health and illness in order to assist the patient to make the best healthcare decisions. Engaging the patient in shared decision-making is the first step of the process that progresses to a review of available care options and continued assessment of the patient's priorities. Therefore, Choices *B*, *C*, and *D* are incorrect.

49. A: Concerns with the guardianship are associated with the patient's loss of autonomy.

50. D: The CMA should follow the "PASS" acronym for proper use of a fire extinguisher: Pull the pin, aim at the base of the fire, squeeze the trigger, and sweep from side to side until the flames are extinguished. CMAs are, in fact, authorized to use extinguishers, and finding someone else to do it would waste precious time that could be used to extinguish the fire. The other directions have elements of the "PASS" acronym but are not in the right order or worded correctly.

51. A: Wounds that occurred more than eight hours ago are prone to the development of tetanus. The development of tetanus is a risk factor for stellate wounds that result from close contact gunshot injury, punctuate wounds of any type, and wounds with compromised tissue. Therefore, Choices *B*, *C*, and *D* are incorrect.

52. A: Closing all the facility doors will help confine the fire. The hallways should always remain uncluttered and emergency exits unblocked for general workplace safety. Activating the emergency response system and rescuing patients are part of the RACE acronym but will not directly affect the confinement of the fire.

53. A: The tiger top (red/black) tube contains silica which promotes clotting of the blood to allow analysis of the clotting factors. The red top tube (glass) does not contain any additive and is commonly used for serological studies; therefore, Choice *B* is incorrect. The purple top tube contains EDTA which is

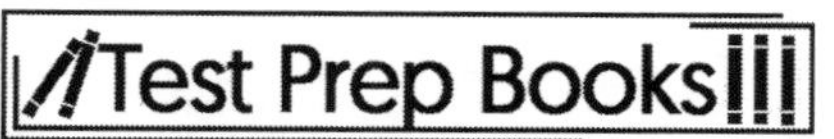

an anticoagulant, and this tube is commonly used for hematological studies; therefore, Choice *C* is incorrect. The light blue tube also contains an anticoagulant, sodium citrate, which prepares the sample for Prothrombin time (PT), partial thromboplastin time (PTT), and fibrinogen studies; therefore, Choice *D* is incorrect.

54. B: A hematologist is a doctor who specializes in the diagnosis and treatment of hematological or blood disorders such as sickle cell anemia. A hepatologist specializes in hepatic or liver disorders. A cardiologist deals with the heart and cardiovascular system but not specifically blood disorders. An immunologist takes care of disorders of the immune system, which involves the white blood cells of the blood but is not blood-specific.

55. D: All the data is included in the pre-admission documentation; however, if the EHR does not contain adequate data to support the medical necessity for the admission, the patient is responsible for all care costs. Therefore, Choice *D* is the highest priority among the four choices.

56. C: Epidemiology is the study of health symptom clusters and patterns of disease outbreak in a community.

57. C: Hypertension is caused by narrowing of the blood vessels by fatty deposits and is associated with fluid volume excess, which means that appropriate food choices should contain moderate amounts of animal fats and small amounts of sodium. Salad dressings, cheese, and canned soups all contain significant amounts of sodium and should be avoided; therefore, Choices *A, B,* and *D* are incorrect.

58. B: The database entries should include the problem, the date of onset, the interventions, and the date of resolution of the problem. The problem list is a chronological record of the patient's progress from the time of the current interventions, which means that details such as the patient's weight and previous medications have already been considered in the development of the problem list. Therefore, Choices *A*, *C*, and *D* are incorrect.

59. D: The three categories of notifiable diseases are outbreak, infectious, and noninfectious; therefore, Choices *A, B,* and *C* are incorrect.

60. D: CHAMPVA insurance coverage covers only the dependents of veterans who are 100% disabled as a result of their active duty, or the dependents of deceased veterans who were 100% disabled as a result of their active duty. Therefore, Choices *A*, *B*, and *C* are incorrect.

61. D: The Hawthorne effect occurs when research participants tell researchers what they want to hear instead of providing accurate answers. Adding an additional section of subjects who receive an inactive substance that resembles the research treatment means that the researcher can have greater confidence in the results. The remaining choices are elements of the RCT study design, but none of these choices treats the Hawthorne effect; therefore, Choices *A*, *B*, and *C* are incorrect.

62. B: Dysfunction of the hepatocyte mitochondria results in increased levels of ammonia in the blood, which damages the astrocytes, resulting in cerebral edema and eventually increased intracranial pressure. The remaining choices are not associated with Reye's syndrome, so Choices *A, C,* and *D* are incorrect.

63. A: The first step to culturally congruent practice is the assessment and acknowledgment of one's own biases and stereotypes. Without this self-awareness, the CMAs actions can be unduly influenced by these personal beliefs. Cultural awareness is necessary to gain the knowledge and skills needed to implement culturally competent patient care. Therefore, Choices *B, C,* and *D* are incorrect.

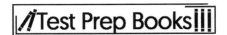

64. D: The meaningful use initiative is a government-funded incentive program that requires the development and implementation of the EHR. It is based on the assumption that the use of the EHR will positively impact the quality of patient care. The meaningful use initiative rewards are determined by the implementation of the EHR, rather than by patient outcomes. The nurse should be aware that there are other government-funded programs that reward providers for improved outcomes and that this is why medical record models that facilitate outcomes assessment are commonly used by providers. However, Choice *A* is incorrect. The implementation of the EHR may improve patient care error rates; however, that is not the basis for the meaningful use initiative; therefore, Choice *B* is incorrect. The meaningful use plan does not require a specific medical record model, but the literature seems to suggest that the POMR is superior to the SOMR regarding outcomes measurement; therefore, Choice *C* is incorrect.

65. C: Patients are not required to waive possible compensation for possible injuries. Informed consent forms should not include any waiver of the patient's rights. The remainder of the choices, Choices *A, B,* and *D*, are essential elements of informed consent and therefore are incorrect.

66. A: Central America is considered a high-risk area for "traveler's diarrhea," while the remaining areas are associated with an intermediate risk. Therefore, Choices *B, C,* and *D* are incorrect.

67. B: Mensuration is the process of measuring and includes parameters such as height and weight, and fundal height. Range of motion is assessed by the process of manipulation; therefore, Choice *A* is incorrect. Bowel sounds are assessed by the process of auscultation; therefore, Choice *C* is incorrect. Body symmetry is assessed by the process of inspection; therefore, Choice *D* is incorrect.

68. A: Fluticasone with Salmeterol (trade name: Advair Diskus) is an inhaled powder that is contained in a disk structure. The disk has a mouthpiece and a lever that positions the individual dose. The patient is instructed to inhale and exhale slowly before positioning the lips firmly around the mouthpiece. After the medication has been inhaled, the patient should hold their breath for 10 seconds before slowly exhaling. The patient is instructed to rinse the mouth with water *without swallowing* after the medication is inhaled. Rinsing the medication from the oral cavity reduces the incidence of thrush, which may develop as a result of the residual medication in the mouth; therefore, Choice *B* is incorrect. Choice *C* identifies the procedure for using an inhaler that is used for medications other than Advair; therefore, Choice *C* is incorrect. This medication is inhaled into the lungs, which means that food intake is not required; therefore, Choice *D* is incorrect.

69. D: Venous ulcers are often located on the medial malleolus and are superficial with irregular borders and copious secretions. Choices *A, B,* and *C* are associated with arterial ulcers and are therefore incorrect.

70. D: Developmental anticipatory guidance includes the assessment of physical and cognitive benchmarks. The nurse provides families with comparison data so that they are able to monitor the child's maturation and support the child's continued progress. Choice *A* is appropriate to anticipatory guidance for crisis management and is therefore incorrect. Delayed grief reaction may be associated with anticipatory guidance for crisis management or end-of-life care; however, it is not associated with developmental norms; therefore, Choice *B* is incorrect. Patient expectations for treatment success are

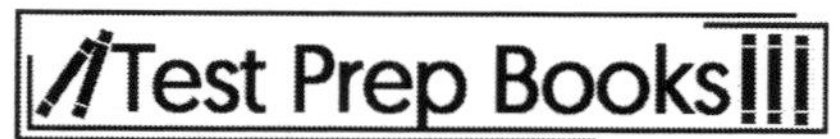

most commonly associated with disease progression rather than developmental norms; therefore, Choice *C* is incorrect.

71. B: The only appropriate action is to instruct the mother to contact the poison control center. Transporting the child to the hospital or agency without any additional information about the poison can delay appropriate treatment; therefore, Choices *A* and *D* are incorrect. Vomiting is contraindicated unless it is verified as a safe intervention for the identified poison; therefore, Choice C is incorrect. identified poison; therefore Choice *C* is incorrect.

72. C: The CMA is responsible for obtaining preauthorization for all care and procedures. The CMA is also responsible for documentation that supports the necessary and reasonable standard in order to eliminate denials for care and reimbursement delays. The CMA understands that all covered expenses are billed to the workers' compensation commercial carrier. Services and care that are not directly associated with the patient's employment are submitted to the patient's third-party payer in accordance with that contract; therefore, Choice *A* is incorrect. The workers' compensation commercial carrier will assign a claims adjustor to all covered employees, and that adjustor will issue preauthorization for details of the patient's care, including the assignment of a primary care physician. That means that the patient may not see their own primary care physician; therefore, Choice *B* is incorrect. The CMA understands that the workers' compensation claim forms are completed as paper documents and are submitted directly to the commercial carrier; therefore, Choice *D* is incorrect.

73. D: The cost of the analog insulins is widely debated. Proponents argue that cost is irrelevant and in line with other new drugs. Others believe that the benefits do not justify the costs. The remaining choices are not widely debated, so Choices *A*, *B*, and *C* are incorrect.

74. B: St. John's Wort may provide some improvement in depressive symptoms, but there is also evidence that regular use of the substance decreases the effectiveness of digoxin; therefore, the CMA should report this remark to the charge supervisor. Limiting prepackaged foods and cooking without salt limits sodium intake, which is appropriate for a patient with hypertension. Recognizing that syncope is a possible side effect is also appropriate; therefore, Choices *A, C,* and *D* are incorrect.

75. C: Insurance regulations define an established patient as an individual who has been seen by at least one provider in the previous three years and has an EHR generated by that agency. Choice *A* is therefore incorrect because the previous encounter was more than three years ago. If a provider cares for the patient in the hospital, the documentation of that care would be included in the patient's hospital record; however, the patient would not have a current record within the agency. That means that if the patient were to schedule an agency appointment with the provider, the patient would be considered a new patient; therefore, Choice *B* is incorrect. A patient referred to a provider in the agency is considered a new patient, rather than an established patient; therefore, Choice *D* is incorrect.

76. C: Ginseng can potentially increase blood pressure and decrease the effectiveness of warfarin. Many over-the-counter preparations and herbal substances can alter the action of prescription medications. Therefore, patients should be encouraged to discuss all over-the-counter substances with their provider. Walking 20 minutes per day is an appropriate goal for this patient; therefore, Choice *A* is incorrect. Adequate blood pressure control and decreased use of salt are also essential to the patient's recovery from the MI; therefore, Choices *B* and *D* are incorrect.

77. D: HMOs enroll members from a single geographic area, which may be localized to a city or a state. In the staff model, the physicians are employees of the HMO, and all patient care is provided in facilities owned by the HMO. In the group model, all physicians are salaried employees from a single specialty group that negotiates per capita care rates with the HMO; therefore, the reimbursement rates for the two models are not the same, so Choice *A* is incorrect. In the network group the HMO contracts with several physician groups to provide care for members. These providers care for non-member patients as well as member patients; therefore, Choice *C* is incorrect.

78. D: Transition of care requires many changes that almost always lead to a slight or major decline in quality of care. This can be mediated with strict standard operating procedures for transition and high levels of communication between caregivers.

79. C: Sanitization is the process of inactivating or inhibiting, but not eliminating, pathogens from a surface such as surgical instruments. Disinfectants are required to remove 99.9 percent of the *specific* susceptible agents; for instance, solution A may be effective agent B and C but not against agent D. Therefore, the solution is not 100 percent effective in eliminating infective agents from a surface. Sterilization is more effective than disinfection because 100 percent of all infectious agents are removed from an object; therefore, Choices *A, B,* and *D* are incorrect.

80. B: The Z-tract injection technique is used when the prescribed medication can potentially irritate or discolor the skin on contact. The retraction and release of the subcutaneous tissue decrease the possibility of any leakage of the medication onto the skin surface following the injection. Intradermal injections, not intramuscular injections, are used for allergy testing; therefore, Choice *A* is incorrect. Intramuscular injections are used to maximize absorption; however, the Z-tract technique is specifically designed to avoid skin irritation. Therefore, Choice *C* is incorrect. The Z-tract technique will not affect the pain associated with the intramuscular injection.

81. A: One of the assessment criteria for patient behavior, especially in children and adolescents, is the patient's developmental level. There is evidence that alterations in behavior are often associated with developmental delays. The purpose of behavioral anticipatory guidance is to provide parents and families with expected behavior that coincides with the patient's developmental level. This form of anticipatory guidance is not limited to abnormal behavior; therefore, Choice *B* is incorrect. Developmental anticipatory guidance is used to assess normal developmental data as well as deviations from normal development; therefore, Choice *C* is incorrect. There is no research evidence that indicates that behavioral anticipatory guidance is less valid than developmental anticipatory guidance in the elderly patient; therefore, Choice *D* is incorrect.

82. B: Indirect contact occurs when a susceptible person comes in contact with an organism that is present on an inanimate object, such as a child's toy. Shaking hands is considered as one-to-one or direct contact, while sneezing could spread infection by droplet or direct contact depending on the circumstances. HIV is most commonly spread by the exchange of blood and body fluids through close physical contact; therefore, Choices *A, C,* and *D* are incorrect.

83. D: Hypokalemia is associated with a prolonged P-R interval, which represents the time from the SA node firing to contraction of the ventricles. The remaining manifestations are associated with hyperkalemia; therefore, Choices *A, B,* and *C* are incorrect.

84. C: Reduced practice requires physician oversight only for prescriptive practice. Restricted practice requires physician oversight for all aspects of NP practice. Unrestricted practice places no restrictions on NP practice. Therefore, Choices *A* and *D* are incorrect. Choice *B* does not define a specific practice model; therefore, it is incorrect.

85. A: A graded drug response is measured on a continuous scale. For instance, diuretic therapy increases urinary output, and the amount of the output is measurable and theoretically continuous. A quantal drug response is one that either occurs or does not occur; therefore, Choice *B* is incorrect. Graded responses vary from one patient to the next because of individual differences in the patients' metabolism of the drugs; therefore, Choice *C* is incorrect. A quantal response can be either positive or negative depending on the specific drug; therefore, Choice **D** is incorrect.

86. D:

$$Tabs\colon \frac{1\ tab}{80\ mg} \times \frac{1000\ mg}{1\ g} \times \frac{0.16\ g}{1} = 2\ tabs$$

Therefore, Choices *A, B,* and *C* are incorrect.

87. C: Barrett esophagus is associated with the development of esophageal adenocarcinoma; therefore, continued PPI therapy is recommended. Adverse effects of proton pump inhibitors (PPI) include non-traumatic fractures, *C. difficile* diarrhea, and acute interstitial nephritis. With consideration of these adverse effects and the success of the treatments for peptic ulcer disease, *H. pylori* infection, and gastro-esophageal reflux disease (GERD), PPI therapy is not recommended for the remaining conditions. Therefore, Choices *A*, *B*, and *D* are incorrect.

88. B: Asian populations have an increased incidence of lactose intolerance, which means that the CMA will consider appropriate alterations to the nutritional plan of care.

89. B: Elias is choosing to further his education, which is a component of lifelong learning. While this may lead to promotion, specializing in a particular field of nursing, or work-life balance, pursuing an advanced degree is directly related to maintaining competence in his field. Nurses should expect to continue their education throughout the course of their careers, as technology, regulations, and other external factors influence the shape of the industry.

90. A: Pure-tone audiometry measures the patient's ability to hear tones at a certain decibel level. The results are compared to normal values to identify right/left deficits in the patient's hearing. It is a subjective test where the patient signals when and if the tone is audible. The speech discrimination test measures the patient's ability to repeat words that are spoken through earphones at decibel levels consistent with hearing threshold levels that were previously identified; therefore, Choice *B* is incorrect. The otoacoustic emission test is an objective test that measures the response of the inner ear to a generated sound. This test is often used to assess hearing deficits in infants; therefore, Choice *C* is incorrect. The auditory brainstem response test measures the integrity of the neural pathway to and from the brain; therefore, Choice *D* is incorrect.

91. A: The TB skin test results for individuals with no known risk factors for the disease are identified as positive when the induration reaches 15 mm in diameter. The result in HIV+ patients and immunocompromised individuals is considered positive when the indurated area reaches 5 mm in diameter, so Choices *B* and *C* are incorrect. Test results for individuals with one or more risk factors, such as arriving in the United States within the last five years, are considered positive when the indurated area measures 10 mm in diameter, so Choice *D* is incorrect.

92. C: Upcoding is the fraudulent practice of reporting a level of care delivered in a patient encounter that is not supported by the EHR or the patient's diagnosis. Upcoding is discoverable in routine audits and the provider may be penalized. The EHR reflects the patient's status as a result of accurate documentation by all providers; therefore, Choice *A* is incorrect. Modifiers are standardized: two numerical or two alpha character symbols are used to refine the definition of the initial code. Therefore, Choice *B* is incorrect. The CPT modifiers are updated by the American Medical Association's CPT Editorial Panel; therefore, Choice *D* is incorrect.

93. B: The Centers for Medicare & Medicaid Services (CMS) reimbursement schedule for institutions reflects the onset of hospital-acquired infections that are regarded as preventable. Pneumonia is considered as hospital-acquired from 48 hours after admission until 14 days after discharge. Therefore, Choices *A* and *C* are incorrect. Patients with community-acquired pneumonia are hospitalized according to the needs of the individual patient, so Choice *D* is incorrect.

94. B: In this case, the healthcare provider considered religious and cultural beliefs of the patient to make her feel comfortable during the exam. Effective cultural considerations improve patient satisfaction scores. In the other options listed, the healthcare providers act inconsiderately, insultingly, and make assumptions about the patient's culture.

95. A: Anti-viral therapy will be started immediately after exposure, without waiting for further specialty consultation if the exposed person is pregnant due to the risk of the unborn fetus. HIV testing will be conducted at frequent intervals to monitor for the presence of evidence of infection; therefore, Choice *B* is incorrect. The precautions listed in Choice *C* are necessary to prevent possible contamination in the event that the exposure has resulted in infection of the exposed individual by the HIV virus; therefore, Choice *C* is incorrect. Renal, hepatic, and hematology studies are monitored to assess any effects of the HIV virus and/or the effects of anti-viral medications if ordered; therefore, Choice *D* is incorrect.

96. D: Patients being started on sumatriptan should receive the first dose under provider supervision to monitor the patient for any unanticipated cardiovascular response in a patient without any history of CV disease. All elderly patients should have an ECG prior to the initiation of the therapy. The remaining choices are not associated with the effects of sumatriptan; therefore, Choices *A*, *B*, and *C* are incorrect.

97. C: The randomized controlled trial (RCT) is regarded as the research design that best controls researcher bias. RCTs tend to be expensive and large-scale; however, the number of subjects often corresponds with the quality of the results. The level of confidence in observational studies is proportional to the control of bias in the specific design, but the evidence is generally considered to be of low quality; therefore, Choice *A* is incorrect. Variable or imprecise estimates of effect size that require additional investigation before the results of the research can be directly applicable are considered as only moderate-quality evidence; therefore, Choice *B* is incorrect. Case controlled analytics are also considered to be moderate-quality evidence; therefore, Choice *D* is incorrect.

98. C: The Hgb A1c test measures the percentage of the hemoglobin molecules that are "coated" or glycosylated with glucose. The hemoglobin molecule is a protein on the RBC, and the RBC has a lifespan of 120 days; therefore, the resulting blood glucose value reflects the patient's blood sugar for the previous 120 days. The blood glucose test only measures the amount of glucose present in the blood at

the time that the sample is obtained. The hemoglobin A1c lab test is a random sample that does not require fasting; therefore, Choice *A* is incorrect. The blood glucose sample may be drawn at any time. The fasting blood glucose level requires an eight-hour fast, and the two-hour postprandial blood sugar must be drawn precisely two hours after a meal; therefore, Choice *B* is incorrect. The blood glucose sample may be collected by finger-stick or venipuncture; therefore, Choice *D* is incorrect.

99. D: Abrupt weight loss or weight gain are common in individuals who abuse drugs because of the effect on the GI system and the brain. GI symptoms such as nausea, vomiting, and constipation may decrease food intake, while the "high" produced by the drugs produces overeating in some individuals. Individuals that abuse alcohol may become malnourished due to inappropriate food intake. However, the weight changes occur more slowly over time. Depression, potentially violent behavior and lack of interest in family and activities are common signs of both alcohol and drug abuse; therefore, Choices *A*, *B*, and *C* are incorrect.

100. D: The highest level of Maslow's hierarchy of needs is self-actualization, in which one achieves their full potential, including creative pursuits. Prestige, a feeling of accomplishment, and self-esteem are all part of the esteem needs, one level below the top and part of the psychological needs section.

101. A: The nurse should identify the patient's reason for requesting the appointment, consult the appointment matrix to be sure that the provider is available, and determine whether the agency is open on the intended date. The patient's height and weight are not required for scheduling an appointment.

102. C: U-500 Humulin® R insulin has a longer duration of action, which means that the peak action is 15 to 18 hours after injection. The patient needs to be aware of this peak timing. This insulin cannot be given intravenously, and it cannot be mixed with other insulins in the same syringe, so Choices *A* and *B* are incorrect. The vial must be discarded 30 days after opening, not 14 days, so Choice *D* is incorrect.

103. C: The risk/benefit for testing in men indicates that the symptoms of the disease in men are more easily recognized, and screening for the disease does not increase the control of the disease. Therefore, testing is not recommended. Women are more commonly asymptomatic than men, which means that the disease is more advanced when diagnosed; therefore, Choice *A* is incorrect. Nucleic acid testing is more specific than antibody testing, but it is also more expensive, and in many cases neither of the tests is required for diagnosis because the patient's presenting symptoms are diagnostic. Therefore, Choice *B* is incorrect. Women with untreated chlamydia risk significant damage to the entire reproductive system, which may become systemic as in the case of pelvic inflammatory disease, so Choice *D* is incorrect.

104. A: Glaucoma occurs when the flow of fluid in the anterior portion of the eye is either slowed or blocked. The eventual change in the pressure in the eye can affect the optic nerve, which will lead to vision loss if the pressure is not controlled. The loss of central vision is due to macular degeneration, which is caused by injury to the macula, a small area on the retina that is responsible for maintaining sharp visional images; therefore, Choice *B* is incorrect. Clouding of the lens is the defect associated with cataract formation, which is most often due to aging and is commonly treated by phacoemulsification surgery, which dissolves and removes the diseased lens and implants the new lens; therefore, Choice *C* is incorrect. Diabetic retinopathy results from the effects of hypertension and increased blood glucose levels on the blood vessels in the retina, which result in swelling of the retina that causes abnormal transmission of impulses to the brain; therefore, Choice *D* is incorrect..

105. C: The normal serum potassium level is 3.5 – 5.0 mEq/L. Elevated potassium levels are manifested by peripheral paresthesias, elevated, peaked T waves, and increased impulse conduction time across the heart, resulting in a widened QRS complex on the ECG. This value represents a severe elevation of the serum potassium level; therefore, Choice *A* is incorrect. Anorexia and a shortened Q-T interval on the ECG are associated with hypercalcemia and elevated calcium level; therefore, Choice *B* is incorrect. Prolonged P-R interval and the presence of U waves are alterations associated with hypokalemia, or a serum potassium level that is less than 3.5 mEq/L; therefore, Choice *D* is incorrect.

106. A: Rapid reactions are often the result of infusing the fluid too quickly or using small hand veins when a larger vein should be used. These reactions can be avoided by adhering to the recommended administration instructions. First dose reactions occur after the first dose and may or may not occur after subsequent doses. Any patients that exhibit these reactions must be closely monitored for worsening reactions, so Choice *B* is incorrect. Providers are cautioned to initiate drug therapies at the lowest therapeutic dose to avoid early reactions; therefore, Choice *C* is incorrect. Intermediate reactions occur after multiple doses in susceptible individuals; therefore, Choice *D* is incorrect.

107. C: An event that requires intervention to prevent permanent damage is considered to be an adverse drug reaction (ADR) by the FDA. Intractable vomiting following chemotherapy is identified as an expected side effect of the treatment and is not reportable as an ADR; therefore, Choice *A* is incorrect. Harmful self-inflicted behaviors are not identified as ADRs by the FDA; therefore, Choice *B* is incorrect. The American Society of Healthcare Pharmacists has proposed that any unexpected or undesired outcome that requires the alteration of the drug dosage should be defined as an ADR. However, currently, the FDA defines the outcomes more narrowly. Therefore, Choice *D* is incorrect.

108. B: Right-sided heart failure is caused by weakness of the right atrium and the right ventricle. Patients will have neck distention; however, central venous pressure is a more precise measurement of the patient's fluid volume status. An increased respiratory rate and dyspnea on exertion are related to left-sided heart failure, which is associated with altered respiratory function; therefore, Choices *A* and *D* are incorrect. The patient with right-sided heart failure has hypervolemia, and the serum sodium would be decreased, not increased; therefore, Choice *C* is incorrect.

109. D: The metric system is used for all numerical documentation in the electronic health record, which means that the CMA will multiply 8 ounces times the conversion factor of 30, which is the number of milliliters per ounce, to identify the appropriate number, 240 milliliters. Choices *A* and *C* are household measures and are therefore incorrect. Choice *B* is equal to 300 milliliters, which is more than the actual intake; therefore, Choice *B* is incorrect.

110. B: In the event of a seizure, the provider will protect the patient's head from injury and assist the patient to the side-lying recovery position once the seizure is over; however, the insertion of tongue depressors is contraindicated because the oral cavity may be damaged, and there is clear research evidence that the patient's tongue will not obstruct the airway. The patient, especially the patient's head, should be protected from injury during the seizure; however, the provider should not restrain the patient in any way. The remaining choices demonstrate safe practice and do not require additional instruction; therefore, Choices *A, C,* and *D* are incorrect.

111. B: The cost-saving potential for the bundled payment option is based on three assumptions: bundled payments will result in less expensive care, providers and payers will divide excess revenue generated by the plan, and providers will not be compensated for complications of covered conditions,

which results in additional savings. Although not identified as the financial focus of the reimbursement plan, improved patient outcomes are also identified as possible favorable outcomes; therefore, Choice *A* is incorrect. The authors of the reimbursement plan expect that patients will receive more care and cost-effective care with improved patient outcomes; therefore, Choice *C* is incorrect. One of the basic assumptions of the cost-saving plan is that providers will not be reimbursed for complications of care; therefore, Choice *D* is incorrect.

112. C: With the normal aging process, the gastric mucosa loses some of the capability to protect against the formation of ulcers due to aging effects on the immune system, and when this process is associated with other existing comorbidities and NSAID use, the incidence of ulcer disease increases. Dry mouth is common in the elderly, but it is due to the effects of medication or disease rather than the aging process; therefore, Choice *A* is incorrect. The upper esophageal sphincter loses tone as a result of aging, which decreases the contractions and contributes to the incidence of gastric reflux; therefore, Choice *B* is incorrect. Malnutrition is not a normal consequence of aging. It may be due to socioeconomic status or other personal issues; therefore, Choice *D* is incorrect.

113. D: Semi-fowler's is the position of choice to facilitate respiration in order to relieve chest pain by maximizing oxygen delivery to the heart. The lithotomy position is required for vaginal and pelvic examinations; therefore, Choice *A* is incorrect. Trendelenburg is the position for shock states when increased blood flow to the brain is required; therefore, Choice B is incorrect. The supine position does not facilitate respiration and is not appropriate for the care of a patient with an MI; therefore, Choice *C* is incorrect.

114. C: The CMA should report his suspicion of substance abuse to HR. Even if he is wrong about the substance abuse, ethically it is the right thing to do. Gossiping to fellow employees does nothing and could be more damaging. Ignoring it and/or not doing anything about it could result in serious patient harm, and the CMA may be named in the case if any litigation were to arise out of the matter. Substance abusers need help with stress and addiction management. By reporting and addressing the problem of substance abuse, those who are addicted can find help to overcoming their addiction.

115. C: The FDA approves drugs for OTC use. This approval also indicates that the drug administration directions are appropriate for adult consumers. All legend drugs are approved by the FDA; therefore, Choice *A* is incorrect. Only legend drugs that have a significant risk for injury or death have a black box warning. OTC drugs are not associated with the same risks; therefore, Choice *B* is incorrect. All prescription drugs are legend drugs, and opioids require a prescription; therefore, Choice *D* is incorrect.

116. B: Tuberculosis, varicella, herpes zoster, and rubella are transmitted by airborne transmission, which means that all who come in contact with the patient must use a particulate respirator capable of filtering the infective molecules which are smaller than five microns. Diphtheria and Adenovirus are spread by droplet infection of causative agents that are larger than five microns, which means that a well-fitting surgical mask is adequate protection against contamination. Therefore, Choices *A* and *C* are incorrect. Contact precautions are required for the care of patients infected with ***Clostridium difficile*** (*C. diff*); however, masks of any type are not recommended; therefore, Choice *D* is incorrect.

117. C: If the diagnosis is bacterial meningitis, the glucose content of the CSF will be less than 45 mg/dL because the glucose is being consumed by bacteria for metabolic processes. The intercranial pressure, not the glucose level, is verified with a monometer, so Choice *A* is incorrect. Proteins levels are not associated with the glucose level, so Choice *B* is incorrect. Ketoacidosis is assessed by testing the serum, not the CSF, so Choice *D* is incorrect.

118. B: HIPAA was enacted to protect patient privacy and confidentiality as well as to decrease inefficiencies and reduce paperwork to speed up the claims process. Human laboratory specimens meeting federal standards is part of the Clinical Laboratory Improvement Act (CLIA) of 1988.

119. B: Tobramycin is ototoxic and should be avoided in children whether or not the tympanic membrane is intact. The remaining choices, Choices *A*, *C*, and *D*, are recommended therapies for this condition.

120. D: Equality of healthcare means that all people are treated equally. For instance, patients should be added to donor lists based only their medical needs. Equitable healthcare refers to the proper management of scarce resources, which can be illustrated by the use of donated organs. The difference can be explained by viewing equality at the level of the individual patient, and equity at the level of the provider. Therefore, Choices *A, B,* and *C* are incorrect.

121. C: The DNP degree is the clinical practice degree that requires additional clinical experience to prepare the APRN for leadership roles in the clinical setting. A PhD degree requires additional study of research methods and application of the results of the research to practice. Although there is a clear difference between the degrees, in many practice settings, there is little distinction between the functions of APRNs with either degree. For example, both degrees are seen in nursing education faculty members. An exception to this would be in large research universities where nursing faculty are expected to conduct and disseminate the research that guides nursing practice. The APRNs in these positions will hold the PhD degree.

122. B: Medicaid is intended to provide healthcare services for low-income individuals and families. Medicaid is jointly funded by the federal and state governments; however, the plan is administered by the individual states; therefore, Choice *A* is incorrect. Although a large number of providers do accept Medicaid reimbursement, physicians are not legally obligated to do so; therefore, Choice *C* is incorrect. The Affordable Care Act revised the requirements for Medicaid eligibility, which resulted in a significant increase in the number of Medicaid recipients; therefore, Choice *D* is incorrect.

123. B: The problem list in the POMR demonstrates the effect of the interventions on the resolution of the individual problems. This chronological record can be used as an outcome measure that is an essential element of the meaningful use standard. The SOMR does not specifically track the resolution of individual problems and therefore is less useful for outcomes assessment than the POMR. Any provider that renders care for the patient documents that care in the SOMR; therefore, Choice *A* is incorrect. There is no evidence that the SOMR generates less paper. In fact, the opposite may be true because each provider maintains a separate entry in the medical record; therefore, Choice *C* is incorrect. The POMR is a chronological compilation of the patient care documentation by all disciplines; therefore, Choice *D* is incorrect.

124. D: One cup of split pea soup contains 4.8 g of fiber. One cup of strawberries contains 3 g of fiber, two pieces of whole wheat bread contain 3.8 g of fiber, and one ounce of dry roasted almonds contains 3 g of fiber.

125. D: A glomus tumor is a tumor located under the nail of a finger or a toe. The condition can be associated with conductive hearing loss. Ménière's disease is a disease of the inner ear and is associated with sensorineural hearing loss, so Choice *A* is incorrect. Arnold-Chiari malformations are forms of spina bifida that are associated with sensorineural hearing loss, so Choice *B* is incorrect. Sensorineural hearing loss is a rare but possible manifestation of multiple sclerosis, so Choice *C* is incorrect.

126: C: Buccal medications are absorbed at a predictable rate into the systemic circulation via the internal jugular vein; therefore, the medication is not present in the stomach and will not be affected by the acid environment of the stomach. Because the palate and gums are less absorptive than the oral mucosa, the medications are formulated to provide predictable rates of absorption; therefore, Choice *A* is incorrect. In contrast to buccal medications, sublingual medications that are surrounded by the oral mucosa are immediately absorbed into the systemic circulation; therefore, Choice *B* is incorrect. Both sublingual and buccal medications can be used to exert local effects such as resolving mucosal ulcers or for systemic effects such as the treatment of angina by nitroglycerin; therefore, Choice *D* is incorrect.

127. C: Ondansetron blocks the reuptake or absorption of serotonin, which increases serotonin levels. Procarbazine decreases the breakdown of serotonin, but it does not affect absorption, so Choice *A* is incorrect. Fenfluramine increases the release of serotonin, so Choice *B* is incorrect. Lithium is a serotonin agonist, so Choice *D* is incorrect.

128. B: Neuropathic pain is caused by damage to the nervous system, as opposed to pain that is a neurologic response to pain in other body tissues. Common examples of neuropathic pain include post-herpetic pain syndrome, diabetic neuropathy, and phantom limb syndrome following amputation. Nociceptive pain is the result of stimulation of the nociceptive pain receptors from all areas of the body, not just the hollow organs; therefore, Choice *A* is incorrect. It is recommended that chronic nociceptive pain be treated with acetaminophen initially, and pharmacologic treatment should only advance to NSAIDs and then opioid analgesics as necessary. Therefore, Choice *C* is incorrect. Most commonly, neuropathic pain is not alleviated by opioid analgesics, and the possibility of opioid dependence in the treatment of chronic pain syndromes limits their usefulness, so Choice *D* is incorrect.

129. A: The concurrent use of spironolactone with simvastatin is contraindicated because the interaction between the two drugs causes a significant increase in the simvastatin levels. There are no reported interactions among spironolactone and KCl, Clorazepate, or metronidazole. Therefore, Choices *B*, *C*, and *D* are incorrect.

130. C: A carotid endarterectomy is often performed in patients with clogged or narrowed carotid arteries to prevent a stroke from a dislodged clot. Myocardial infarction, or a heart attack, can happen as a result of a clot but is not the biggest concern with atherosclerotic carotid arteries, which are very close to the brain where strokes occur. A pulmonary embolism is another condition involving clots but also is not the greatest concern directly related to carotid arteries. Though the carotid arteries are located in the neck, similar to the thyroid gland, they do not have anything to do with hyperthyroidism.

131. D: This question can be answered with a "yes" or a "no," so it is a closed question. An exploratory question is a specific type of open-ended question in which a subject is dissected and investigated in depth. A rhetorical question is one that is asked that does not require any answer at all; it is simply asked for the sake of being asked. An example of a rhetorical answer would be, "Is it ever going to stop raining?" The person asking logically knows that the rain always stops eventually. They are venting their frustration about the rain and impatience for better weather by asking a rhetorical question. Open-ended questions require the person to give a more detailed answer than just "yes" or "no." An example would be asking the patient what they are feeling, inviting a descriptive and detailed answer.

132. D: Bupropion results in the development of, or worsening of, hypertension in one in every 10 people who take the drug. Acetaminophen may be associated with orthostatic hypotension in susceptible patients; therefore, Choice *A* is incorrect. Dextromethorphan is a cough suppressant that is associated with drowsiness, but there is no reported effect on blood pressure. Dapagliflozin is a sodium-glucose cotransporter-2 (SGLT2) inhibitor that is used for glycemic control in patients with type 2 diabetes. The drug is not associated with HTN; therefore, Choice *C* is incorrect.

133. A: Objective data is information that is observed by the provider, while subjective data is the information that the patient contributes to the health record. The patient supplies the data related to the chief complaint, family history, and the details of the present illness; therefore, Choices *B, C,* and *D* are incorrect.

134. C: Bone health depends on Vitamin D, Vitamin C, and sufficient calcium. The remaining choices are important to other processes; therefore, Choices *A, B,* and *D* are incorrect.

135. C: Understanding the patient concerns validates the patient's viewpoint, which can enhance the patient's self-image. A positive self-image can increase self-efficacy, which is the patient's perception of the ability to succeed. Choice *A* engages the patient with an open-ended question; therefore, Choice *A* is incorrect. Choice *B* asks for clarification, but it will not enhance self-efficacy, so Choice *B* is incorrect. Choice *D* is part of a summary statement that is giving the patient the opportunity to contribute more information, so Choice *D* is incorrect.

136. C: When lifting, proper technique dictates that the load be kept close to the body. Infection prevention requires appropriate personal protective equipment (PPE) if that is a concern. The other three items listed (bending at knees and lifting with legs, wide base, proper posture) are all part of proper lifting technique.

137. C: The Wells score is a multi-step calculation that assesses the likelihood of a pulmonary embolism (PE). The assessment criteria include the presence of clinical signs and symptoms of DVT; a clinical decision that PE is the number one diagnosis or equally likely; a heart rate above 100; a history of immobilization for at least three days or surgery in the previous four weeks; a history of previous, objectively diagnosed PE or DVT; hemoptysis; and a history of malignancy with treatment within the last six months or palliative care. Each of these elements is scored as zero if the element is not present, or from one to three points if it is present. The Wells score cannot confirm the presence of a DVT, so Choice *B* is incorrect. Choices *A* and *D* are not associated with the Wells score and are therefore incorrect.

138. B: Patients with type 1 diabetes have special needs for insulin dosage regulation depending on the specific illness. In general, patients are cautioned to not skip doses. However, the provider will identify a detailed plan for insulin administration and blood glucose monitoring for each patient. There may be patient-specific recommendations for the situations identified in the remaining choices. However, the "sick day" plan is most commonly identified with the care of the diabetic patient. Therefore, Choices *A, C,* and *D* are incorrect.

139. D: Insulin shock is a state of hypoglycemia and is manifested by sweating, anxiety, shakiness, and hunger. Diabetic ketoacidosis is a state of hyperglycemia and is manifested by malaise, weakness,

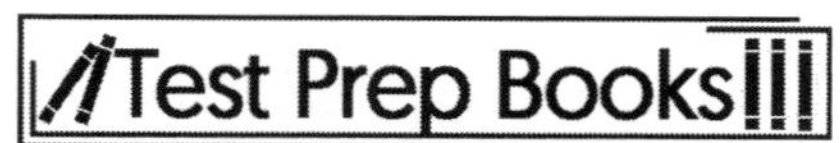

fatigability, and GI symptoms that include abdominal pain, anorexia, nausea, and vomiting. Therefore, Choices *A, B*, and *C* are incorrect.

140. C: Fat will be used as an energy source when there is insufficient insulin to use glucose for energy production. If this condition exists for any extended period of time, the byproducts of the processed fats will accumulate in the blood. These ketones, or waste products, rapidly accumulate in the blood and the urine resulting in ketoacidosis. Small amounts of the ketones may be excreted with respiration as the lungs attempt to lower the levels in the circulating blood volume. This action results in the fruity odor of the exhaled air, which is a classic symptom of ketoacidosis. The remaining choices are manifestations of insulin shock, which are due to the effect of hypoglycemia on the nervous system; therefore, Choices *A, B,* and *D* are incorrect.

141. D: Federally assisted care institutions are held to mandatory compliance with the communication standards of the CLAS criteria, such as the provision of skilled interpreters. The remaining standards are focused on providing culturally sensitive care but do not require mandatory compliance and reporting; therefore, Choices *A*, *B*, and *C* are incorrect.

142. B: Mandatory restrictions for administration of the drug are included when the incidence of adverse effects is affected by the route of administration. Drug labels only contain black box warnings when significant risk of injury or death is among the adverse effects; therefore, Choice *A* is incorrect. The black box information is intended for providers; however, the providers are then responsible for sharing the content with the patient and explaining the implications for the patient's care. Therefore, Choice *C* is incorrect. Black box warnings include rare potential complications in addition to the most common significant concerns; therefore, Choice *D* is incorrect.

143. A: An elevated C-reactive protein level (CRP) is an indicator of the presence of an inflammatory process that has been identified as a risk factor for coronary artery disease. It also may indicate the presence of arthritis, pancreatitis, and kidney failure. The CRP is a serum test, not a stool test, which must be used to identify blood loss; therefore, Choice *B* is incorrect. Antibiotic sensitivity is identified by skin testing; therefore, Choice *C* is incorrect. Pregnancy tests measure the levels of human chorionic gonadotropin hormone, not the C-reactive protein; therefore, Choice *D* is incorrect.

144. B: If a physician believes that a procedure or treatment is necessary, but it is not a covered expense, the physician assumes financial responsibility for all costs associated with that treatment or procedure. Preauthorization is required for all treatments; pre-certification is required for hospital admission. Therefore, Choices *A* and *C* are incorrect. Preauthorization applies to all patients insured by MCOs as stipulated by the individual plans; therefore, Choice *D* is incorrect.

145. C: The red bone marrow is the active site for production of stem cells, which are converted into white blood cells to combat infection. The system does protect the spleen, store calcium, and make new bone tissue; however, these activities are not associated with the function of the immune system. Therefore, Choices *A, B,* and *D* are incorrect.

146. D: The results indicated uncompensated respiratory acidosis because the pH and the pCO2 are going in opposite directions, the pCO2 is elevated, the HCOs is normal, and the pH is acidic and abnormal. Choices *A, B,* and *C* are incorrect.

147. B: Wisdom is the virtue that is developed if the ego conflict of integrity vs. despair is positively overcome. Fidelity is the virtue that comes after identity vs. role confusion is positively overcome. Caring is the virtue that is developed after the ego conflict of generativity vs. stagnation is positively overcome. Love is the virtue that comes out of a positive outcome of the intimacy vs. isolation conflict.

148: D: The SDS includes potential hazards associated with the substance in order to protect employees from harm due to misuse. The SDS is issued by the manufacturer and will not contain any local information; therefore, Choice *A* is incorrect. Agency policies regarding the use of hazardous substances may address personnel issues. However, the SDS strictly applies to the individual hazardous substances; therefore, Choice *B* is incorrect. Consumer products containing potentially hazardous materials contain safety labels that may contain first-aid instructions; however, the SDS is not required of consumer products; therefore, Choice *C* is incorrect.

149. A: Most prescription drugs are not labeled for pediatric patients, which increases the incidence of off-label use of prescription drugs. The PREA encourages researchers to provide the evidence for labeling drugs for use in normal pediatric patients and in the case of rare pediatric disease. The Pediatric Research Equity Act supports the expansion of drug testing in pediatric populations research that can provide evidence-based practice guidelines for pediatric providers; therefore, Choice *B* is incorrect. Pediatric patients are not simply "small adults" where drug therapies are concerned. There is evidence that more than dosages require revision prior to accepted use of the drug in pediatric patients; therefore, Choice *C* is incorrect. FDA approval is required for drug therapy in pediatric populations; therefore, Choice *D* is incorrect.

150. A: The TB test is evaluated by assessing the ***wheal*,** or indurated area at the site of the injection. Although a positive test may present as a reddened area surrounding the wheal, only the indurated area is measured and reported. The patient must return to the clinical agency for assessment of the results within 48 to 72 hours of the injection of the allergen, regardless of the presence or absence of redness at the site; therefore, the CMA must report the patient's remarks so that the licensed provider can reinforce the testing protocol. The remaining statements are appropriate and do not require intervention by the supervisor; therefore, Choices *B, C,* and *D* are incorrect.

151. B: When a patient has been adequately informed about a procedure or decision and signs a document granting their permission to commence, it is called informed consent. Expressed or verbal consent is when the patient consents merely with a gesture such as a nod or verbally agrees. Implied consent is when there is not necessarily any formal agreement made verbally, through gestures or through writing, but consent is assumed. Usually, implied consent is used in emergency situations or for small, minor procedures.

152. B: The patient is in the knee-chest position for a sigmoidoscopy in order to allow the insertion of the sigmoidoscope. The lithotomy position is appropriate for the vaginal examination, the lateral position is appropriate for the administration of the Fleet's enema, and the Fowler's position is appropriate for the EKG; therefore, Choices *A, C,* and *D* are correctly stated.

153. C: Bulimic patients consume large amounts of food in a short period of time and then self-induce vomiting to prevent weight gain by disposing of the food. Stomach acids that are raised each time the patient vomits damage the mucous membrane of the mouth and the enamel layer of the teeth. Men and women are affected by eating disorders; however, more women than men are bulimic. Therefore, Choice *A* is incorrect. The bulimic patient consumes large amounts of food, but that intake is immediately followed by vomiting. The anorexic patient refuses to ingest any food; therefore, Choice *B* is incorrect. Eating disorders are difficult to treat and relapses are common, which means that long-term

health effects are common. Effects can range from mild malnutrition to heart failure and death; therefore, Choice *D* is incorrect.

154. C: Nitroglycerin is formulated for sublingual (under the tongue) administration. The medication dissolves rapidly into the circulation and acts to dilate the coronary arteries in order to relieve the pain of angina. The remaining choices are not appropriate to the administration of nitroglycerin; therefore, Choices *A, B,* and *C* are incorrect.

155. D: Aging is identified as the leading cause of altered binding of drugs at receptor sites, but thyrotoxicosis also causes alterations at the receptor sites which can enhance or inhibit the pharmacodynamics of a specific drug. The additional endocrine disorders do not have the same effect at the cellular receptor sites; therefore, Choices *A, B,* and *C* are incorrect.

156. D: The CMA must maintain a professional image, as they are a representative of a respected profession: medical assisting. Posting gossip-type information as well as photos that could violate HIPAA contribute to an unprofessional—not to mention immature—image of CMAs and should be avoided. The consequences could be serious for the CMA as far as their employment and ability to practice are concerned.

157. B: The ABN is the form that is sent to patients enrolled in original Medicare plans when a claim is denied by Medicare. Members of Medicare Advantage programs receive a Medicare Notice of Non-coverage when the CMA identifies the claim that is likely to be denied. Therefore, Choice *A* is incorrect. A patient's request for therapy that does meet the necessary and reasonable status may be appealed and approved; therefore, Choice *C* is incorrect. Primary care providers only notify patients of primary care procedures that may be denied, not hospital procedures; therefore, Choice *D* is incorrect.

158. B: The heart rate, respiratory rate, and blood pressure BP are all elevated above normal for a 12-year-old child. The other choices demonstrate normal values for the specific patient. The newborn has the most rapid heart rate and respiratory rate, which gradually decrease as the child matures; therefore, Choices *A, C,* and *D* are incorrect.

159. A: Humans contract Lyme disease by contact with deer ticks that are infected with the spirochete Borrelia burgdorferi. The causative agent is carried by the vector, the tick, that obtains the organism by a blood meal from the infected source, the deer, to the susceptible human, causing the illness. Legionnaires disease is a severe form of pneumonia that is an airborne infection caused by the bacterium legionella. It was first identified in a hotel in Philadelphia where the infection was spread through the hotel's ventilation system; therefore, Choice *B* is incorrect. Varicella, chickenpox, is caused by the varicella zoster virus and can be spread through airborne, droplet, and contact exposure; therefore, Choice *C* is incorrect. Impetigo is caused by direct or indirect contact with objects that are contaminated with one of the causative organisms, Streptococcus pyogenes or Staphylococcus aureus; therefore, Choice *D* is incorrect.

160. B: By paraphrasing what the patient says, the CMA is using the reflection technique to assess the patient's level of understanding. Restatement means to repeat exactly what the patient says back to them. Clarification involves questions and repeating back the essential meaning to the patient. Feedback involves more of a reaction to what the patient says with a desire to improve the relationship and further communications.

161. D: Children are at risk for cerebral edema secondary to the fluid volume replacement used to reverse the dehydration. The replacement volume in HHS is greater than the replacement volume in DKA. The remaining choices are manifestations of DKA; therefore, Choices *A, B*, and *C* are incorrect.

162. A: Passed under President Barack Obama's term, the Patient Protection and Affordable Care Act of 2010 reformed individual health insurance markets and expanded Medicaid coverage. Overall, it cut uninsured patient numbers by approximately half. It is the largest healthcare reform since Medicaid and Medicare programs were developed in the 1960s.

163. A: Collecting laboratory specimens for analysis is an activity that is within the scope of practice of the CMA. Evaluation, interpretation of results and constructing elements of the plan of care all require the expertise of licensed providers including physicians and nurses. Therefore, Choices *B, C*, and *D* are incorrect.

164. C: Emphysema results in the failure of the alveoli and trapping of air in the distal airways, with resulting obstruction to the flow of air. Pneumonia is an infective process that may include the accumulation of secretions in the larger airways; however, air is not trapped in the airways. Small cell cancer is a neoplastic disorder that will affect lung function depending upon the size and location of the malignancy. Asthma is an allergic response to environmental antigens that is manifested by the stricture or closure of the airways; therefore, Choices *A, B,* and *D* are incorrect.

165. A: Patients who consistently miss appointments or cancel without rescheduling the appointment may be considered non-compliant with the healthcare plan and may be dismissed by the provider after proper notice is provided. Therefore, Choice *A* is correct. The CMA attempts to reschedule all missed appointments, including those identified as "no-shows." The patient's attendance pattern is not reported to the insurer, so Choices *B* and *D* are incorrect. However, the provider may impose a fee for the missed appointments.

166. B: Bruising is the most common initial assessment finding in child abuse because physical abuse is the most common form of abuse. Disruptive behavior and bed wetting may not be evident in the initial assessment. In addition, the abused child may or may not verbalize the details of the abuse. The CMA also understands that the results of abuse are not all visible, and the reports of the parent or care provider are not always accurate. Therefore, Choices *A, C*, and *D* are incorrect.

167. A: These are direct components of preparing for a local or nearby disaster, which sets the foundation for disaster management.

168. B: Paroxetine is a psychotropic drug used to treat mood disorders such as depression and anxiety disorders. Diclofenac is a non-steroidal anti-inflammatory drug, rather than an opioid analgesic, which is used to treat mild to moderate pain such as the pain associated with osteoarthritis and rheumatoid arthritis; therefore, Choice *A* is incorrect. Hydroxyzine is an antihistamine with antianxiety effects; therefore, Choice *C* is incorrect. Ondansetron is an anti-emetic used for post-operative nausea and nausea associated with chemotherapy; therefore, Choice *D* is incorrect.

169. C: Individual patient identifiers are necessary to provide treatment of the patient and avoid progression of the disease. Therefore, Choices *A, B,* and *D* are incorrect.

170. C: The CMA should send the patient a letter by certified mail and include the signed receipt of the patient's EHR. The CMA should not find the patient face-to-face or send them a list with their provider's

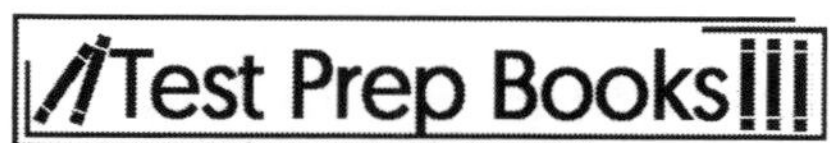

complaints, making Choices *A* and *B* incorrect. The information should be sent by mail, not email, making Choice *D* incorrect.

171. A: The patient is demonstrating "undoing"—a defense mechanism that attempts to undo a wrong or bad action with the opposite action. Denial is a defense mechanism in which a person simply denies a reality because they do not want to deal with potentially painful emotions. Sublimation is a defense mechanism in which negative impulses are channeled into positive action. Repression is a defense mechanism in which a person unconsciously avoids thoughts about something painful, similar to the conscious act of suppression.

172. B: Although there may be agency-specific instructions, magnesium or calcium-containing medications are withheld to avoid interference with the scanned images. The scan is only able to identify bone density. Arthritic changes will not be visualized or evaluated. Therefore, Choice *A* is incorrect. Bone density testing is recommended for all at-risk populations, including elderly men; therefore, Choice *C* is incorrect. Fasting for this scan is not required or recommended; therefore, Choice *D* is incorrect.

173. A: Common law is based on precedents, or previously decided court cases. Civil law involves disputes between individuals and community members. Criminal law involves consequences for those who commit crimes. Statutory law is based on laws passed through legislative action.

174. D: Tertiary prevention measures are focused on decreasing the impact of the disease on quality of life. A blood transfusion for a patient with sickle cell disease will not cure the disease; however, the infusion of red blood cells (RBCs) can decrease tissue hypoxia and pain by replacing the sickled red blood cells with cells that are carrying the normal oxygen load. The MMR vaccination and the PKU screening are examples of primary prevention; therefore, Choice *A* and Choice *C* are incorrect. Application of the Pavlik harness for the treatment of DDH is an example of secondary prevention that focuses on early intervention of an identified condition; therefore, Choice *B* is incorrect.

175. B: The first time the patient voids, the urine is discarded, and the 24-hour testing period begins. This ensures that only the urine produced during the testing period is included in the analysis. The individual urine samples are collected in one container and are not submitted as individual specimens; therefore, Choice *A* is incorrect. The urine collection is usually refrigerated; however, the first voided sample must be discarded in order that only the urine produced during the 24-hour test period is analyzed. Therefore, Choice *C* is incorrect. The 24-hour urine collection does not require a sterile specimen; therefore, Choice *D* is incorrect.

176. B: Although drug companies are not allowed to profit from the protocol, they are allowed to recoup actual costs, which are often beyond the patient's ability to pay for the therapy.

177. D: According to the DEA, Schedule I drugs have a high potential for abuse and should not be accepted for use under medical supervision. Other Schedule I drugs include heroin, LSD, ecstasy, and bath salts. Schedule II drugs also have a high potential for abuse but, according to the DEA, have medically accepted reasons for use.

178. C: A patient's health information is to remain private and confidential, according to the Health Insurance Portability and Accountability Act, commonly known as HIPAA. The other three items listed, Genetic Information Nondiscrimination Act (GINA) of 2008, Health Information Technology for Economic and Clinical Health (HITECH), and Public Health and Welfare Disclosure, do not have to do exclusively with patient privacy. HITECH involves patient access to their own medical record, GINA was enacted to prevent patients from being discriminated against based on their genetics, and Public Health and Welfare Disclosure has to do with disease prevention within a population.

179. C: When research studies are complete, they should be officially disseminated to colleagues in the field through academic and scholarly publications. This gives credence to the study and allows it to influence both future research and current fieldwork. Receiving funds and interpreting data are earlier stages of a research project. Participant data does not necessarily need to be destroyed as long as it remains safeguarded and the participants give their permission for their data to remain with study materials.

180. C: The CMA will immediately report the potassium level of 2.8 mEq/L, which requires intervention to avoid the development of cardiac arrhythmias. The hemoglobin A1c is minimally elevated, but this result does not require immediate intervention; therefore, Choice *A* is incorrect. Choices *B* and *D* are within normal limits and do not require intervention.

181. C: High blood pressure is represented by a systolic measurement of 140 or higher and a diastolic measurement of 90 or higher (140/90). Low blood pressure would be 90 systolic and 60 diastolic or lower, so Choice *A* is incorrect. Normal blood pressure would be 120 systolic and 80 diastolic or lower, so Choice *B* is incorrect. Dangerously high blood pressure would be 180 systolic and 120 diastolic or higher, so Choice *D* is incorrect.

182. C: In most cases, patients are asked to sign a consent to release their personal health information for certain purposes before they receive treatment. These purposes include treatment, claims and billing for insurance companies, and training and educational activities with staff. Thus, the sharing of a patient's medical information during training would not be in violation of the Health Insurance Portability and Accountability Act (HIPAA)—assuming that the patient signed such consent. Choice *A* would be in violation of HIPAA because the grandfather did not provide consent to discuss his case outside of the facility. Choice *B* would be in violation of HIPAA because healthcare workers have no authority to access medical records of patients who are not under their care. Choice *D* would violate HIPAA as well as other federal regulations that protect patients' personal information regarding addictions, and violators could be criminally penalized.

183. B: According to the Centers for Disease Control and Prevention (CDC), a man or woman is overweight with a body mass index (BMI) between 25 and 29.9. A person is obese with a BMI of 30 or higher, so Choice A is incorrect. A person is a healthy weight with a BMI between 18.5 and 24.9, so Choice C is incorrect. A person is underweight with a BMI below 18.5, so Choice D is incorrect.

184. D: The main purpose of Current Procedural Terminology (CPT) modifiers is to add certain details to the original report so that the patient encounter is more accurately reflected. These details, in turn, will decrease the potential for denial of coverage. Choice *A* is incorrect because CPT modifiers are not designed to correct mistakes *per se* in the original report. Choice *B* is incorrect because the main purpose of CPT modifiers is not to increase the healthcare institution's revenue. Choice *C* is incorrect because describing a higher level of care than the patient actually received in order to increase reimbursement is a type of fraud known as upcoding.

185. A: The prefix *bucc-* means cheek, as in the buccal cavity, which consists of the cheek, tongue, and palate; the suffix *-plegia* means paralysis, as in hemiplegia, which is paralysis on one side of the body. In

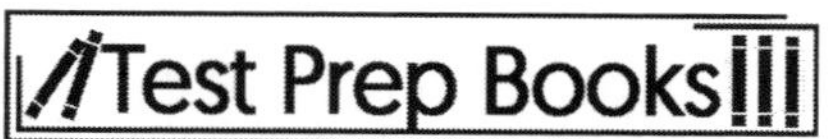

Choice *B*, *andr-* means male, as in androgens, which are male sex hormones; *-emia* means a blood condition, as in anemia. In Choice *C*, *lyso-* means breaking down, as in lysosomes, which break down old cell parts; *-blast* means budding, as in myeloblast, a type of immature white blood cell that develops, or buds off, in the bone marrow. In Choice *D*, *cutane-* means skin, as in cutaneous membrane; *-penia* means a deficiency, as in thrombocytopenia, a deficiency of platelets.

186. B: The chain of infection proceeds from the reservoir (such as the lungs of a person with influenza) to the portal of exit (sneezing by the infected person) to the mode of transmission (direct contact by another person with the influenza virus) to the portal of entry (such as the nose of the other person) to the susceptible host (the person newly infected with the virus). Choices *A*, *C*, and *D* are incorrect because they each show elements of the chain of infection in an incorrect sequence.

187. D: President George W. Bush signed the Genetic Information Nondiscrimination Act in 2008 to prevent health insurers and employers from discriminating against people based on genetic flaws or perceived flaws. Choices *A*, *B*, and *C* are incorrect because they give the wrong names and years for this legislation.

188. B: The Level II Healthcare Common Procedure Coding System (HCPCS) is used to file health plan claims for any supplies, medications, devices, or transportation provided to the patient. Choice *A* is incorrect because the coding system that is used to file claims for medical services—such as surgeries, radiological therapies, laboratory tests, or diagnostic procedures—is the Current Procedural Terminology (CPT) system. Choice *C* is incorrect because the HCPCS codes are not meant for classifying medical services in electronic medical records. Choice *D* is incorrect because the International Classification of Diseases (ICD) is the World Health Organization's system for classifying diseases and diagnoses.

189. D: The Occupational Safety and Health Administration (OSHA) was created in 1970 as the main federal government agency that has responsibility for ensuring the health and safety of Americans in their places of employment through the enforcement of federal regulations and laws. OSHA is an agency within the Department of Labor, but the department as a whole has numerous other responsibilities, so Choice *A* is incorrect. The Department of Health and Human Services (HHS) is responsible for enhancing the health and well-being of all Americans—not just workers—by providing various services, so Choice *B* is incorrect. The Centers for Disease Control and Prevention is an agency within HHS that is tasked with protecting public health through the control and prevention of infectious diseases, injuries, and disabilities and through education and research, so Choice *C* is incorrect.

190. C: The standard length of time to schedule a new patient appointment is 30–45 minutes. When scheduling the appointment, the CMA should verify that the patient understands the appointment details, including any pre-appointment paperwork that needs to be completed. The CMA also must obtain the patient's demographic information, the name of the referring physician, and any other information deemed to be relevant by the provider. Choices *A*, *B*, and *D* are incorrect because they give appointment times that are either too short or too long.

191. A: Whenever a healthcare worker is exposed to an infectious pathogen, the healthcare institution is responsible for immediately implementing its post-exposure plan, or post-exposure protocol, which is a set of guidelines that must be followed for each type of infection to take care of the worker and prevent further infection. In the case of hepatitis B, the plan might include a blood test to verify infection in the worker, an injection of immunoglobulin to prevent illness, administration of a vaccine, and/or administration of an antiviral medication. Choice *B* is incorrect because hepatitis B is spread primarily through sexual contact, the sharing of needles, and accidental needle sticks, so isolation is not of primary importance. Choice *C* is incorrect because, although the institution will want to eventually report the incident to the Occupational Safety and Health Administration (OSHA), that is not the most important immediate action to take. Choice *D* is incorrect because vaccination may be a part of the post-exposure plan, but the full plan needs to be followed.

192. B: In the images of the draping body positions, the lithotomy position is shown by number 6, the Fowler's position by number 2, the supine position by number 3, and the Sim's position by number 1. Choices *A*, *C*, and *D* are incorrect because they each have wrong numbers for all or most of the positions.

193. B: Self-actualization—the feeling of having achieved one's full potential in life—is the top, most complicated human need in Maslow's hierarchy. Choice *A* is incorrect because being esteemed—feeling accomplished and respected—is the second-to-the-top need in Maslow's hierarchy. Choice *C* is incorrect because the need to feel loved and to belong is in the middle of Maslow's hierarchy. Choice *D* is incorrect because physiological needs—such as food, water, warmth, and rest—are the most basic needs and form the base of Maslow's hierarchy pyramid.

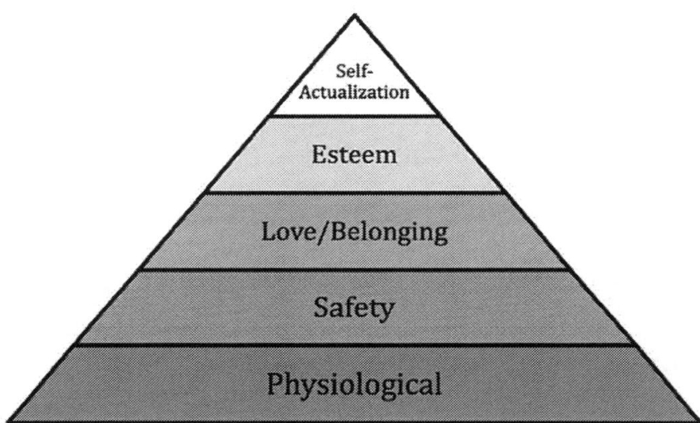

194. C: During the course of a normal pregnancy, women typically receive the second pelvic exam during the third trimester to assess the development of the fetus and the status of the woman's reproductive system. Then, after birth, a postpartum pelvic exam is performed to assess the return of the reproductive organs to their nonpregnant state. Choices *A*, *B*, and *D* are incorrect because they give times that are either too early or too late for the second pelvic exam.

195. D: A surgical scrub, which is performed to reduce infectious agents on the skin before surgical procedures, consists of a timed five-minute washing of the hands, fingernails, and forearms with antimicrobial soap and water. Choice *A* is incorrect because it gives no time, and it mentions sanitizer solution rather than antimicrobial soap. Choice *B* is incorrect because it mentions sanitizer solution rather than antimicrobial soap, and it mentions sterilization, which involves the killing of all microorganisms, including their spores. Surgical scrubbing does not involve sterilization; it involves disinfection, which is the reduction of microorganisms to a minimum. Choice *C* is incorrect because it gives the wrong time, and it does not mention antimicrobial soap.

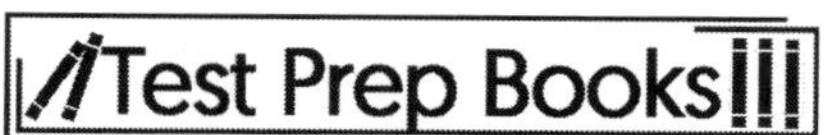

196. C: For an individual to be considered an "established" patient, he or she must have been seen by an agency provider within the previous three years and have a current medical record. Choices *A*, *B*, and *D* are incorrect because they give time periods that are either too short or too long.

197. B: According to the Controlled Substances Act, many drugs with high potential for abuse, possibly leading to severe psychological and physical dependency, are classified as Schedule II. However, under certain circumstances and with medical supervision, these substances may have some medical applications. Schedule II drugs include oxycodone, fentanyl, cocaine, methamphetamine, and hydromorphone. Choice *A* is incorrect because Schedule I drugs, such as LSD, heroin, and peyote, have high potential for abuse and no currently accepted medical applications. Choice *C* is incorrect because Schedule III drugs, such as Tylenol (acetaminophen) with codeine and anabolic steroids, are considered to have moderate to low potential for abuse and dependence. Choice *D* is incorrect because Schedule IV drugs, such Ambien (zolpidem) and Xanax (alprazolam), are all considered to have low potential for abuse and dependence.

198. C: In sublimation, a person redirects the energy that they use to put in a negative activity, such as getting drunk or high, into a positive activity, such as exercising or meditating. Choice *A* is incorrect because denial is the rejection of certain unpleasant facts in order to avoid dealing with them. Choice *B* is incorrect because undoing is the attempt to right a wrong, such as a father taking his child out for ice cream after unfairly scolding him. Choice *D* is incorrect because transference is the redirection of positive or negative feelings about one person onto another person.

199. C: An absolute contraindication refers to a circumstance in which the use of a certain drug or drug combination could result in adverse effects that are potentially fatal. Choice *A* is incorrect because side effects are typically minor, temporary reactions to drugs. Choice *B* is incorrect because, although adverse effects refer to serious reactions to drugs that may or may not be life-threatening, the term is not precise enough to characterize the circumstance of the given example. Choice *D* is incorrect because relative contraindications refer to circumstances in which the potential for adverse effects must be weighed against the expected therapeutic benefits of drugs, and the decision whether to use a drug would depend on the particular case.

200. A: When administering a drug to a patient, the provider needs to verify that six things about the patient and drug are correct, or right. These things are called the six rights of medication administration. The provider should verify that the right patient is receiving the drug; that the right drug, right dosage, and right route are being used; that the drug is being given at the right time; and that the right documentation is completed. Choice *B* is incorrect because there are six rights, not 10. Choices *C* and *D* are incorrect because the six rights are not called a checklist.

Practice Test #2

1. What is a benefit of providing a digital patient portal for a practice's EHR?
   a. Patients can renew prescriptions online.
   b. Patients can digitally sign an ROI.
   c. Patients can check the process of an insurance claim.
   d. Patients can schedule appointments online.

2. What is the acronym for stroke symptoms?
   a. ARM
   b. STROKE
   c. FAST
   d. TIME

3. Which of the following is the federal act that requires a patient's health information to be kept confidential?
   a. Health Information Personal Accountability Act
   b. Health Insurance Private Access Act
   c. Health Information Privacy and Accountability Act
   d. Health Insurance Portability and Accountability Act

4. Which of the following is a right established in the Patient Self-Determination Act?
   a. The right to accept or refuse treatment
   b. The right to choose a healthcare provider
   c. The right to end one's life
   d. The right to determine one's medication

5. The CMA is working with a patient who has just received new orders for insulin glargine. The CMA knows that this is which type of insulin?
   a. Intermediate-acting
   b. Short-acting
   c. Long-acting
   d. Rapid-acting

6. Define the term *insurance eligibility*.
   a. The patient can receive insurance from a provider of their choice.
   b. The practice is certified to bill patients insured by Medicare or Medicaid.
   c. The patient is currently receiving coverage from their insurance provider.
   d. The practice has confirmed that the insurance provider will pay for the procedure.

7. The CMA is unfamiliar with a term but sees that it begins with the prefix *onco-*. With which of the following would this term be associated?
   a. Lymphatic system
   b. Blood
   c. Genetics
   d. Tumors

8. Which statement provides the strongest feedback that a patient understood the CMA's education on their medication?
   a. "So I can go back to work on Monday?"
   b. "So I take the medication, and I will get better?"
   c. "Does this mean I need another appointment?"
   d. "Yeah, yeah, one in the morning, two before bed."

9. Which of the following programs provides medical insurance to active-duty members of the United States military?
   a. CHAMPVA
   b. TRICARE
   c. VA
   d. CHCBP

10. Which of the following is a component of blood that is adversely impacted by low blood iron levels?
   a. Hemoglobin
   b. Hematocrit
   c. Platelets
   d. Plasma

11. Which of the following statements made by a patient may indicate their levothyroxine is therapeutic?
   a. "Is there anything I could do to increase my energy levels?"
   b. "May I have an order for a stool softener?"
   c. "I apply lotion several times a day."
   d. "I am feeling warmer than usual."

12. Which of the following patients would least likely be recommended for yearly lung cancer screenings?
   a. A 65-year-old male patient who has smoked two packs per day for 40 years
   b. A 55-year-old patient who has smoked one pack per day for the past 25 years
   c. A 75-year-old patient who began smoking one pack per day at 30 years of age and quit smoking 20 years ago
   d. A 50-year-old patient who started smoking one pack per day at the age of 20 and quit smoking 10 years ago

13. Which of the following typically receives the bill for healthcare services covered by workers' compensation?
   a. Employer's insurance
   b. Patient's insurance
   c. Medicare
   d. The employer

14. Which of the following is a dosage form that can be split, crushed, or opened?
   a. Immediate-release tablet
   b. Enteric-coated tablet
   c. Long-acting tablet
   d. Modified-release tablet

15. To what extent is a medical practice able to guarantee the security of patient information when delivered to the patient electronically?
    a. All digital communications are secure if encrypted.
    b. All digital communications are secure if a patient password is required for access.
    c. Digital communications are mostly secure but can be compromised by human error.
    d. Digital communications are not secure, and physical access to patient information is preferred.

16. Which of the following statements is true about Healthcare Maintenance Organizations (HMOs)?
    a. They only pay for in-network healthcare.
    b. They only pay for preventative healthcare.
    c. They only pay for healthcare within a specific state.
    d. They only pay for preexisting conditions.

17. A law enforcement official contacts a medical practice and seeks health information in order to provide appropriate accommodations to an individual in their custody. Should the medical assistant provide that information?
    a. Yes, because medical professionals should comply with requests made by legal officials.
    b. No, because there is no proof the individual is in the official's custody.
    c. No, because this situation does not describe a clear risk of harm to the individual.
    d. No, because a signed ROI has not been presented.

18. Which of the following is the most significant indicator of possible identity theft?
    a. A change of the patient's address
    b. Documents with different information
    c. Outdated documents
    d. Frequent change in insurance information

19. Which of the following should a healthcare practice request that a new patient provide prior to their visit?
    a. A credit report
    b. Insurance information
    c. Medical history questionnaire
    d. Emergency contact number

20. When discussing breast cancer prevention and screening with a female patient who has regular periods, what is the recommended timing for breast self-examination?
    a. As the menstrual period is ending
    b. In the middle of the menstrual cycle
    c. At the beginning of the menstrual period
    d. On the same day each month

21. Which financial statistic describes a healthcare practice's profit from patient services?
    a. Excess margin
    b. Operating margin
    c. Average payment period
    d. Accounts receivable

22. The CMA is completing intake on a patient who is being treated for an animal bite. It would be most important to ask this patient about the status of which immunization?

a. Tuberculosis
b. Meningococcal
c. Tetanus
d. Hepatitis B

23. What is an insurance deductible?

a. A discount on healthcare received from in-network physicians
b. The amount a patient must pay out of pocket before insurance will pay
c. A service offered at reduced cost as part of financial assistance
d. An amount removed from wages to pay a debt

24. Which of the following fraudulent activities is referred to as a kickback?

a. Receiving payment in exchange for a patient referral
b. Receiving payment from a patient in exchange for performing an unnecessary service
c. A physician selling insurance coverage
d. Selling drug prescriptions without diagnosis

25. How can a medical assistant best support an illiterate adult patient presenting for an annual physical exam?

a. Spend time one-on-one with the patient to complete their medical history forms.
b. Provide education on how the patient can receive literacy education.
c. Invite the patient to seek help from others while completing forms in the waiting room.
d. Indicate that the patient should complete their medical history when visiting with their physician.

26. Which of the following illegal activities is a type of prescription fraud?

a. Selling prescribed medication to others
b. Lying about symptoms to receive medication
c. Performing self-harm to seek medication
d. Writing an unnecessary prescription

27. Which of the following is NOT a reason Release of Information (ROI) forms are important?

a. They ensure the provider is not liable for breaches in data privacy.
b. They enable continuity of care across multiple providers.
c. They inform the patient about who has access to their health information.
d. ROIs are a legal requirement when sharing health information.

28. The CMA is preparing to perform a venipuncture to obtain blood for laboratory testing. Which of the following is NOT an effective method to prevent blood hemolysis?

a. Make sure the tourniquet remains in place while preparing for the procedure.
b. Pull the plunger back gently when attempting to draw from the venipuncture site.
c. Ensure the venipuncture site dries completely after prepping the area.
d. Immediately invert anticoagulant-containing tubes after obtaining the sample.

29. What information should a CMA send to the laboratory department when scheduling a patient's appointment for a blood draw?
    a. Complete medical history
    b. Allergen information
    c. Current vital records
    d. Mental health diagnoses

30. Which of the following side effects would the CMA recognize as being most concerning for a patient receiving ciprofloxacin?
    a. Nausea
    b. General malaise
    c. Trouble swallowing
    d. Diarrhea

31. A patient with breast cancer is being evaluated for follow-up after receiving chemotherapy. Which statement made by the patient would be most concerning?
    a. "I have been walking for 30 minutes a day, three times a week."
    b. "I cannot stand the taste of meat since starting treatment."
    c. "I was feeling a little nauseated this week, but ginger tea really helped!"
    d. "My friend recommended I go to acupuncture therapy, so I started that this week."

32. A patient receives orders to walk "*ad libitum*." Which of the following statements by the CMA to the patient would accurately reinforce the physician's order?
    a. "You should walk only when it is required."
    b. "You may walk whenever you would like."
    c. "Be sure to walk frequently each day."
    d. "Make sure to walk slowly."

33. What is another word for long-term conditions or illnesses?
    a. Emergent
    b. Chronic
    c. Acute
    d. Urgent

34. While assisting with dietary counseling for a patient recently diagnosed with end-stage renal disease, the CMA knows teaching was successful when the patient states which of the following?
    a. "Examples of foods I should include in my diet are bananas, spinach, and milk."
    b. "I know that one six-ounce glass of juice is about 150 milliliters."
    c. "I need to be careful not to eat too much salt."
    d. "I will need to limit the amount of protein I am eating each day."

35. While reviewing medications with a patient, they report they are currently taking gabapentin. Which active problem listed in the patient's medical record would most likely be the indication for use for this drug?
    a. Swelling
    b. High blood pressure
    c. Nerve pain
    d. High blood sugar

36. How often should a CMA follow up on claims submitted to insurance providers?
   a. Weekly
   b. Monthly
   c. Every 90 days
   d. Annually

37. The medical assistant is taking care of a patient who has a serious head injury. Which symptoms would they NOT expect the patient to have?
   a. Unequal pupils
   b. Shortness of breath
   c. Persistent vomiting
   d. Restlessness and irritability

38. The CMA is preparing a vaccine for administration. It has been a very busy day, and while withdrawing the solution from the vial, the CMA realizes they selected the wrong vial. After drawing up the correct vaccine, what is the most appropriate action?
   a. They are not required to do anything because the vaccine had not yet been delivered.
   b. They should reflect on their process to identify ways to improve safety.
   c. They should notify their supervisor about what happened.
   d. They should notify the patient of what happened.

39. Which of the following situations requires a mandatory report for child abuse?
   a. A 12-year-old male reports the bruise on his thigh was caused by his mother.
   b. A 14-year-old female confides engaging in sexual activity with her 15-year-old boyfriend.
   c. A father tells his 6-year-old son he will spank the child if he doesn't behave.
   d. A mother enrolls her 9-year-old daughter in a child beauty pageant with provocative costumes.

40. A patient who recently had a stroke is slurring their speech. The medical assistant can help them communicate by doing which of the following?
   a. Ask the family to communicate with the patient.
   b. Get the patient a pen and paper.
   c. Ask the nurse to communicate with the patient.
   d. Speak loudly.

41. A patient is being treated after sustaining a deep laceration of the right leg during a fall. What is the name of the instrument the physician will use to guide the needle during closure of the wound?
   a. Tweezers
   b. Scissors
   c. Scalpel
   d. Driver

42. Which organ system is the largest?
   a. Cardiovascular
   b. Integumentary
   c. Musculoskeletal
   d. Pulmonary

43. Upon assessment, the CMA measures a one-month-old infant's respiratory rate to be 48 breaths per minute. What is the most appropriate next step the CMA should take?
   a. Document the reading in the patient's record.
   b. Notify the physician immediately.
   c. Ask a colleague to confirm the measurement.
   d. Observe for additional signs of patient distress.

44. Which of the following is the best option for erasing confidential digital records?
   a. Hire a certified digital sanitization service.
   b. Delete the files, and empty the computer's recycle bin.
   c. Utilize an open-source disk cleaning software.
   d. Transfer the files to an external storage unit and destroy that storage device.

45. Which of the following would NOT be commonly associated with prednisone use?
   a. Irritability
   b. Anorexia
   c. Insomnia
   d. Bruising easily

46. Which of the following is a CPT code?
   a. 99211
   b. G0008
   c. Z00.129
   d. X72.XXXD

47. What does SBAR stand for?
   a. Situation, background, assessment, and recommendation
   b. Situation, background, allergies, and results
   c. Situation, breathing, assessment, and results
   d. Situation, breathing, allergies, recommendation

48. The CMA is performing an intramuscular injection on a six-month-old infant. Which injection site is the preferred location for this patient?
   a. Deltoid muscle
   b. Vastus lateralis muscle
   c. Dorsogluteal muscle
   d. Ventrogluteal muscle

49. Which of the following medications seen in an adolescent patient's record is a stimulant medication used to treat attention-deficit/hyperactivity disorder (ADHD)?
   a. Atomoxetine
   b. Guanfacine
   c. Methylphenidate
   d. Clonidine

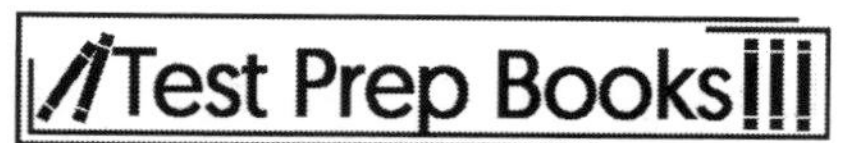

50. A medical assistant is explaining the management of type 2 diabetes to a patient with cognitive disabilities. What is the most appropriate way to educate the patient?
   a. Provide a full education to the patient's primary caregiver, so they can educate the patient.
   b. Ask the patient's primary caregiver for advice on the patient's preferred learning style.
   c. Simplify the information using a comparison to an activity the patient likes, such as a game or a sport.
   d. Speak slowly and require the patient to repeat what you have said to confirm their understanding.

51. Which of the following medications is NOT considered an NSAID?
   a. Ibuprofen
   b. Aspirin
   c. Naproxen
   d. Acetaminophen

52. A female four-year-old is present at the medical practice with her father for a scheduled check-up. She is due for two vaccinations. When the child sees the needles, she begins screaming that her mother said she would not get more shots. Whose consent is required to vaccinate the child?
   a. The child
   b. The present parent
   c. The primary physician
   d. Both parents

53. What is the most important reason for a healthcare practice to collect co-pays and other payments when the patient presents for their appointment?
   a. This improves the practice's accounts receivable ratio.
   b. Staff will not need to follow-up with patients about payments.
   c. This increases the practice's access to liquid cash.
   d. The practice can cancel appointments with patients who won't pay.

54. Which of the following documents are NOT needed when filing an insurance appeal?
   a. An explanation of benefits denying coverage
   b. An advance directive
   c. Patient's medical history
   d. Laboratory test results

55. Which over-the-counter medication has a maximum daily dose of 4000 milligrams daily?
   a. Ibuprofen
   b. Tylenol
   c. Aspirin
   d. Naproxen

56. A teenage patient who recently started fluoxetine treatment has returned for follow-up. Which question is most important to ask this patient?
   a. "Have you had any thoughts of harming yourself?"
   b. "When was your last bowel movement?"
   c. "How is your appetite since starting treatment?"
   d. "Have you experienced any shortness of breath since starting treatment?"

57. Which of the following tasks is most likely to be completed by a primary care physician?
    a. Measuring blood pressure
    b. Recording vitals
    c. Billing the insurance provider
    d. Recommending a lifestyle change

58. The CMA knows that which of the following is the most impactful way to prevent the spread of infection in the healthcare setting?
    a. Disinfecting surfaces
    b. Wearing a face mask
    c. Washing hands
    d. Staying home when sick

59. The CMA documents a patient's pulse as "4+." Which of the following findings is associated with this documentation?
    a. Diminished pulse
    b. Bounding pulse
    c. Strong pulse
    d. Absent pulse

60. Which of the following actions is most effective when communicating with a patient who suffers from hearing loss?
    a. Use written communication when possible
    b. Speak in a louder, higher voice
    c. Speak into the patient's more affected ear
    d. Stand at the head of the bed when speaking

61. If a patient's axillary temperature is 101.2 degrees Fahrenheit, what is their body temperature?
    a. 100.2 degrees Fahrenheit
    b. 98.6 degrees Fahrenheit
    c. 102.2 degrees Fahrenheit
    d. 101.2 degrees Fahrenheit

62. Which of the following shows the correct order for removing PPE?
    a. Mask, goggles, gown, gloves
    b. Gloves, gown, mask, goggles
    c. Gloves, goggles, gown, mask
    d. Goggles, mask, gown, gloves

63. The CMA is preparing a female patient for a general pelvic examination. Which position is the most appropriate for this procedure?
    a. Supine
    b. Fowler's
    c. Sims
    d. Lithotomy

64. Oral thrush is caused by which class of infectious organism?
   a. Virus
   b. Fungus
   c. Bacteria
   d. Parasite

65. Which of the following job duties is most likely a task performed by the CMA?
   a. Diagnosing a patient's illness
   b. Explaining laboratory results
   c. Collecting the patient's medical history
   d. Providing assistance during an outpatient procedure

66. In preparing to obtain a blood sample, the CMA knows which site is generally the preferred anatomical region for phlebotomy?
   a. Inner forearm
   b. Inner elbow
   c. Top of the hand
   d. Top of the forearm

67. When is a healthcare provider required to report an ICD-10-CM code to Medicare?
   a. After performing a billable procedure
   b. When seeking precertification for a procedure
   c. When billing for durable medical equipment
   d. When billing for each patient encounter

68. Which statement best describes illegal abandonment of a child?
   a. A child left in a "baby box"
   b. A child who does not receive sufficient food for normative development
   c. A child left alone for weeks at a time, without a parent or caregiver providing supervision
   d. A child who does not receive medical attention for an illness

69. Mononucleosis is an infection associated with which of the following viruses?
   a. Rhinovirus
   b. Epstein-Barr
   c. Adenovirus
   d. Varicella-zoster

70. In which of the following situations might the legal doctrine *respondeat superior* apply?
   a. A nurse does not respond to an emergency alert, and a patient in their care experiences a medical crisis. The employer disciplines the nurse.
   b. Multiple employees violate HIPAA by sharing confidential patient information with their spouses. The employer does not discipline the employees.
   c. A medical assistant receives a subpoena to testify about witnessing alleged criminal activity by a patient in the workplace.
   d. The relative of a deceased patient writes an insulting letter to the local newspaper about the medical practice.

71. A patient with limited mobility who is at risk for deep vein thrombosis (DVT) should be given which medical device to help reduce risk?
   a. Walker
   b. Trapeze bar
   c. Wedge and cushions
   d. Sequential compression devices

72. While administering a vaccine, a colleague is inadvertently stuck with a used needle. What should the CMA assist the colleague to do first?
   a. Notify the physician or supervisor.
   b. Go to the emergency room for evaluation.
   c. Wash the area with soap and water.
   d. Draw bloodwork on both the colleague and patient.

73. Define the acronym *ABN*.
   a. Alternative Benefit Notice
   b. Automatic Beneficiary Note
   c. Active Benefit Negotiated
   d. Advance Beneficiary Notice

74. While assessing a patient's blood pressure manually, the CMA begins to slowly release air from the cuff while listening for a series of distinct sounds. The first of these sounds is associated with which of the following?
   a. Point of maximal impulse
   b. Systolic blood pressure
   c. Diastolic blood pressure
   d. Pulse pressure

75. A patient is recommended a treatment plan that is expected to cost $25,000. Their deductible is $2,000, and their co-insurance is 25%. How much will the patient owe to the healthcare provider after insurance?
   a. $7,750
   b. $6,250
   c. $5,750
   d. $4,250

76. Which of the following employees of a healthcare organization is likely NOT a mandated reporter?
   a. Medical assistant
   b. Medical coder
   c. Physician's assistant
   d. Nurse practitioner

77. The CMA is reviewing a patient's chart and comes across an unfamiliar medical term in the physician's notes. This term is used to describe the patient's condition and ends in the suffix *-algia*. Based on their knowledge of medical terminology, the CMA knows that this term is describing which of the following?
   a. A condition involving the musculoskeletal system
   b. A condition that causes pain
   c. A condition that causes stiffness
   d. A condition involving inflammation

78. What is the best way to prevent the spread of germs?
   a. Wear a properly fitted mask when around patients
   b. Wear gloves and a gown during each patient interaction
   c. Handwash with soap and water frequently
   d. Wipe down work areas with disinfectant at regular intervals

79. What is the best physical distance to maintain when calming down an escalated patient?
   a. Close
   b. Arm's reach
   c. Three steps away
   d. As far as possible

80. The lungs are part of which body system?
   a. Pulmonary
   b. Cardiovascular
   c. Musculoskeletal
   d. Neurological

81. The medical assistant is the first to discover unusual bruising on a newly admitted patient. When asked what happened, the patient states that their daughter struck them while she was drunk. It is your legal obligation to notify which of the following?
   a. Coworkers
   b. Adult Protective Services
   c. The MD
   d. The patient's family

82. While placing leads for an electrocardiogram, leads V1 and V2 are placed to the right and left of the sternum, at the ___________ intercostal space.
   a. 9th
   b. 5th
   c. 2nd
   d. 4th

83. What is the precertification process?
   a. Getting informed consent from the patient prior to a procedure
   b. Obtaining an ROI to send information to an insurance provider
   c. Asking an insurance provider if a service or procedure will be covered
   d. Renewing a physician's license prior to expiration

84. A patient has a tibia fracture in their left leg and was told that they cannot bear any weight on that side. Which crutch gait would be most appropriate to educate the patient on?
   a. Two-point crutch gait
   b. Swing-through crutch gait
   c. Swing-to crutch gait
   d. Three-point crutch gait

85. What is a benefit of contacting patients to confirm their appointment the day before their appointment is scheduled?
   a. The practice is more likely to receive the co-pay on the date of the visit.
   b. The patient is more likely to bring their medication to the visit.
   c. The patient is more likely to attend the appointment.
   d. The practice can confirm how long the appointment will take.

86. Which technique used during intramuscular injection can help to ensure medication remains in the muscle?
   a. Hold the needle at a 90-degree angle during administration.
   b. Aspirate prior to injecting the medication.
   c. Pull the skin away from the injection site before injection.
   d. Choose the appropriate needle size for the patient.

87. The CMA is performing initial intake for a new patient. The patient is measured to be 124.4 kilograms. If the patient asks what their weight would be in pounds, what number would the CMA provide (rounded to the nearest whole number)?
   a. 57
   b. 60
   c. 270
   d. 274

88. What is the function of a modifier when coding with CPT?
   a. To upcode the service due to additional complexity
   b. To indicate the code has been changed by the NCCI
   c. To provide additional information about the service
   d. To bundle several related codes to a single claim

89. Which gland secretes growth hormones?
   a. Thyroid
   b. Pancreas
   c. Ovaries
   d. Pituitary

90. Which of the following behaviors best describes a CMA who is actively listening to a patient?
   a. Looking at their computer screen and nodding when the patient speaks
   b. Folding hands in lap and making frequent eye contact with the patient
   c. Asking questions to confirm the patient's symptoms
   d. Checking the office schedule to see how much time the CMA has allotted for the conversation

91. Which breath sound, present on inspiration and expiration, is associated with narrowing bronchi?
   a. Wheeze
   b. Crackle
   c. Rhonchi
   d. Stridor

92. What is the purpose of the HCPCS Level I set of medical codes?
   a. Identifying equipment used in healthcare
   b. Listing procedures performed by the provider
   c. Indicating diagnosed illnesses
   d. Coding experimental or provisional treatments

93. Which step in the handwashing process below is incorrect?
   a. Turn on the warm water.
   b. Place soap in the palm of the hand.
   c. Rub hands and wash for at least 10 seconds.
   d. Rinse hands with fingers pointing down.

94. Which of the following is an example of a modifiable risk factor for falls?
   a. Dementia
   b. Stroke history
   c. History of falls
   d. Incontinence

95. A patient's account becomes an account receivable at which point in the financial process?
   a. Upon discharge from the healthcare practice
   b. After receiving the first payment for service
   c. Once the first bill for services provided is sent
   d. When the bill is sent to a collections service

96. Which of the following intramuscular injection sites is NOT typically recommended due to the risk of nerve injury?
   a. Dorsogluteal muscle
   b. Deltoid muscle
   c. Vastus lateralis muscle
   d. Ventrogluteal muscle

97. The CMA is preparing to provide instructions to a female patient regarding a clean-catch urine specimen. The CMA should include which of the following instructions?
   a. "Ensure that you collect the first stream of urine for your sample."
   b. "Wipe the outer area of the vulva with the provided wipe."
   c. "Place the cup a few centimeters away from the urethra and try to fill half the specimen cup."
   d. "Make sure you are not touching the labia or vulva while urinating into the specimen cup."

98. Which of the following statements made by the CMA would be appropriate to teach a patient regarding safe use of a walker?
   a. "When walking, lead each step with the stronger leg first. Follow up by bringing the weaker or injured leg forward."
   b. "To stand up from a chair, place feet hips distance apart and brace yourself by placing both hands on the grips of the walker for stability."
   c. "To sit down in a chair, back up until the legs are a foot distant from the seat of the chair and place hands on the armrests before gently lowering into the chair."
   d. "To step up on a curb, place the walker fully on the elevated surface. First, step up with the stronger leg and follow with the weaker or injured leg."

99. The CMA is setting up the examination room in preparation for a patient who is scheduled for a yearly gynecological examination and Pap smear. Which of the following instruments and supplies would NOT typically be required for this type of visit?
   a. Speculum
   b. Suture kit
   c. Cotton-tipped applicator sticks
   d. Specimen bottle

100. Which of the following is NOT a natural barrier against infection in the human body?
   a. Inflammatory response
   b. Skin
   c. Stomach acid
   d. Mucous membranes

101. The medical assistant is taking care of a patient who is about to undergo an arm amputation. The patient will neither discuss nor acknowledge their upcoming surgery. This is a defense mechanism known as:
   a. denial
   b. regression
   c. acting out
   d. projection

102. The CMA is currently working with an orientee. Shortly after rooming a patient, they receive notification that the patient is experiencing a nosebleed. After the nosebleed is controlled, it is noted that there is blood on the floor and examination table where the patient was sitting. Which action by the orientee would warrant intervention by the preceptor?
   a. The orientee is observed putting on gloves and a face shield prior to beginning cleanup.
   b. The orientee soaks up the liquid blood with towels.
   c. The orientee uses a detergent containing bleach to disinfect the contaminated areas.
   d. The orientee ensures that all towels are disposed of in the waste bin.

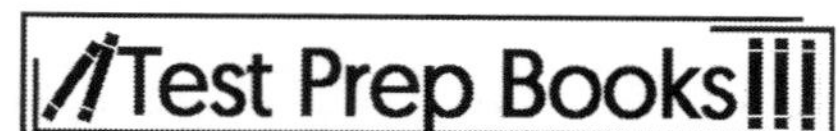

103. A resident's orders state that they should remain in the Semi-Fowler's position. What does this mean?

a. The resident should remain on their stomach.
b. The resident should remain flat on their back.
c. The resident should remain on their back with the head of their bed raised between 30 and 45 degrees.
d. The resident should remain on their back with the head of their bed raised above 60 degrees.

104. Which of the following contact methods is most effective in reducing the frequency of no-show appointments for a healthcare practice?

a. Phone call
b. Email
c. Social media
d. Text message

105. What are the five vital signs?

a. Heart rate, temperature, blood pressure, respiratory rate, pain
b. Temperature, urinary output, heart rate, blood pressure, respiratory rate
c. Blood pressure, heart rate, blood glucose, respiratory rate, urinary output
d. Blood pressure, lung sounds, blood glucose, heart rate, pain

106. A patient receiving treatment with alendronate should prioritize appropriate intake of which of the following vitamins?

a. Vitamin A
b. Vitamin B12
c. Vitamin C
d. Vitamin D

107. The medical assistant is taking care of a postpartum woman who is bleeding uncontrollably. The uncontrollable bleeding could be:

a. a stroke.
b. a hemorrhage
c. a episode of hematemesis.
d. a normal effect of giving birth.

108. An insurance provider denies authorization to cover a patient's prescription of an expensive name-brand medication. What is the best way a CMA can provide support to this patient's treatment plan?

a. Request authorization of a generic medication with similar benefits.
b. Refer the patient to financial counseling to help budget for the expense.
c. Encourage the patient to use OTC medications for symptom management.
d. Help the patient submit an appeal to their insurance provider.

109. The CMA has received an order to assist with the removal of sutures on a patient's lower abdomen. In the middle of the procedure, it is noted that there is an area near the middle of the wound where the edges appear to be separating. Which of the following would NOT be an appropriate action by the CMA?
   a. Apply wound closure strips to the affected area.
   b. Notify the physician.
   c. Apply antibiotic ointment to the area.
   d. Stop the suture removal procedure.

110. The CMA is preparing to administer a Mantoux test. On which part of the body is this test typically performed?
   a. Hand
   b. Face
   c. Arm
   d. Neck

111. The CMA can safely choose liquid hand sanitizer to perform hand hygiene in which situation?
   a. After eating lunch
   b. Before caring for a patient with *Clostridium difficile* (*C. diff*)
   c. After using the restroom
   d. After applying lotion to hands

112. A patient returns to the clinic for follow-up one week after a cholecystectomy. During intake, the patient says they have had a dull, achy pain in the back of their left leg for a few days. The CMA recognizes that this could potentially be a sign of which postoperative complication?
   a. Pulmonary embolism
   b. Deep vein thrombosis
   c. Infection
   d. Post-cholecystectomy syndrome

113. Why should a healthcare practice collect ethnic and racial demographic data during new patient registration?
   a. To understand whether the patient is more or less likely to require financial assistance
   b. To meet requirements set forth by federal regulations
   c. To improve medical record management when tracking illnesses
   d. To determine if additional supports will be required when providing services

114. Which of the following patients is LEAST likely to notify the CMA that they have a restriction on the location where a venipuncture can be performed?
   a. A 62-year-old female patient with a history of breast cancer
   b. A 58-year-old male patient in treatment for end-stage renal disease
   c. A 24-year-old male patient receiving long-term daily intravenous antibiotic therapy
   d. A 53-year-old female patient with a history of congestive heart failure

115. Which example of communication below protects resident rights and is HIPAA-compliant?
   a. The medical assistant talking with the patient's nurse about recent MRI results
   b. The medical assistant talking to their friend, an NA on another unit, about their patient's recent complaints
   c. The medical assistant looking up the medical record of a friend who is admitted on a unit on another floor
   d. The medical assistant letting their friend know they are taking care of their uncle and discussing his care

116. When taking a patient's blood pressure on the upper arm, the arrow should be aligned with which of the following?
   a. The radial artery
   b. The brachial artery
   c. The femoral artery
   d. The popliteal artery

117. Which of the following is a test that provides information about a patient's blood sugar over the last three months?
   a. 24-hour urine test
   b. Fasting blood glucose level
   c. Glucose tolerance test
   d. Hemoglobin A1C

118. Which of the following is NOT a function of a living will?
   a. Designate power of attorney
   b. Provide autonomy to an unconscious patient
   c. Indicate the patient's wishes if in a comatose state
   d. Express the patient's desire not to be resuscitated

119. Which of the following requires only a gown and gloves?
   a. Reverse Isolation
   b. Advanced Droplet Precautions
   c. Airborne Precautions
   d. Standard Precautions

120. How does the concept of standard of care apply to medical malpractice lawsuits?
   a. It states that harm has been done if the provided treatment was not successful.
   b. Practitioners who treat an illness with non-standard procedures can be found negligent.
   c. A medical practice can be found negligent if their activities do not match the current standard of care for an illness.
   d. It states that the physician must diagnose the patient's illness prior to treating the illness.

121. What data does an aging of accounts report provide to a healthcare practice?
   a. The average age of patients provided service by the practice
   b. The total money owed by patients or insurance to the practice
   c. A description of how long patients or insurance have owed payments
   d. A trajectory for when a new practice will achieve profitability

122. The CMA is obtaining vital signs on a confused female geriatric patient. Which of the following observations would be most concerning for elder abuse?
   a. The patient's clothing is worn and dirty, and she has a strong body odor.
   b. The patient is startled and jumps when the CMA applies the blood pressure cuff.
   c. The patient is tearful and asks her caregiver where her husband is.
   d. There is a bruise on her right elbow where the caregiver reports the patient fell last week.

123. Which situation describes a case where the patient provides implied consent?
   a. Performing CPR on someone who is unresponsive
   b. A parent nodding before you clean their child's wound
   c. Receiving verbal consent to release information to another healthcare provider
   d. A surgeon performing a scheduled procedure on a patient

124. Which type of precaution would be used for a patient with a *Clostridium difficile* infection?
   a. Droplet
   b. Airborne
   c. Contact
   d. Standard precautions only

125. Is it ethically appropriate for a medical assistant to receive a personal gift from a patient?
   a. Yes, if the gift is under $100.
   b. Yes, if the patient is no longer receiving services from the CMA.
   c. No, because gifts are identical to bribes for preferential treatment.
   d. No, because receiving a gift weakens professional boundaries.

126. A patient mentions taking escitalopram. To which drug class does this medication belong?
   a. Serotonin-norepinephrine reuptake inhibitors
   b. Tricyclic antidepressants
   c. Monoamine oxidase inhibitors
   d. Selective serotonin reuptake inhibitors

127. Which of the following is NOT a culturally appropriate support for a Muslim patient who wishes to participate in their daily prayers while at the healthcare provider's office?
   a. Look up the direction in which they ought to pray.
   b. Encourage them to use part of the waiting room, if space is available.
   c. Allow the patient to use an empty examination room for their prayers, if available.
   d. Ask at what times the patient wishes to pray, and then schedule their tests around those periods.

128. Which of the following cancers is NOT typically associated with human papillomavirus?
   a. Oropharyngeal cancer
   b. Cervical cancer
   c. Anal cancer
   d. Breast cancer

129. Which new symptom reported by the patient taking furosemide may indicate that they are experiencing a potential treatment complication relating to potassium levels?
   a. Weakness
   b. Diarrhea
   c. Headaches
   d. Seizures

130. After a blood sample is placed in the centrifuge, the top layer, which is closest to the opening of the vial, is which of the following blood components?
   a. Plasma
   b. Leukocytes
   c. Platelets
   d. Erythrocytes

131. When is an operative note written, and by which staff member?
   a. While preparing for the surgery, and by the primary surgeon
   b. Prior to scheduling the surgery, and by the diagnosing physician
   c. During the surgery, and by an operating room technician
   d. After the surgery is complete, and by the primary surgeon

132. A teenager arrived for follow-up after being treated for a fracture of the radius. Which part of the patient's body was injured?
   a. Arm
   b. Leg
   c. Head
   d. Torso

133. While the CMA is reviewing a patient's discharge sheet and new orders, the patient states, "I don't remember the doctor mentioning that medicine. I think it was another one, but I can't remember the name." Which response by the CMA would be most appropriate?
   a. "I would be happy to print and review a handout about this new medication."
   b. "Your doctor has entered these and has asked me to review them with you."
   c. "May I step out of the room and confirm these orders with your doctor?"
   d. "I know doctor visits can be overwhelming. I am here to help you understand your new medicines."

134. The CMA is performing initial intake for a new patient. The patient is measured to be 124.4 kilograms. If the patient asks what their weight would be in pounds, what number would the CMA provide (rounded to the nearest whole number)?
   a. 57
   b. 60
   c. 270
   d. 274

135. The CMA is asked to assist the physician during a procedure to open and drain a large pus-filled lesion on a patient's underarm. Which medical term most appropriately describes this patient's lesion?

a. Abscess
b. Pustule
c. Comedone
d. Carbuncle

136. Jaundice of the skin would be associated with which color?

a. Red
b. Blue
c. Purple
d. Yellow

137. What is the most important piece of information for a medical assistant to provide when answering the phone?

a. Name of the healthcare practice
b. Medical assistant's name
c. List of healthcare providers
d. New patient availability

138. Which suffix is associated with a class of medications used to lower blood cholesterol levels?

a. -statin
b. -sartan
c. -olol
d. -mab

139. To which law enforcement agency should a CMA report suspected health insurance fraud?

a. FBI
b. CIA
c. IRS
d. CMS

140. Which of the following medical terms best describes a respiratory rate that is faster than normal?

a. Hyperpnea
b. Hyperoxia
c. Tachypnea
d. Hyperventilation

141. The CMA is assisting to room and prepare a patient to be seen for a follow-up appointment with the physician. While reviewing current medications, which of the following statements made by the CMA would best gauge the patient's overall medication compliance?

a. "Are you taking your medications as prescribed?"
b. "Can you tell me about the medicines you are taking?"
c. "Have you started or stopped any medications since your last visit?"
d. "Are there any medications you are having difficulty taking?"

142. Which of the following is NOT a routine appointment?
   a. Taking a blood draw with a phlebotomist
   b. Visiting a family physician for a physical examination
   c. Seeking relief for an earache
   d. Seeing a doctor for a medication refill

143. Which statement made by a four-year-old patient's mother may indicate a need for further dietary teaching?
   a. "I do try to offer a variety of foods, but she is pretty picky."
   b. "We sit down together for most meals, but sometimes it takes her an hour to clean her plate."
   c. "She drinks mostly water but likes milk or juice every once in a while."
   d. "She doesn't really like meat, but she will eat cheese and peanut butter."

144. A CMA is with a patient with a known respiratory infection. The patient is on droplet precautions. What is the minimum PPE required when caring for this patient?
   a. Gloves, gown, and an N-95 respirator
   b. A gown, eyewear, gloves, and a disposable mask
   c. Gloves and a disposable mask
   d. A disposable mask, sterile gloves, and eyewear

145. When repositioning a patient in the supine position, it is important for the medical assistant to make sure which areas of the body have additional padding underneath them?
   a. Calves
   b. Middle of the back
   c. Heels
   d. Upper thigh

146. A patient's rectal temperature is measured at 100.6 degrees Fahrenheit. If the CMA measured this patient's temperature orally, what temperature (in Fahrenheit) would be expected?
   a. 100.3–100.9
   b. 101.1–101.6
   c. 99.6–100.1
   d. 98.6–99.1

147. A patient had a heart attack one month ago. His wife tells the medical assistant privately that he doesn't remember having it. This is a defense mechanism known as:
   a. denial.
   b. repression.
   c. dissociation.
   d. grief.

148. Which anatomical site is most commonly used to palpate pulse in a responsive adult?
   a. Brachial
   b. Carotid
   c. Radial
   d. Apical

149. HIPAA is a law designed to protect the patient's:
   a. dignity.
   b. iIdentity.
   c. physician.
   d. family .

150. While reviewing a patient's record, the CMA recognizes that which of the following medications is an oral hypoglycemic medication?
   a. Regular insulin
   b. Atorvastatin
   c. Lisinopril
   d. Metformin

151. Which of the following tasks would a CMA most likely do as part of end-of-day reconciliation?
   a. Review the next day's schedule.
   b. Print and mail patient bills.
   c. Sanitize the healthcare practice's examination rooms.
   d. Balance the front desk cash from patient co-pays.

152. Which of the following is an assistive device for mobility?
   a. Physical therapy
   b. Occupational therapy
   c. Crutches
   d. Restraints

153. The medical assistant is caring for a resident who is hearing impaired. What is one step the medical assistant can take to aid in communication with the resident?
   a. Talk to the resident while his back is turned.
   b. Stay in the resident's line of vision while speaking with him.
   c. Talk quietly so as to maintain a calm environment.
   d. Use Braille to communicate with the resident.

154. A 41-year-old female patient expresses the belief that abortion is wrong to a medical assistant during a routine yearly physical. What is the most appropriate response?
   a. Agree, regardless of personal beliefs, to build rapport with the patient.
   b. Express personal beliefs as long as the conversation remains civil.
   c. Provide neutral, factual information on the topic, such as the state's laws on the subject.
   d. Ignore the statement and focus the conversation on the patient's health.

155. Which of the following is NOT a reason why itemized statements are important in healthcare?
   a. They define which services are covered by the insurance provider.
   b. They explain the cost of provided services.
   c. They simplify resolution of disputes about service cost.
   d. They verify that the patient received the correct services.

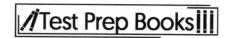

156. Why should a CMA ask for a patient's date of birth (DOB) when providing customer service over the telephone?

a. Age is a significant factor in an individual's health.
b. Providing DOB helps ensure the speaker is who they claim to be.
c. Collecting patient information over the phone reduces the information needed when they arrive for an appointment.
d. The patient's DOB is required by CMS for patient identification.

157. A patient has been given an order for ondansetron. The route of administration is written "ODT." How should the patient take this medication?

a. By swallowing the tablet
b. By allowing the tablet to dissolve in the mouth
c. By placing the tablet under the tongue
d. By placing the tablet in the cheek

158. Under HIPAA, when can a patient request an amendment of their health information?

a. When they disagree with the physician's diagnosis
b. When the EHR has a factual inaccuracy
c. When a second provider has provided an alternative diagnosis
d. When the patient is transferring to the care of a new healthcare provider

159. A female patient reports experiencing pain on the right outside part of her hip. Which medical term describes the location of the patient's pain?

a. Lateral
b. Dorsal
c. Ventral
d. Medial

160. While reviewing medications, a patient reports taking Klonopin. Which of the following medications listed in the patient's chart is the generic form of this drug?

a. Clonidine
b. Lorazepam
c. Clonazepam
d. Clindamycin

161. Define the act of *writing off* a bill owed to the healthcare practice.

a. Forgiving a bill due to the patient's life circumstances
b. Reporting the bill as a loss on the healthcare practice's taxes
c. Sending a bill payment notice to the patient
d. Removing a patient's overdue account due to bankruptcy filing

162. The CMA is working with a 64-year-old male patient. During a conversation about current medications, the patient suddenly collapses. The CMA attempts to rouse the patient without success, and the patient is observed taking a few gasping breaths. The CMA is unsure if there is a pulse or not. What is the most appropriate next action after calling for assistance?
   a. Begin chest compressions.
   b. Assess pulse from another pulse point.
   c. Give two rescue breaths.
   d. Perform sternal rub.

163. The CMA is assisting the physician to reinforce teaching regarding at-home blood sugar testing. Which of the following teaching strategies tends to be most appropriate for this type of teaching?
   a. Demonstration
   b. Teach-back
   c. Video tutorial
   d. Written handout

164. In reviewing a patient's medication list, which of the following over-the-counter medications would be concerning for a patient taking lisinopril?
   a. Ibuprofen
   b. Tylenol
   c. Omeprazole
   d. Vitamin C

165. The medical assistant is caring for a patient who recently had a heart attack and has been placed on a cardiac diet. How would the medical assistant most accurately describe this diet to the patient?
   a. High in sodium, low in cholesterol and fat
   b. Increased carbohydrate and water intake, low in sodium and fat
   c. Low in sodium, fat, and cholesterol
   d. Increased carbohydrate intake, decreased water intake, low in cholesterol

166. Which of the following could result in a false low blood pressure measurement?
   a. Positioning the extremity above the level of the heart
   b. Using a cuff that is too small
   c. Having a patient with a full bladder
   d. Performing the test in a doctor's office

167. The medical assistant is taking care of a patient who has influenza. Which transmission-based precaution should they take?
   a. Airborne precaution
   b. Contact precaution
   c. Standard precaution
   d. Droplet precaution

168. Which of the following healthcare providers is most likely to add a discharge summary to a patient's EHR?

a. Drug rehabilitation facility
b. OB/GYN specialist's office
c. Family physician's practice
d. Laboratory department

169. A patient is visiting the clinic with suspected influenza. Which personal protective equipment (PPE) should be used by the CMA upon entering the exam room where the patient is waiting?

a. Respirator mask only
b. Surgical mask only
c. Gloves and surgical mask
d. Gloves and respirator mask

170. The CMA is coaching a diabetic patient regarding diet. After being asked to review their diet from the previous day, the patient reports having one piece of whole-grain toast with margarine and an apple. Which of the following statements made by the CMA would be LEAST appropriate?

a. "Whole-grain products can help reduce cholesterol levels and insulin spikes."
b. "It is best to avoid eating bread and fruit together in a single meal."
c. "What have your blood sugar readings been this past month?"
d. "Consider adding lean protein, such as egg whites or turkey sausage, to this meal next time."

171. What is the appropriate angle to administer a subcutaneous injection in an infant's thigh?

a. 90 degrees
b. 45 degrees
c. 60 degrees
d. 75 degrees

172. The CMA reviews a patient's discharge paperwork and sees a new medication that has been ordered to be taken "TID." Which statement by the patient indicates the patient is taking their new medication correctly?

a. "I take that one in the morning and at night."
b. "I have been taking that one with breakfast, lunch, and dinner."
c. "I take that medicine whenever I feel like I need it."
d. "I take this medication every other day."

173. The CMA is performing intake on a patient who is recovering from nonalcoholic pancreatitis. Which of the following describes the function of the pancreas?

a. Helps with the digestion of fat and helps regulate blood clotting
b. Absorbs water and nutrients to be used by the body
c. Helps with blood sugar regulation and produces enzymes for digestion
d. Filters blood and assists in waste removal from the body

174. How are growth charts used as part of the EHR?

a. They describe the increase or decrease in a practice's patient population over time.
b. They track the size of growths—such as a lipoma—over time.
c. They record a child's size in relation to the child's age.
d. They measure emotional growth through tracking a patient's treatment objectives.

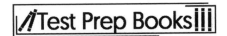

175. A patient’s family member is observed being verbally threatening to the patient and regularly causing them to feel fearful and worthless. This is an example of what kind of abuse?
    a. Physical abuse
    b. Sexual abuse
    c. Emotional/mental abuse
    d. Financial abuse

176. When preparing a patient for safe use of crutches, the CMA instructs the patient to align the handgrips with which anatomical location?
    a. The hip flexor
    b. The waist
    c. The top of the pelvis
    d. The top of the greater trochanter

177. Which of the following vital sign measurements taken on an adult patient receiving metoprolol may signal that the patient’s dose may need to be decreased?
    a. A temperature of 99.9 degrees Fahrenheit
    b. A pulse rate of 56 beats per minute
    c. A blood pressure measurement of 180/110
    d. A respiration rate of 22 breaths per minute

178. The medical assistant walks into a patient’s room and witnesses the patient violently convulsing with rigid muscles. The patient is completely unconscious. The medical assistant notifies the nurse immediately and recognizes this is what type of seizure?
    a. Myoclonic
    b. Absence
    c. Grand mal
    d. Tonic

179. The medical assistant is speaking with a patient when she notices that the patient is having trouble forming thoughts into sentences and one side of his face appears to be drooping. What emergency condition is likely occurring in the patient?
    a. Meningitis
    b. Migraine
    c. Seizure
    d. Stroke

180. What is the e-prescribing process?
    a. The patient electronically contacts their healthcare provider to request new prescriptions.
    b. The healthcare provider sends the patient's prescriptions electronically to their pharmacy.
    c. The pharmacy accesses the patient's EHR to determine when to automatically refill a prescription.
    d. The healthcare provider integrates their EHR system with a partner pharmacy's EHR system.

181. To obtain as much information as possible, which approach would be best to use when interviewing patients?
   a. Focus on closed-ended questions to obtain specific, relevant information.
   b. Use mainly open-ended questions to allow patients to express themselves.
   c. Emphasize probing questions to clarify responses and resolve contradictions.
   d. Use a mix of closed- and open-ended questions to get a range of information.

182. What is the name of the type of patient consent that is often used in emergency departments to provide care?
   a. Informed consent
   b. Implied consent
   c. Expressed consent
   d. Emergency consent

183. Regarding the documentation of care, which choice best reflects the types of items that should be included in the patient's social history?
   a. Number and health of friends and relatives; types of regular social activities
   b. Alcohol, smoking, and drug use; living arrangements; marital status; occupation
   c. Chief complaint; review of symptoms; past medical history; family history
   d. Occupation history; compliance with treatment; test and examination results

184. In what type of circumstance must a CMA provide a patient with an advanced beneficiary notice (ABN)?
   a. When the standard of care is not met for original Medicare coverage
   b. When the standard of care is not met for Medicare Advantage coverage
   c. When the standard of care is not met for private insurance coverage
   d. When the standard of care is not met for any type of insurance coverage

185. Which screening test is useful in decreasing the incidence and mortality of cancer and is generally recommended once every three years for women aged 21 to 65?
   a. HPV
   b. PAP
   c. Colonoscopy
   d. Mammogram

186. Which term accurately describes a cleaning process that kills or inactivates most infectious bacteria and viruses on hard surfaces?
   a. Sanitization
   b. Disinfection
   c. Sterilization
   d. Medical asepsis

187. A CMA may have to pay compensation to a patient if the patient sues the CMA for some kind of professional negligence and the CMA loses the case in court. What is the precise term for this type of legal situation?
   a. Tort
   b. Libel
   c. Liability
   d. Slander

188. Which statement is most accurate about people who have health insurance that is covered by Medicaid?
   a. People who have annual incomes that are below a certain level
   b. People who have low incomes or belong to disadvantaged groups
   c. People in racial or ethnic groups that are historically disadvantaged
   d. People who are 65 or older or who have certain serious health conditions

189. The type of sign shown below is typically what colors?

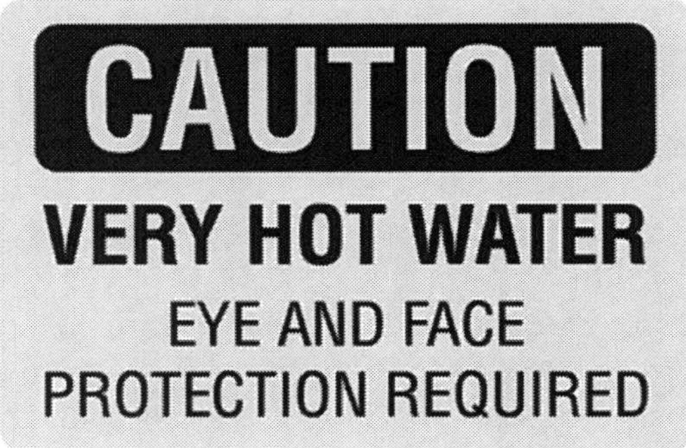

   a. Gray and black
   b. Orange and black
   c. Yellow and black
   d. Colors may vary.

190. Which choice is NOT a common urgent or emergent condition that can typically be accommodated with a same-day appointment?
   a. Muscle strains and sprains
   b. Fever greater than 100 °F in children
   c. Severe pain without bleeding or fainting
   d. Diarrhea that has lasted more than three days

191. Warning signs, such as the example shown below, are generally used for what purpose in healthcare settings?

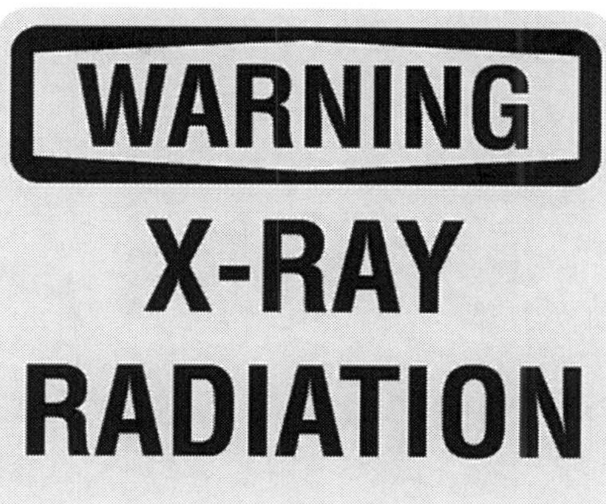

a. To identify hazards related to radiation exposure
b. To identify hazards related to medical equipment
c. To indicate the potential for moderate-level harm
d. To indicate the potential for serious injury or death

192. Which statement does NOT give an accurate explanation for why wounds on the feet take a long time to heal—and may not heal at all—in people with diabetes?

a. Hyperglycemia affects the immune system, hindering the body's natural healing processes.
b. Hyperglycemia causes blood vessels to constrict, reducing circulation of blood and oxygen to the feet.
c. Insulin deficiency causes excess salt concentration in blood, irritating wounds and preventing healing.
d. Neuropathy limits sensation in the feet, so people with diabetes may not be aware of the presence of wounds.

193. A CMA feels uncomfortable and doesn't know what to say to a patient who is newly diagnosed with a terminal illness. What is probably the best thing for the CMA to do in this situation?

a. The CMA should say anything at all so that the patient knows she cares.
b. The CMA should tell the patient not to worry and that everything will be okay.
c. The CMA should just sit there, show no emotion, and listen to the patient.
d. The CMA doesn't have to talk but might hug or hold hands with the patient.

194. At what age does an infant typically begin to recognize familiar faces?

a. Three months
b. Six months
c. Nine months
d. One year

195. What is the name of the body system that is specifically responsible for the production of blood cells?
   a. Hematopoietic system
   b. Cardiovascular system
   c. Lymphatic system
   d. Circulatory system

196. What is the best general definition of a patient portal?
   a. A website that gives patients access to their personal health information
   b. A website that allows patients to send direct messages to their doctors
   c. A website from which patients can download medical-related forms
   d. A website on which patients can make payments for medical services

197. If a provider wanted a medication to be absorbed slowly and gradually into the patient's body, which would be the preferred route of administration?
   a. Z-tract injection
   b. Oral administration
   c. Intramuscular injection
   d. Subcutaneous injection

198. What would probably be the best response of a CMA to a patient who is very agitated and angry that he has not received his pain medication after repeatedly asking for it?
   a. "I know you're in pain. Let's call your nurse while I'm here, and then I'll check on you afterward."
   b. "I understand you're in pain. I will be sure to tell your nurse. After you get the med, I'll check back with you."
   c. "Please calm down because getting angry will make your situation worse. I'll be sure to tell your nurse."
   d. "I'm sure your nurse is aware that you requested the pain medication. She'll be here as soon as she can."

199. Which choice provides the most accurate description of MedWatch?
   a. The Food and Drug Administration's system for the public to report drug reactions and drug failures; providers use a different system for medical errors.
   b. The Food and Drug Administration's system for providers and the public to report medical errors, drug reactions, product quality problems, and drug failures
   c. The National Institutes of Health's online system for providers to access the latest publications in medical research and archives of medical news
   d. The National Institutes of Health's online system for the public to access the latest regulations, reports, and other updates concerning healthcare

200. Which federal agency is the best source for obtaining Vaccine Information Statements, which document the benefits and risks associated with particular vaccines?
   a. National Institutes of Health
   b. Food and Drug Administration
   c. Agency for Healthcare Research and Quality
   d. Centers for Disease Control and Prevention

Answer Explanations #2

1. D: A patient portal generally provides access to the patient's health information and provides the ability to message providers or schedule new appointments. Therefore, Choice *D* is correct. It does not generally provide access to financial or insurance information, so Choice *C* is incorrect. Choice *A* is incorrect because if a new prescription is required, the patient must meet with a provider to receive the prescription. Choice *B* is incorrect because an ROI should be signed in person, not online.

2. C: FAST is the acronym for stroke symptoms. It stands for *face*, *arms*, *speech*, and *time*. *Face* refers to facial droop on one side of the face. *Arms* refers to sudden weakness or inability to move the arm, usually just on one side. *Speech* refers to the slurring of words, and *time* refers to the importance of getting the patient to a hospital in a timely manner because the risk for significant brain damage increases the longer the patient goes untreated.

3. D: Choice *D* is correct. HIPAA stands for Health Information Portability and Accountability Act. This act is sometimes incorrectly called HIPPA; it is important for medical assistants to remember that there is no separate HIPPA law.

4. A: The Patient Self-Determination Act (PSDA) ensures the end-of-life rights of a patient, including their right to refuse treatment for an illness. Choice *B* is a patient's right but is not governed by the PSDA; therefore, Choice *B* is incorrect. Choices *C* and *D* are not legally recognized as patient rights and are incorrect. Euthanasia is illegal in most jurisdictions, and patients may not prescribe themselves medications—that is the role of a physician.

5. C: Insulin glargine (Lantus) is an example of a long-acting insulin type, remaining in effect for approximately 24 hours. Choice *A* is incorrect because intermediate insulins (e.g., human isophane insulin [NPH]) last a shorter duration of time at approximately 12–18 hours. Choice *B* is incorrect because short-acting insulins (e.g., regular insulin [Humulin R]) last a shorter time period (between 4 and 8 hours). Choice *D* is incorrect because rapid-acting insulins (e.g., insulin lispro [Humalog]) have a more rapid onset (can be within 15 minutes).

6. C: Choice *C* is correct because a patient is eligible to receive services if their insurance is current and they are in good standing with the provider. Choice *A* is incorrect because the described status does not have a technical definition. Choice *B* describes *enrollment* in a government-sponsored healthcare program. Therefore, Choice *B* is incorrect. Choice *D* is incorrect because authorization for a single procedure is precertification, not eligibility.

7. D: The prefix *onco-* relates to the study of tumors. Choices *A* is incorrect because the prefix *lymph-* is associated with the lymphatic system. Choice *B* is incorrect because the prefix *heme-* is associated with blood. Choice *C* is incorrect because the study of genetics is associated with the suffix *-gen* or *-gene*.

8. D: Restating the received information in the patient's own words is a strong indicator that the patient understood the CMA's directions. Choices *A* and *B* indicate a low level of understanding because they express impatience rather than comprehension. Choice *C* is incorrect because the question does not relate to the patient's medication.

9. B: TRICARE is the Department of Defense's program that provides medical coverage to active-duty service members, retirees, and their families. Choice *B* is correct. Choice *A* is incorrect because

CHAMPVA is a program that assists the families of deceased, disabled veterans. Choice *C* is incorrect because the Department of Veterans Affairs (VA) is not a medical coverage program. Choice *D* is incorrect because the Continued Healthcare Benefit Program (CHCBP) is a program related to TRICARE that provides temporary medical coverage after leaving the military.

10. A: Hemoglobin is the iron-containing protein that is responsible for facilitating oxygen and carbon dioxide transfer throughout the body. Hemoglobin levels are dependent on the level of available iron in the body. Choice *B* is incorrect because hematocrit is not a component of blood but is the percentage of red blood cells that make up the total volume of whole blood. Choice *C* is incorrect because platelets (the component of blood that assist with clotting) increase with low iron levels. Choice *D* is incorrect because plasma (the liquid portion of blood made up of water, salt, and enzymes) is not significantly impacted by iron levels.

11. D: Choice *D* is the only choice that may indicate a patient's levothyroxine medication is effective. Levothyroxine is a synthetic thyroid hormone used for the treatment of hypothyroidism. Feeling warmer than usual may indicate a decrease in sensitivity to cold associated with hypothyroidism. Choice *A* is incorrect because fatigue is a symptom of hypothyroidism and would not indicate therapeutic treatment levels. Choice *B* is incorrect because stool softeners would indicate that the patient continues to have constipation, which is another side effect of hypothyroidism. Choice *C* is incorrect because applying lotion frequently may indicate that the patient continues to have dry skin, which is yet another symptom of hypothyroidism, indicating that the treatment is not therapeutic.

12. C: Choice *C* is the correct answer because this patient quit smoking more than 15 years ago, which falls outside of current guidelines for yearly lung cancer screenings. Choices *A*, *B*, and *D* are incorrect because these patients all fall within current guidelines for yearly lung cancer screenings. Guidelines include all of the following: individuals between 50 and 80 years of age, fairly healthy medical status, current smokers (or individuals who quit smoking within the last 15 years), and at least 20 pack-years of smoking history.

13. A: An employer is required to pay for healthcare expenses incurred due to on-the-job illnesses or injuries. Typically, the employer has an insurance policy that pays for these expenses. Therefore, Choice *A* is correct. Choices *B* and *C* are incorrect because neither of these forms of healthcare pay for workers' compensation. Choice *D* is incorrect because employers pay the expenses directly very infrequently.

14. A: Choice *A* is correct because it is the only example of a dosage form that can sometimes be split, crushed, or opened (as recommended by the physician and/or pharmacy). Choices *B*, *C*, and *D* are incorrect because these are all examples of dosage forms that should never be split, crushed, or opened because it would alter the absorption of the drug.

15. C: Digital communications—such as email—and certified electronic healthcare record (EHR) systems are generally secure for accessing and transmitting confidential patient information. However, no system is foolproof, and it is important that the medical assistant educates patients about the risks of data management when using an EHR.

16. A: An HMO is a type of insurance provider that negotiates contracts with healthcare providers to ensure reduced prices for their insured customers within a network of approved providers. Choices *B, C,* and *D* are incorrect because those statements are not true of all HMOs.

17. D: Even if the request is being made by a government or legal official, it is neither moral nor legal to provide confidential health information without the patient's consent. Therefore, Choices *A, B,* and *C* are incorrect.

18. B: Choice *B* is the strongest indicator of identity theft because if a patient has had a life event which changed one or several pieces of their personal information, their new documents should still match one another. Choices *A, C,* and *D* are more easily explained through life events and, therefore, are incorrect.

19. C: Completing standardized medical history questionnaires ahead of time speeds up the patient's appointment and helps the physician provide higher-quality care. Choice *C* is correct. Choice *A* is incorrect because a healthcare practice does not need their patients' credit reports. Choices *B* and *D* are incorrect because this information can be received in person at the appointment.

20. A: Choice *A* is the correct answer. Breast self-examination is recommended to be performed at approximately the same point during the menstrual cycle because hormone levels lead to changes in the breast tissue throughout the month. The end of the menstrual cycle is when tissue is less sensitive and less prone to inflammation; therefore, this will provide consistency, increased patient comfort, and smoother breast tissue. Choice *B* is not the best recommendation because the middle of the menstrual cycle can be a more challenging point for many women to identify. Choice *C* is less recommended because breast tissue tends to be more sensitive and engorged; therefore, this would not be the most comfortable and reliable timing for breast self-examination. Choice *D* is not the most appropriate recommendation because menstrual cycle length varies considerably from patient to patient and from month to month. Recommending the same date each month can lead to self-examination at different points within the menstrual cycle, which will reduce the consistency of breast tissue and lead to less reliable results.

21. B: The operating margin is a ratio that describes how much income the healthcare practice is generating against its operating expenses. Therefore, Choice *B* is correct. Choice *A* is incorrect because the excess margin includes sources of income other than patient care. Choices *C* and *D* are incorrect because these terms do not describe the practice's profitability.

22. C: Choice *C* is the correct answer because tetanus can be transmitted by animal or human bites. If the status is unknown or it has been more than 10 years since the last tetanus vaccine, another will be administered. Choice *A* is incorrect because the tuberculosis vaccine (BCG) is not widely used in the United States and is not an associated risk following an animal bite. Choice *B* is incorrect because meningitis is not a significant risk following an animal bite. Choice *D* is incorrect because a hepatitis B risk would be associated with human bites, not animal bites.

23. B: The deductible is a specified quantity that the patient is expected to pay before the insurance provider will begin providing assistance with healthcare expenses. Choice *B* is correct. Choices *A, C,* and *D* do not fit the definition of a deductible; therefore, they are incorrect.

24. A: A kickback is when a healthcare provider receives payment for referring a patient to another healthcare provider. Choice *A* is correct. Choices *B, C,* and *D* are not kickbacks because they do not involve patient referral.

25. A: Choice *A* is correct because it demonstrates respect to the patient by showing that completing their forms is a worthwhile use of the medical assistant's time. Choices *C* and *D* are disrespectful because they pass the support on to another person. Further, Choice *C* violates the patient's right to privacy. Choice *B* provides a useful support, but one that is not timely for facilitating the present visit.

26. D: Prescription fraud is when an authorized healthcare provider writes a prescription for a medication that they know is not necessary to treat the patient's illnesses. Choice *D* is correct. Choices *A, B,* and *C* are incorrect because they describe illegal activities related to abusing prescribed medication rather than the fraudulent writing of a prescription.

27. A: A signed ROI does not absolve the healthcare provider of responsibility to prevent access to the patient's private health information—it just gives permission to share information with specified parties. Choices *B, C,* and *D* are all valid reasons why a healthcare provider must use ROIs.

28. A: Choice *A* is the correct choice because having a tourniquet in place or having the patient ball their fist for an extended period of time can lead to sample hemolysis. Choice *B* is incorrect because pulling back the plunger gently prevents damage to the sample from forceful suction. Choice *C* is incorrect because drying the venipuncture site completely after cleaning the area can prevent chemically damaging the blood sample. Choice *D* is incorrect because anticoagulant-containing vials should be immediately inverted at least six to eight times in order to ensure that the anticoagulant additive is thoroughly mixed with the sample.

29. B: Choice *B* is correct because the laboratory needs to know allergen information to ensure patient safety. For example, an allergy to latex can cause an allergic reaction with some types of disposable gloves. Choices *A, C,* and *D* are each incorrect because they share excessive health information, which is not needed by the phlebotomist to perform a blood draw.

30. C: Choice *C* would be most concerning because trouble swallowing could be an early sign of anaphylaxis. Nausea, malaise, and diarrhea are incorrect because they do not typically represent an immediate danger to the patient.

31. D: Choice *D* is the most concerning because acupuncture is an alternative therapy method that involves placing very small needles in the skin over different parts of the body to manage health conditions. This treatment is generally safe; however, there is a contraindication for use in individuals at risk for bleeding or infection. Chemotherapy treatments often inhibit the bone marrow production of blood cells (including red blood cells, platelets, and white blood cells). Therefore, any patient undergoing chemotherapy would be advised to work closely with their doctor to monitor blood levels before considering acupuncture. Choice *A* is incorrect because gentle activity, such as walking, is highly encouraged for chemotherapy patients because it can help with maintaining energy and mental wellness during treatment. Choice *B* is incorrect because taste changes are a very common and expected side effect of chemotherapy. This statement would warrant follow-up to determine if a patient is able to maintain dietary intake, but this is not the most concerning statement. Choice *C* is not the most concerning statement because nausea is another very common side effect of chemotherapy treatment, and ginger tea is a generally safe and effective complementary way to manage nausea. Although this symptom and treatment are generally not unexpected or concerning, the CMA would still record any symptom reported by the patient as well as any home remedies used to manage symptoms.

32. B: Choice *B* is the most accurate representation of the physician's order because *ad libitum* means "as desired" or "as tolerated." Choice *A* is incorrect because the order does not restrict walking. Choice

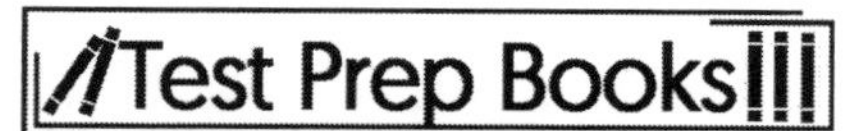

C is incorrect because the order does not indicate how often the patient should walk each day. Choice *D* is incorrect because the order does not indicate anything about the intensity of walking.

33. B: Chronic illnesses or conditions are long-term. Emergent refers to conditions that are immediately life threatening. Acute illnesses are present but usually short-term, and urgent conditions require help as soon as possible.

34. C: Choice *C* is the correct answer because dietary guidelines for end-stage renal disease include limiting salt intake. Choice *A* is incorrect because patients should avoid high potassium foods such as bananas, spinach, and milk. Choice *B* is incorrect because one ounce of fluid is equal to approximately 30 milliliters, which would make a six-ounce glass of juice approximately 180 milliliters. Choice *D* is incorrect because patients in end-stage renal disease often require more protein each day.

35. C: Nerve pain is one of the indications for use of gabapentin (brand name Neurontin). Choices *A* and *B* are incorrect because gabapentin does not treat swelling or high blood pressure. Choice *D* is incorrect because gabapentin does not treat high blood sugar. However, diabetic patients do sometimes receive gabapentin for management of diabetic peripheral neuropathy, which causes nerve pain, tingling, and numbness.

36. A: A follow-up with the insurance provider every seven days is best practice because this ensures timely notification of a delayed or denied claim and gives the healthcare practice ample time to either resubmit the claim (for simple denials, like incorrect billing codes) or appeal the decision. It's important to do so swiftly so that an appeal is submitted within the payer's appeal window. Choices *B, C,* and *D* are each too infrequent and, therefore, are incorrect.

37. B: Shortness of breath is not an expected symptom associated with a traumatic brain injury. The remaining choices of unequal pupils, persistent vomiting, restlessness, and irritability are all examples of symptoms commonly associated with a brain injury. Other symptoms that may indicate a serious head injury are convulsion, facial or skull fracture, inability to move limbs, severe headaches, loss of consciousness, slurred speech, distorted vision, and clear fluid from the ears, nose, or mouth.

38. C: This scenario depicts a medication error that did not result in harm to the patient because it was caught prior to administration. Even though the vaccine had not been delivered, Choice *C* is the most appropriate response when there is any situation in which a medication error could have occurred. A supervisor should be notified, and an incident report should be completed. Choice *A* is incorrect because even though the medication didn't make it to the patient, it should be reported to identify what systematic factors may have contributed to the medication error. Choice *B* is not wrong, but this action would not be the priority in this situation because an incident report should still be filed. Choice *D* is incorrect because the patient had not received the inappropriate vaccine.

39. A: Allegations of physical abuse by a parent must always be reported to the local authorities. The exact procedure for doing so will vary depending on the organization and the jurisdiction. Choice *B* is incorrect because sexual activity with a similar-age partner is not abuse. Choice *C* is incorrect because spanking is controversial but generally not illegal. Choice *D* is incorrect because participation in pageants does not indicate abuse is taking place.

40. B: Providing the patient with a pen and paper can facilitate their communication by allowing them to write while they are having difficulty speaking. Speaking loudly is not necessary, as there is no mention of hardness of hearing. It is also not necessary to rely on the RN or the family to communicate with the patient.

41. D: A needle driver is a specialized instrument used by the physician to guide a suture needle during closure of a wound. Choice *A* is incorrect because tweezers are another type of grasping tool that is used for tasks such as packing a wound. Choice *B* is incorrect because scissors are used for cutting things such as wound packing material or suture thread. Choice *C* is incorrect because scalpels are used to incise tissue.

42. B: The integumentary system is the largest body system. It includes the skin, hair, nails, and some exocrine glands.

43. A: Choice *A* is the most appropriate response because the expected respiratory range for a one-month-old infant would be between 25 and 55 breaths per minute. 48 breaths per minute is within normal limits; therefore, the most appropriate response by the CMA would be to document the reading in the patient's medical record. Choices *B* and *D* are not the most appropriate responses because the measurement was appropriate for the patient's age, and there is no indication of distress or need to notify the physician immediately. If the patient in this example was a teenager or adult, however, this measurement would be considered critically out of range and would warrant further assessment and immediate reporting to the physician. Choice *C* is not the most appropriate choice because there is no indication that the CMA is unsure of their measurement, and this reading is not out of range for this patient. However, it is important to note that asking a colleague to confirm a measurement is a valid option to choose in any situation in which a result is unclear or the CMA is unsure of the measurement.

44. A: Hiring a certified service provider gives the strongest guarantee that the files will be deleted and no remnant of them will remain on the server or storage device. Choices *B* and *D* do not address the possibility that the files could be recovered after deletion. Choice *C* is inappropriate because open-source software—while cost efficient—is generally not certified for use with confidential material.

45. B: Choice *B* is the correct answer because prednisone (a steroid medication) is NOT commonly associated with anorexia. Steroid medications are associated with increased appetite. Choices *A*, *C*, and *D* are incorrect because these are all commonly associated side effects of prednisone and steroid use.

46. A: All CPT codes begin with a numeral. Therefore, Choice *A* is correct. Choice *B* provides an HCPCS Level II code. Choices *C* and *D* provide ICD-10-CM codes. Therefore, Choices *B, C,* and *D* are all incorrect.

47. A: *Situation, background, assessment, and recommendation* is the correct meaning of the acronym SBAR, which is used in patient handoff reports.

48. B: The vastus lateralis muscle, located on the lateral thigh, is the correct answer because this location is the preferred site for intramuscular injections in infants due to the size of the muscle and the ease of delivery. Choice *A* is incorrect because this muscle is less developed, and safe administration in this age group would be challenging. Choices *C* and *D* are incorrect because these sites present major challenges for safe administration due to positioning and the tendency of infants to squirm.

49. C: Choice *C* is the correct answer because it is the only stimulant ADHD medication. Choice *A* is incorrect because atomoxetine (Strattera) is a nonstimulant norepinephrine modulator medication. Choices *B* and *D* are incorrect because guanfacine (Intuniv) and clonidine (Catapres) are examples of nonstimulant alpha agonist medications.

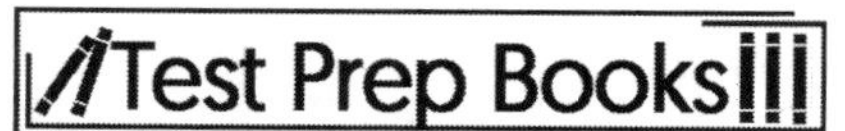

50. B: Choice *B* is correct because it utilizes the caregiver as a resource, rather than offloading the task to them. Choice *A* is incorrect because it is important that the medical assistant provides the information directly, rather than relying on a non-expert. Choices *C* and *D* are incorrect because they make assumptions about the extent of the patient's cognitive disabilities. Further, rote memorization as in Choice D is disrespectful to the individual and often does not lead to internalization of the information.

51. D: Acetaminophen is the correct answer because this is the only listed medication that is NOT considered a nonsteroidal anti-inflammatory drug (NSAID). Choices *A*, *B*, and *C* are incorrect because they are all NSAIDs.

52. D: Best practice is to ensure both parents consent to the vaccination of their child. In most situations, a single parent present in combination with a history of providing medical care to the family is sufficient to vaccinate the child with the present parent's consent, as demonstrated in Choice *B*. However, the child's words indicate otherwise, so it is best to be thorough and obtain consent from both parents. Legally, this situation's permissions vary depending on the practice's jurisdiction. Choice *A* is incorrect because a minor's permission is generally not required to provide medical services. Choice *C* is incorrect because the physician is not the child's legal guardian.

53. B: Choice *B* is correct because reducing administrative overhead reduces the healthcare practice's expenses and increases the amount of staff time and energy available to serve patients. Choices *A* and *C* are incorrect because improving these metrics does not improve the quality of service; therefore, these metrics are less important than Choice *B*. Choice *D* is incorrect because a healthcare practice should not cancel a patient's appointment without exploring alternative methods to pay for the service.

54. B: Completing an advance directive is not part of the insurance appeal process. Therefore, Choice *B* is correct. Choices *A, C,* and *D* are incorrect because each choice identifies a piece of documentation which may help the patient present their case with the insurance provider.

55. B: Tylenol (acetaminophen) is the correct answer because there is a maximum recommended dose of 4000 mg (4 g) per day of this medication. Exceeding the maximum dosing recommendations can result in liver toxicity. Choices *A, C,* and *D* are incorrect because these medications do not have a recommended maximum daily dose of 4000 mg per day.

56. A: Choice *A* is the most appropriate answer because Prozac (fluoxetine) is an antidepressant. Studies have shown that individuals 24 years of age and younger who take antidepressants can become suicidal after starting antidepressant therapy. Generally, antidepressants take four to six weeks for full effect, and during this time, patients are at significantly increased risk for suicide. It is important to educate patients and identify patients at risk. Choice *B* is not the most important question, although diarrhea is not uncommon with fluoxetine treatment. However, diarrhea is typically not a life-threatening side effect. Choice *C* is incorrect because, although nausea can occur with fluoxetine treatment, changes in appetite would not be an immediate life-threatening concern for a patient starting an antidepressant medication such as fluoxetine. Choice *D* is incorrect because shortness of breath is not a common life-threatening potential side effect of fluoxetine.

57. D: Choice *D* is correct because a lifestyle change recommendation is done by the patient's physician as a part of treating an illness. Choices *A, B,* and *C* all describe tasks that might be performed by a nurse, a medical assistant, or another member of the healthcare practice's support team.

58. C: Properly and frequently washing hands is the single most effective means of preventing the spread of infection in the healthcare setting. Choices *A*, *B*, and *D* are all ways to prevent infection, but these are not the most impactful ways to prevent the spread of infection.

59. B: Choice *B* is correct because the documentation of a pulse amplitude of 4+ would be associated with a bounding pulse (cannot be occluded during palpation). Choice *A* is incorrect because a diminished (or thready) pulse is associated with an amplitude of 1+. Choice *C* is incorrect because a strong pulse (or full, normal pulse) is most associated with an amplitude of 3+. Choice *D* is incorrect because an absent pulse would be graded at an amplitude of 0.

60. A: When caring for a patient with hearing loss, it is best to use written communication when possible. Patients with hearing loss may pretend to hear or understand out of shame or embarrassment and therefore may not get adequate care or communication. Using written communication helps to eliminate opportunity for miscommunication. Choice *B* is incorrect because the medical assistant should speak clearly in a normal volume and tone. Choice *C* is incorrect because the medical assistant should direct their head and voice towards the patient's unaffected ear. Choice *D* is incorrect because the medical assistant should stand directly in the patient's eyeline, allowing them to read lips more easily.

61. C: The patient's body temperature is 102.2 degrees Fahrenheit. One degree Fahrenheit is added to the axillary temperature to obtain a patient's body temperature.

62. C: The correct order to remove PPE is gloves, goggles, gown, and then mask. When removing the equipment, make sure to remove equipment by holding onto the non-contaminated parts and properly disposing of the equipment. The remaining choices do not show PPE removal in the correct order.

63. D: The lithotomy position (patient lying on back with legs in stirrups) is a common position used to perform general female pelvic examinations because it provides visualization of the vaginal and perianal areas and facilitates the insertion of speculum for exam. Choice *A* is incorrect because the supine position (patient lying on their back) does not provide visualization or access to the vagina for pelvic examinations. Choice *B* is incorrect because the Fowler's position (lying with upper body partially elevated) would limit visibility and access to the vaginal area. Choice *C* is incorrect because, although the Sims position can be useful for rectal examinations as well as for evaluation of vaginal prolapse, this left-lying position with knee bent is not regularly used for general pelvic exams.

64. B: Oral thrush is caused by *Candida albicans,* a fungal organism. Choices *A*, *C*, and *D* are incorrect because these infectious organisms do not cause oral thrush.

65. C: A medical assistant is most likely to act as a support staff member in the healthcare organization, providing clinical assistance only as needed. Collecting the patient's medical history is the best example of a typical job duty. Choices *A* and *B* are generally performed by the patient's healthcare provider. Choice *D* is incorrect because medical assistants are generally not involved in surgery procedures.

66. B: The preferred anatomical location for obtaining a blood sample via phlebotomy is the inner elbow (antecubital fossa). The reason this is an ideal location is that the more proximal (closer) the vein is to the heart, the bigger in diameter it tends to be. In addition, the veins are closer to the surface in this location, and they tend to be more stable during venipuncture. Choice *C* would be the second most-preferred location and would, therefore, be incorrect. Veins on the dorsal (top) surface of the hand do tend to be more visible. However, distal (farther from the shoulder and heart) veins tend to be smaller in diameter, and the veins of the hand can be subject to more mobility than the antecubital fossa. Also,

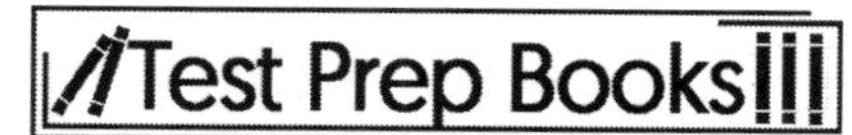

the hand can be much more uncomfortable for the patient. Choices *A* and *D* are incorrect because the veins of the forearm are often deeper, and their size and anchoring can be less predictable.

67. D: The ICD-10-CM code set indicates a patient's diagnosed illnesses. These diagnoses must be reported each time a healthcare service is billed to Medicare. Choices *A* and *B* do not describe all situations in which the ICD-10-CM code set is used. Therefore, Choices *A* and *B* are incorrect. Choice *C* is incorrect because durable medical equipment is billed with the HCPCS Level II codes, category E.

68. C: Child abandonment occurs when parents or legal caregivers leave the child without intent of returning to care for them. Choice *C* accurately describes illegal child abandonment. Although Choice *A* does describe abandonment, "baby boxes" provide a legal way to anonymously abandon an unwanted child in jurisdictions where they are installed. Choices *B* and *D* are incorrect because they describe neglect, not abandonment.

69. B: Mononucleosis is an infectious disease associated with the Epstein-Barr virus (EBV). Rhinovirus is incorrect because this virus is associated with the common cold. Adenovirus is incorrect because this is the virus responsible for an infection that presents like a mild cold or flu. Varicella-zoster virus is incorrect because this is the virus associated with shingles (herpes zoster).

70. B: *Respondeat superior* is a legal doctrine that describes when an employer is responsible for the actions of their employees. This applies to Choice *B* because by not disciplining the employees, the employer has indicated their violation of HIPAA was acceptable. Choice *A* is an example of negligence and therefore incorrect. Choices *C* and *D* are incorrect because no connection is described between employee behavior and the employer's actions.

71. D: A patient who is at risk of developing a DVT should be given sequential compression devices (SCDs) to help promote blood flow and circulation, especially in patients who are confined to their beds. Patients who are more mobile can be given anti-embolism stockings to help reduce risk of developing a DVT. The remaining choices are not devices that help reduce the risk of developing a DVT.

72. C: Washing the area with soap and water is the most critical first step to take after a needle stick injury because this can assist in reducing the risk of blood-borne pathogen transmission. Choice *A* would be the next step to take after washing the area; therefore, this would not be the correct choice. Later interventions may include a medical evaluation, drawing of bloodwork from the caregiver and patient involved, and prophylactic treatment. Therefore, Choices *B* and *D* are incorrect.

73. D: An ABN is an Advance Beneficiary Notice. The function of this notice is to inform the patient that the specified services are not covered by Medicare or other governmental assistance. Choice *D* is correct. Choices *A, B,* and *C* are incorrect because these do not represent actual terms used in medical practice.

74. B: Systolic blood pressure (the numerator, or top number, of a blood pressure measurement) is associated with the first sound auscultated as air is released from a blood pressure cuff. These sounds—the first of five phases of Korotkoff's sounds—represent the force of the contracting heart muscle. Choice *A* is incorrect because the point of maximal impulse is the area on the chest wall—typically the 5th intercostal space, midclavicular line—where the pumping of the heart is most easily palpated. Choice *C,* diastolic blood pressure (the denominator, or bottom number, of a blood pressure measurement) is associated with the fifth and final phase of Korotkoff's sounds and is the point when the tapping sounds can no longer be heard. Choice *D* is incorrect because pulse pressure is the systolic blood pressure measurement minus the diastolic measurement. Pulse pressure can provide information about the flexibility and strength of the heart muscle.

75. A: The order of operations for this billing situation is to first reduce the total bill by the patient's deductible. Then, multiply the remainder by the patient's co-insurance. The result is how much the patient owes after meeting their deductible. In this case, the result is $5,750. Add the deductible—$2,000—to this result to determine the total cost the patient will owe the healthcare provider. The total is $7,750. Therefore, Choice *A* is correct. Choice *B* is incorrect because the deductible was not subtracted from the total bill. Choice *C* is incorrect because the deductible was not added to the multiplied amount. Choice *D* is incorrect because the deductible was subtracted after multiplying the patient's co-insurance by the total bill.

76. B: In the medical field every individual who interacts directly with vulnerable individuals—such as children—is mandated to report suspected abuse or neglect of those individuals. Choice *B* is correct because medical coder is an administrative position which generally does not interact directly with patients.

77. B: Choice *B* is correct because the suffix *-algia* means "pain." Choices *A*, *C*, and *D* are incorrect because this suffix does not indicate a location and does not necessarily involve stiffness or inflammation.

78. C: The best way to prevent the spread of germs is regular handwashing with soap and water, including before and after seeing patients and when hands are visibly dirty. The remaining choices may be appropriate to help reduce infection depending on the patient's condition, but they are not the best way to prevent spread of germs.

79. C: A medium distance—in this case, a few steps away—is best for de-escalation because it balances being close enough for emotional appeals with being distant enough to avoid crowding the escalated individual. Choices *A* and *B* risk escalating the individual further because they may feel the CMA's position is confrontational. Keeping too much distance is less effective because it makes communication difficult; therefore, Choice *D* is incorrect.

80. A: The lungs are part of the pulmonary system, which also includes the airways and diaphragm. The cardiovascular system includes the heart and blood vessels. The musculoskeletal system includes muscles, bones, and soft tissues such as cartilage and tendons. The neurological system is composed of the brain and spinal cord.

81. B: Medical assistants have a duty to report suspected abuse to state authorities, or Adult Protective Services.

82. D: Choice *D* is correct because leads V1 and V2 are placed to the right and left of the sternum at the 4th intercostal space. Choice *B* is incorrect because V4 would be placed over the 5th intercostal space at the midclavicular line. V3 is placed between V2 and V4. V5 and V6 are lined up next to V4, with V5 at the anterior axillary line and V6 at the mid-axillary line. Limb leads are placed on each extremity. Choices *A* and *C* are incorrect because leads are not placed at these locations.

83. C: Precertification—sometimes called prior authorization—is the process of certifying that an insurance provider will cover a procedure if the healthcare provider performs the procedure. Choice *C* is

correct. Precertification does not apply to the other processes; therefore, Choices *A, B,* and *D* are incorrect.

84. D: A patient who is unable to bear weight on one leg, either due to fractures, pain, or amputation, should use a three-point crutch gait. Choice *A* is incorrect because a two-point crutch gait is used for poor coordination and weakness in both legs. Choice *B* is incorrect because a swing-through crutch gait is used for inability for both legs to bear weight. Choice *C* is incorrect because a swing-to crutch gait is used for weakness in both legs.

85. C: Appointment confirmation is an important part of the scheduling process because it improves patient attendance; therefore, Choice *C* is correct. Choices *B* and *D* are incorrect because appointment confirmation does not involve the discussion of the patient's health conditions. Choice *A* is incorrect because confirming the patient's attendance does not correlate with receipt of co-pays.

86. C: Choice *C* is the correct answer because pulling the skin away from the injection site prior to performing the injection—called the Z-track method—prevents the medication from oozing from the muscle site back through the needle "track." Choices *A, B,* and *D* are incorrect because these techniques do not help to ensure that the medication remains in the muscle. Choice *A* helps to ensure that the injection reaches the muscle. Choice *B* is traditionally used to assess for injection into a blood vessel. Choice *D* ensures that the medication safely reaches the muscle and helps to avoid unnecessary discomfort during injection.

87. D: Choice *D* is correct because 1 kilogram equals approximately 2.2 pounds. That makes the patient's weight 273.68 pounds, which becomes 274 when rounded to the nearest whole number. Choice *A* is incorrect because the weight in kilograms is not divided by 2.2 to get the weight in pounds. Choice *B* is incorrect because dividing the weight in kilograms by 2.2 and rounding the answer to 60 would be rounding to the nearest ten instead of the nearest whole number. Choice *C* is incorrect because rounding down to 270 would be rounding to the nearest ten instead of the nearest whole number.

88. C: Choice *C* is correct because CPT modifiers are used to provide additional information to the insurance provider when submitting a claim. Choice *A* is incorrect because upcoding is a type of medical fraud that does not require the use of modifiers to perform. Choice *B* is incorrect because the National Correct Coding Initiative publishes edits to code sets, rather than modifiers to existing codes. Choice *D* is incorrect because modifiers are not used exclusively for bundling.

89. D: The pituitary gland secretes growth hormones. The thyroid secretes thyroid hormones, which help to regulate metabolism and contribute to brain development. The pancreas secretes insulin and digestive enzymes. Ovaries secrete the sex hormones progesterone and estrogen.

90. B: Body language that indicates active listening includes frequent eye contact and minimal movement. This tells the patient that the CMA is focused on what the patient is saying, not their computer, schedule, or other concerns. Choices *A, C,* and *D* are incorrect.

91. A: Wheezes are high-pitched sounds with a musical quality that are associated with airway narrowing at the level of the bronchi. Crackles, as the name implies, are a series of popping or crackling sounds that can be associated with a variety of pulmonary diseases. Crackles can be classified as fine or coarse and are associated with alveoli snapping shut during inspiration. Rhonchi are lower in pitch and resemble the sound of snoring. These sounds are typically associated with excessive secretions in the airway. Stridor is the sound associated with narrowing of the upper airway, at the level of the trachea. This sound, although similar to wheezing, typically occurs only during inspiration.

92. B: The Healthcare Common Procedural Coding System (HCPCS) Level I codes are more commonly known as the Current Procedural Terminology (CPT) codes. These codes are used to bill services and procedures to insurance providers. Therefore, Choice *B* is correct. Choice *A* is incorrect because medical equipment is coded by HCPCS Level II. Choice *C* is incorrect because diagnoses are coded with the ICD-10-CM code set. Choice *D* is incorrect because experimental procedures may be coded using a variety of sets depending on the nature of the procedure; the most common set used is CPT Category III.

93. C: When performing proper handwashing, the hands should be rubbed together for at least 20 seconds, not 10 seconds. The other answer choices are correct steps in the handwashing process.

94. D: Incontinence is the correct answer because incontinence can be modified in a variety of ways, including pelvic floor therapy, absorbent undergarments, medical devices (condom catheter), and medications. Choices *A*, *B*, and *C* are incorrect because these are examples of unmodifiable risk factors of falls. They cannot be changed with medical or other interventions.

95. C: The phrase *accounts receivable* describes all accounts where a patient has received service, but the healthcare practice has not yet received payment for that service. Choice *C* is correct. Choice *A* is incorrect because patient discharge does not impact the payment process. Choices *B* and *D* are incorrect because the patient account has already been an account receivable when payment is received or if collection is requested.

96. A: The dorsogluteal muscle is the correct answer because this site is typically NOT recommended for general use due to its proximity to the sciatic nerve. This site has an increased risk for nerve injury, including varying degrees of paresthesia or paralysis of the distal leg. Choices *B, C,* and *D* are incorrect because these sites have been shown to be more reliably safe for intramuscular injection.

97. C: Choice *C* is correct because the patient should be instructed to place the cup over the urethra without touching the skin and attempt to fill the cup approximately halfway full. Choice *A* is incorrect because a clean-catch specimen is collected by having the patient start to urinate and then stop the stream. Then, the specimen cup should be placed under the area where the urethra is located so the patient can provide the sample. They can finish urinating in the toilet afterward, if applicable. Choice *B* is incorrect because the patient should be instructed to first cleanse the area inside the external vulva in a front-to-back motion. Afterward, they should use another wipe to cleanse the urethra front to back. Choice *D* is incorrect because female patients should use two fingers to hold the labia open to prevent contamination after cleansing.

98. D: Choice *D* is the only true statement regarding safe use of a walker. Choice *A* is incorrect because it is recommended to lead with the weaker or injured leg first when taking a step while walking. Choice *B* is incorrect because patients should avoid using the hand grips for support when standing. Choice *C* is incorrect because patients should be advised to back up until the chair is touching the back of the legs before using the armrests (or back of chair and seat if no armrests) for support and gently lowering into the chair.

99. B: A suture kit is the correct answer because sutures are not typically required for a yearly gynecological examination with a Pap smear. A speculum is incorrect because this tool *is* used during routine pelvic examination to access and view the internal vagina and cervix. Cotton-tipped applicator

sticks and specimen bottles are incorrect because these two items are used to collect and send out surface cells from the cervix to the lab for a Pap smear test.

100. A: The inflammatory response is not a natural barrier against infection, but it is a reaction to organisms that get past the body's natural barriers. Choices *B*, *C*, and *D* are all examples of natural barriers to infection in the human body.

101. A: Denial occurs when a patient refuses to acknowledge something that is painful. Regression is reverting to an earlier stage of development. Acting out occurs when a patient engages in a behavior that is unusual for that person. Projection occurs when a patient attributes their own negative feelings or characteristics to another person.

102. D: Choice *D* warrants intervention by the preceptor because the orientee should dispose of any contaminated towels in a biohazard waste container. Choices *A, B,* and *C* do not require intervention. The orientee correctly chose to don PPE before cleaning the spill. They also correctly used towels to soak up the bulk of the spill before using a bleach-containing cleaning detergent to disinfect the contaminated areas.

103. C: Semi-Fowler's position means the head of the bed is raised 30 to 45 degrees. Choice *A* is a description of prone positioning. Choice *B* is a description of supine positioning. Choice *D* is a description of High-Fowler's positioning.

104. D: Research has demonstrated that patients are about twice as likely to engage with a text message reminding them of an upcoming appointment in comparison with other communication methods. Choice *D* is correct. Choices *A, B,* and *C* are incorrect because the listed methods are less effective than a text message.

105. A: The five vital signs are heart rate, temperature, blood pressure, respiratory rate, and pain. Pain was recently recognized as the fifth vital sign and should be checked regularly. Although it may be important to measure the other options listed, they are not considered to be main vital signs.

106. D: Fosamax (alendronate) is a medication used to treat osteoporosis. It is especially important for patients receiving this medication to intake adequate amounts of calcium and vitamin D. These vitamins support bone strength and mineralization. Choices *A*, *B*, and *C* are incorrect because these vitamins would not be the highest priority for patients receiving Fosamax (alendronate) treatment.

107. B: A hemorrhage is an episode of uncontrolled bleeding. A stroke is caused by lack of oxygen to the brain. Hematemesis is when a patient vomits blood. Hemorrhaging is not normal during childbirth; it is a rare and abnormal complication.

108. A: Choice *A* is the best answer because if an effective but cheaper drug is available, the insurance provider will likely authorize that expense. While this may not provide as much benefit as the name-brand drug, this still provides the quickest access to treatment for the patient. Choices *B, C,* and *D* are incorrect.

109. C: Choice *C* is the correct answer because it would NOT be appropriate for the CMA to apply antibiotic ointment to the area where the edges appear to be separating until the physician has evaluated the wound and provided orders to do so. Choices *A*, *B*, and *D* are incorrect because these are examples of actions the CMA would perform in the event that an opening is noted during suture removal. The suture removal procedure should be immediately stopped, wound closure strips should be applied to the open area to provide stabilization of the wound, and the physician should be immediately notified.

110. C: Choice *C* is the correct answer because a Mantoux tuberculin skin test (or PPD) is performed on the inner forearm. Choices *A*, *B*, and *D* are incorrect because a PPD test is not performed on the hand, the face, or the neck.

111. B: Choice *B* is correct because hand sanitizer is an appropriate option for hand hygiene when used before caring for a patient with *C. diff*. Soap and water must be used to perform hand hygiene after entering a room or caring for any patient suspected of or confirmed to have *C. diff*. Choices *A* and *C* are incorrect because soap and water is the most appropriate choice for use after eating or using the restroom. This is because alcohol-based hand sanitizers do not removed particulates and should not be used when hands are soiled. Choice *D* is incorrect because alcohol-based hand sanitizers are ineffective at removing grease or residue from hands.

112. B: Deep vein thrombosis (DVT) is a blood clot that can form in the vein and is commonly found in the legs or groin area. DVT typically presents as pain and swelling of the affected limb. Patients undergoing cholecystectomy (gallbladder removal) or any other surgery are at an increased risk for developing blood clots. Choice *A* is incorrect because a pulmonary embolism (PE) is the potential postoperative complication that can occur after a DVT mobilizes and travels to the lungs. Symptoms of PE can present as sudden shortness of breath and a sudden unexplained feeling of dread. Choice *C* is another common postoperative complication that can occur; however, signs tend to begin at the site of surgical incision as opposed to the leg. Signs of infection include fever as well as increased swelling, redness, pain, and drainage at the surgical site. For a cholecystectomy, this can also involve increasing stomach pain, swelling, and vomiting if the GI tract is involved. Choice *D* is incorrect because post-cholecystectomy syndrome is a persistence of presurgical gallbladder symptoms, including nausea, vomiting, indigestion, and spasmodic pain in the abdomen.

113. B: Choice *B* is correct because healthcare practices are required to provide demographic data for their patient population to the Department of Health and Human Services. Choices *A* and *D* are incorrect because these actions can lead to biased conclusions using racial and ethnic data. Choice *C* is incorrect because this data is not used by the CDC when tracking the source of an illness.

114. D: The patient in Choice *D* would be least likely to have a restriction on where a venipuncture could be performed because there are no indications that there is a reason for a restriction. The patient described in Choice *A* may likely be restricted in venipuncture sites due to her history of breast cancer because surgical mastectomy can often lead to lymph node removal and an increased risk of lymphedema of the upper extremities. It would be recommended for this patient to avoid blood pressure and venipuncture to the affected side. The patient described in Choice *B* is in treatment for end-stage renal disease and may have a dialysis fistula in one of his upper extremities. Dialysis fistulas should not be accessed or occluded with a tourniquet. The patient in Choice *C* is receiving long-term daily intravenous antibiotic therapy, which means he may have a central venous catheter (CVC) or peripherally inserted central catheter (PICC). Venipuncture should be avoided in an extremity with a PICC line.

115. A: The Health Insurance Portability and Accountability Act (HIPAA) protects the resident's rights to privacy with their health information. Choice *A* is a proper discussion of patient care as the nurse and

medical assistant are both directly caring for the patient and may discuss relevant results. The remaining choices are incorrect and not HIPAA-compliant because private medical information about a patient is being discussed with individuals who are not involved in the patient's medical care.

116. B: The brachial artery should be aligned with the arrow on the blood pressure cuff. The radial artery is in the wrist, the femoral artery is in the groin, and the popliteal artery is in the foot/ankle region.

117. D: Hemoglobin A1C is a blood test that provides physicians with an average blood sugar level for the last three months. Choice *A* is incorrect because a 24-hour urine test is used to diagnose problems with the kidneys. Choice *B* is incorrect because a single fasting blood glucose level is not adequate to identify risk of or diagnosis of diabetes. Choice *C* is incorrect because a glucose tolerance test is performed to evaluate how the body interacts with glucose and identifies metabolic and hormone issues.

118. A: A living will does not designate power of attorney but instead describes the patient's wishes in situations when they are alive but not conscious. Power of attorney can be designated with a similar document, an advance directive. Choices *B, C,* and *D* are incorrect because they accurately describe functions of a living will.

119. D: Standard Precautions require only a gown and gloves. In Reverse Isolation, gowns, gloves, and medical masks must be worn. Droplet Precautions require surgical masks, gloves, and gowns. Airborne Precautions require an N95 mask, eye protection, a gown, and gloves.

120. C: Standard of care indicates that the healthcare provider's actions are reasonably similar to those of other medical professionals in a given situation. A provider who does not meet a minimal standard of care can be found negligent. Choice *A* is incorrect because the law does not require treatment to be successful. Choice *B* is incorrect because performing an unconventional or experimental treatment may be appropriate if other physicians would act the same. Choice *D* is incorrect because *standard of care* does not describe specific methodologies for practicing medicine—just that one provider's actions must be similar to others'.

121. C: Choice *C* is correct because an aging of accounts report describes how long it takes for the typical payer (whether a patient or an insurance provider) to pay a bill to the healthcare practice. The account ages as the practice waits for payment or engages in the collections process. Choice *A* is incorrect because the aging of accounts does not track patient health information. Choices *B* and *D* are incorrect because the aging of accounts typically focuses on days passed without payment, rather than the quantity owed to the healthcare practice.

122. A: Choice *A* is the most concerning for potential elder abuse in the form of neglect because worn and dirty clothing with strong body odor may indicate a lack of care provided by a caregiver. Choice *B* would not be the most concerning answer, although startling and jumping during examination could possibly be a sign of abuse. However, confused patients can also be easily started or frightened because they are in an unfamiliar setting. Choice *C* is not the most concerning answer because tearfulness and repeatedly asking for a loved one is not uncommon for a confused older adult. Choice *D* mentions a single bruise with an identifiable origin and would not necessarily be indicative of physical abuse because confused patients are at increased risk for falls and injury. It is important to note that elder abuse is very challenging to identify, and any of the answers have the potential to be present in a patient experiencing abuse. It is important for the CMA to be aware and report any signs of suspected abuse.

123. A: The concept of implied consent applies when administering lifesaving care to a patient unable to respond. Choice *A* is correct because the patient was unresponsive. Choice *B* is incorrect because the healthcare provider received explicit consent from the parent. Choice *C* is incorrect because verbal agreement to an ROI does not legally qualify as consent to send confidential information. Choice *D* is incorrect because the surgeon assumed consent. Even if a procedure is scheduled in advance, best practice is to confirm the patient's consent before operating.

124. C: Contact precautions are used for a patient with a *Clostridium difficile* infection. Contact precautions include wearing a gown and gloves to keep the infectious bacteria from spreading to clothing and hands.

125. D: It is best practice for healthcare professionals not to accept personal gifts from patients because this may impact how they exercise professional boundaries with that patient or the patient's family. Choices *A* and *B* are therefore incorrect. Choice *C* is incorrect because gifts are often offered from gratitude, not as an effort to sway the CMA's opinion.

126. D: Escitalopram is an antidepressant medication belonging to the family of selective serotonin reuptake inhibitors (SSRIs). Choice *A* is incorrect because serotonin-norepinephrine reuptake inhibitors (SNRIs) are a different class of antidepressant medications, including duloxetine (Cymbalta) and venlafaxine (Efexor). Choice *B* is incorrect because tricyclic antidepressants are a class of medications that include amitriptyline and nortriptyline. Choice *C* is incorrect because monoamine oxidase inhibitors (MAOIs) are a rarely used class of antidepressant medications, including tranylcypromine and isocarboxazid.

127. B: Choice *B* is correct because the action does not provide the Muslim patient with respectful accommodations or support. Choices *A, C,* and *D* are incorrect because they are each reasonable ways in which a medical assistant might provide the patient with support for their religious practice.

128. D: Choice *D* is correct because this is the only answer that is not associated with human papillomavirus (HPV). Choice *A* is incorrect because HPV is a contributing factor in approximately 60 to 70 percent of all oropharyngeal cancers. Choices *B* and *C* are incorrect because HPV is largely associated with cervical cancer and anal cancers, being directly associated in more than 90 percent of all cases.

129. A: Muscle weakness that is new in onset is one of the potential indicators for decreased potassium. Furosemide is a diuretic and lowers blood pressure and swelling by removing water from the body through the bladder. In doing this, it also removes potassium from the body. Choice *B* is incorrect because low potassium levels would be more associated with constipation. Choices *C* and *D* are incorrect because central nervous system symptoms (e.g., headaches and seizures) are not associated with potassium deficiency, although they can be associated with other electrolyte deficiencies such as magnesium or sodium.

130. A: Plasma, which makes up more than half of the volume of blood, makes up the top layer of a blood sample after it has been centrifuged. Choices *B* and *C* make up the next layer, the buffy coat, which makes up less than one percent of the total volume of blood. Choice *D* is the bottom layer and makes up a little less than half of the total volume of blood.

131. D: An operative note is written by the surgeon who performed the procedure. The note summarizes all details of the procedure after its completion, including diagnosis, intended benefit, and post-operative care. Operative notes are not written by other staff members, because the surgeon is the person responsible for leading the procedure. Choices *A, B,* and *C* are incorrect.

132. A: Choice *A* is correct because the radius is one of the bones of the forearm. Choices *B, C,* and *D* are incorrect because the radius is not located in the leg, the head, or the torso.

133. C: Choice C is the most appropriate response because any time a patient questions anything regarding their care, it is always best to stop and confirm the accuracy of the orders or documentation. Choice *A* is incorrect because it fails to consider a possible error in the record. Choice *B* is incorrect because it fails to validate the patient's concern and does not stop to consider the possibility that the patient is correct. Choice *D* does provide empathy; however, this is not the most appropriate response because it does not address the possibility of a mistaken entry.

134. D: Choice *D* is correct because 1 kilogram equals approximately 2.2 pounds. That makes the patient's weight 273.68 pounds, which becomes 274 when rounded to the nearest whole number. Choice *A* is incorrect because the weight in kilograms is not divided by 2.2 to get the weight in pounds. Choice *B* is incorrect because dividing the weight in kilograms by 2.2 and rounding the answer to 60 would be rounding to the nearest ten instead of the nearest whole number. Choice *C* is incorrect because rounding down to 270 would be rounding to the nearest ten instead of the nearest whole number.

135. A: Abscess is the correct answer because this patient is experiencing a large painful area that has formed beneath the skin. Choice *B* is incorrect because a pustule is a small, inflamed pus-filled lesion. Choice *C* is incorrect because comedones are light- or dark-colored skin lesions that are associated with acne. Choice *D* is incorrect because a *carbuncle* is a collection of pus-filled lesions that are closer to the surface of the skin.

136. D: Jaundice (a sign of potential issues with the liver, gallbladder, or pancreas) is associated with yellow coloring of the skin. Choice *A* is incorrect because red skin coloring is associated with irritation or injury to the skin (erythema). Choice *B* is incorrect because blue coloring is associated with lack of blood flow or oxygen (cyanosis). Choice *C* is incorrect because purple coloring would often be associated with bleeding under the skin (ecchymosis or bruising).

137. A: The most professional response when answering the phone is a simple greeting, starting with the healthcare practice's name. This helps the caller confirm that they have called the correct number. With practice, this should become a habit. Choice *A* is incorrect because the employee's name is less important. Choices *C* and *D* are incorrect because this information does not need to be included in a simple greeting.

138. A: Choice *A* Is correct because this suffix is associated with HMG-CoA reductase inhibitors, which are a class of cholesterol-lowering medications. Choice *B* is incorrect because *-sartan* is associated with the class of medications called angiotensin II receptor antagonists, which are medications used in the treatment of hypertension and heart failure. Choice *C* is incorrect because *-olol* medications are associated with the class of medications called beta-blockers, which are used to manage arrhythmias and hypertension. Choice *D* is incorrect because medications ending in *-mab* are associated with monoclonal antibodies, which are a class of medications typically used in the treatment of autoimmune diseases.

139. A: A claim of health insurance fraud is a federal crime and should be reported to the FBI using the organization's website. Therefore, Choice *A* is correct. Choice *B* is incorrect because the CIA is involved in foreign activities, not domestic activities. Choices *C* and *D* are incorrect because the IRS and the CMS are not law enforcement agencies.

140. C: Tachypnea is the most appropriate medical term associated with a respiratory rate that is faster than normal. Although not always associated with a medical condition, tachypnea can be associated with lung disease, asthma, infection, obesity, or anxiety. Hyperpnea is the state of taking deeper breaths than normal and is a natural state that occurs when there is increased oxygen demand (e.g., exercise). Hyperoxia, or oxygen toxicity, is a state in which too much oxygen is being pushed into the tissues and organs by pressure. This can be most often found in patients on prolonged oxygen therapy (e.g., ICU patients, premature infants), divers, and individuals undergoing hyperbaric oxygen treatment. Hyperventilation is the state of taking rapid deep breaths. Some causes of hyperventilation include anxiety, problems involving the nervous system, and lung injury or disease.

141. B: Choice *B* provides the most information about overall medication compliance because this is an open-ended interview question that does not lead the patient to a specific answer. This question provides an opportunity for the CMA to compare the written record with what the patient is doing. This can potentially identify misuse, overuse, underuse, or medication errors. This also provides a starting point for the CMA to ask clarifying and more specific questions based on the patient's responses. Choice *A* is incorrect because this closed-ended question assumes the patient knows the correct way to take their medication. Choice *C, also a closed-ended question,* does not provide the most information regarding overall compliance because it only asks about starting or stopping medications. Choice *D* also provides limited information about the difficulty of taking medications and does not effectively gauge overall compliance.

142. C: Choice *C* is correct because the patient is seeking immediate care for a new illness. Choices *A* and *B* are incorrect because these appointments are both a routine part of annual healthcare. Choice *D* is incorrect because renewing a prescription is part of routine health maintenance.

143. B: Choice *B* indicates that the mother may need additional teaching about pediatric dietary considerations. Sitting down for family meals can be a great way to encourage healthy habits for young children. However, at four years of age, it would be more realistic to expect a child to remain at the table for up to approximately 20 minutes. Enforcing times longer than are developmentally reasonable could result in adverse emotional and behavioral patterns surrounding eating. In addition, enforcing a rule that an infant or young child should clean their plate sets up a pattern for the patient to begin to ignore their innate hunger and satiety cues. Choice *A* does not require additional teaching. It is not uncommon for children to be picky eaters, and this would only become concerning if the patient was experiencing severe growth and development concerns. Offering a variety of foods is also a great way to encourage children to try new things and develop a wider palate. Choice *C* does not require additional dietary teaching because water and milk are the most appropriate choices of drinks for children. Juice and other sugary drinks are recommended to be limited as much as possible. Choice *D* does not require additional teaching because cheese and peanut butter are good non-meat protein options for a child who does not prefer meat.

144. C: Gloves and a disposable mask are all that are required for droplet precaution; however, additional PPE may be used if desiring extra protection. The key word in this question is *minimum.* Choice *A* is not correct because an N-95 mask is not required. Choice *D* is not correct because sterile gloves are not needed and eyewear is optional. Choice *B* would give the most coverage for protection but it is not the minimum PPE required.

145. C: When a patient is lying flat on their back in the supine position, it is important to pad bony prominences such as the heels, tailbone, elbows, shoulder blades, and head. The remaining choices naturally have more padding and may be uncomfortable to the patient if additional padding is added.

146. C: Choice *C* is correct because a rectal temperature measurement is approximately 0.5–1.0 degrees Fahrenheit higher than the oral route. Choice *A* is incorrect because it would not be expected for an oral temperature to be approximately the same as a rectal temperature. Choice *B* is incorrect because it would not be expected for an oral temperature to be higher than a rectal temperature. Choice *D* is incorrect because it would not be expected for an oral temperature to be 1.5–2.0 degrees Fahrenheit lower than a rectal temperature.

147. B: Repression is a coping mechanism in which a patient forgets a traumatic event that has happened to them. Denial is a coping mechanism in which a patient refuses to acknowledge something that has happened. Dissociation occurs when a patient separates from reality. Grief is a general term that describes a series of stages someone goes through after a significant loss.

148. C: The most common anatomical site for assessing pulse in an adult is the radial artery, which is located at the wrist near the thumb. Choice *A* is incorrect because the brachial artery is the recommended location for measuring pulse in a nonresponsive infant. Choice *B* is incorrect because the carotid artery is recommended for unresponsive adult patients. Choice *D* is incorrect because apical pulse is an auscultated measurement of pulse via the apex, which is located at the very bottom tip of the heart. This method is ideal for cardiac assessment and is also frequently used to obtain pulse measurement in neonates.

149. B: HIPAA is a law that protects a patient's identity. It prevents disclosure of information without the patient's knowledge and consent.

150. D: Metformin is correct because this is the only listed oral hypoglycemic medication. Choice *A* is incorrect because regular insulin is a subcutaneous hypoglycemic. Choice *B* is incorrect because atorvastatin is a medication used to manage high cholesterol. Choice *C* is incorrect because lisinopril is an angiotensin-converting enzyme (ACE inhibitor) used to treat high blood pressure.

151. D: Choice *D* is correct because end-of-day reconciliation is a financial process in which staff confirm that the financial elements of the practice's administration are correct. Choices *A* and *C* do not involve the healthcare practice's finances, and therefore are incorrect. Choice *B* is incorrect because mailing bills is not part of balancing the books.

152. C: Crutches are an example of an assistive device for mobility. Physical and occupational therapies assist with mobility but are not devices. Restraints do not assist with mobility.

153. B: The medical assistant should stay in the resident's line of vision while speaking with him so that the resident can see that the medical assistant is speaking and can receive nonverbal cues. Talking with one's back to the resident and talking quietly both make it difficult for the resident to hear the medical assistant. Braille is used for visually impaired residents.

154. D: It is best that a medical assistant avoids discussing controversial topics—such as abortion or politics—unless directly related to the patient's healthcare needs. This professional boundary improves patient care by increasing patient and provider comfort in the situation. Therefore, Choices *A* and *B* are incorrect. Choice *C* is incorrect because even neutral information still engages in the topic and increases the risk of patient discomfort.

155. A: Choice *A* is correct because an itemized statement from the healthcare provider summarizes all costs incurred. An explanation of benefits from the insurance provider describes what services they have covered. Choices *B, C,* and *D* are incorrect because they describe accurate benefits of an itemized statement.

156. B: Asking for the patient's DOB helps confirm that the CMA has the correct EHR open, and further helps confirm the speaker's identity. It is still important, however, that the CMA avoids disclosing privileged information over the phone. Health information should only be provided in person or through a secure electronic transmission. Choices *A* and *C* are not relevant to the CMA's job duties while answering the phone, and so they are incorrect. Choice *D* is incorrect because CMS does not rely on DOB as a primary means of patient identification.

157. B: Choice *B* is correct because "ODT" is the abbreviation for an orally disintegrating tablet, which is placed in the mouth to dissolve. Choice *A* is incorrect because it is the oral route, which is abbreviated "PO." Choice *C* is incorrect because it is the sublingual route and is abbreviated "SL." Choice *D* is incorrect because it is the buccal route of administration, abbreviated "BUC."

158. B: HIPAA provides patients with the right to request a change to their health records if the patient believes the record is based on incorrect facts. HIPAA does not give patients the right to request amendment of a physician's diagnosis; therefore, Choice *A* is incorrect. Choices *C* and *D* are incorrect because these changes do not require the physician to alter their own records.

159. A: Choice *A* is correct because lateral describes a location that is going on or toward the side of the body and away from the midline. Choice *B* is incorrect because dorsal refers to the back side of the body. Choice *C* is incorrect because ventral refers to the front side of the body. Choice *D* is incorrect because medial refers to something going toward the center of the body as opposed to something moving distally (away) from the center of the body.

160. C: Clonazepam is the generic name for Klonopin, a sedative medication used most commonly to treat seizures and anxiety disorders. Choice *A* is incorrect because clonidine is the generic name for Catepres, which is an antihypertensive medication used to lower blood pressure and heart rate. Choice *B* is incorrect because lorazepam is the generic form of Ativan, which is another sedative medication commonly used to treat seizures and anxiety. Choice *D* is incorrect because clindamycin is an antibiotic used to treat various bacterial infections.

161. B: Writing off a bill describes the process of counting the owed amount as an expense when filing taxes annually. This process treats the overdue payment as lost income. Choice *B* is correct. Choices *A, C,* and *D* are incorrect because they do not describe the loss being reported to the IRS as part of the tax filing process.

162. A: The most appropriate next action would be to begin chest compressions. This patient is unresponsive with gasping breaths and a pulse that cannot be confirmed. This indicates the need for immediate initiation of cardiopulmonary resuscitation (CPR). Choice *B* is incorrect because pulse should be assessed for no more than 10 seconds at the carotid pulse point. If pulse cannot be confirmed within that time, CPR initiation beginning with chest compressions is warranted. Choice *C* is incorrect because the patient does not have a confirmed pulse; therefore, chest compressions are the most appropriate choice. Choice *D* is incorrect because a sternal rub (a painful stimuli that can be used to determine neurological status of a patient) is not appropriate for use when there is no confirmed pulse.

163. B: The teach-back method, a strategy to assess learning by having the patient "teach" the medical provider the presented information or skill, is an effective way to gauge patient understanding. Demonstration, which involves the CMA demonstrating the skill, would not be most effective because it does not provide the patient with the opportunity to practice the skill. Video tutorials would not be the most effective learning strategy for learning skills because they lack return demonstration; however, videos are helpful to supplement patient teaching. They allow patients to review as many times as needed. Written handouts would be the least effective method for learning about blood sugar testing because this method does not provide visual, demonstration, or hands-on learning opportunities.

164. A: Choice *A* is correct because NSAIDs such as ibuprofen decrease the effect of ACE inhibitors (e.g., lisinopril). There are no known interactions between Choices *B*, *C*, and *D* and lisinopril; therefore, these are not the appropriate answers.

165. C: A cardiac diet consists of food that is low in sodium, fat, and cholesterol. Patients with cardiac conditions such as heart disease, recent cardiac events, high cholesterol, and high blood pressure are often placed on his diet. Choice *A* is incorrect because a diet that is high in sodium would cause a patient to retain more water, which can increase blood pressure and put more stress on the heart. Choices *B* and *D* are incorrect because increased carbohydrate and water intake can also raise blood pressure and cause weight gain, which would put more stress on the heart. Water intake should be monitored and only restricted if specifically indicated.

166. A: Positioning the extremity above the level of the heart is the only answer that is associated with a false low blood pressure measurement. Choices *B, C,* and *D* are incorrect because each of these answers is associated with false high blood pressure measurements.

167. D: Patients with influenza should be placed on droplet precautions. The medical assistant should wear at least a mask and gloves. Choice *A* is incorrect because airborne precautions are used for infections such as Tuberculosis, measles, and chickenpox. Choice B is incorrect because contact precautions are used for conditions such as *C. diff*, norovirus, or with patients who are incontinent or have ostomy bags. Choice *C* is incorrect because standard precautions are used to prevent contact by blood, bodily fluids, broken skin, rashes, and mucous membranes that do not have additional known infectious agents.

168. A: A discharge summary is written by the physician after the patient's stay at an in-patient healthcare provider (such as a hospital) to summarize the patient's illnesses, treatment, and after-stay treatment recommendations. They are sent to other healthcare providers to ensure continuity of care. Choice *A* is correct because a treatment facility does complete a discharge summary when a patient leaves their care. The providers listed in Choices *B, C,* and *D* do not typically require a discharge summary after providing healthcare services.

169. B: When entering a patient's room, it is advised to wear a surgical mask. Surgical masks provide protection against droplets, which are produced during talking, breathing, coughing, or sneezing. Choice *A*, a respirator mask, is not required when entering a patient's examination room, but it is recommended when performing any task that could produce aerosols. Aerosol-producing procedures can include tracheostomy care or suctioning. Gloves, as a general rule, should only be donned after entering the examination room, patient room, or the immediate area where care is to be provided. Gloves must also be removed and hand hygiene performed prior to exiting the immediate care area. Therefore, Choices *C* and *D* are incorrect. Gloves are indicated when there is a risk of coming into contact with contaminated surfaces or fluids.

170. B: Choice *B* is the correct answer because this statement would be the least appropriate choice. Dietary guidelines for management of diabetes encourage balanced, individualized nutrition as opposed to blanketed limitations of food choices. Choice *A* is incorrect because whole grains do assist with reduction in cholesterol and insulin levels. Choice *C* is incorrect because asking what a patient's blood sugar readings have been would help identify how the patient's current diet is impacting their blood sugar levels. Choice *D* is incorrect because the addition of protein and fiber to meals helps patients avoid sharp spikes and dips in blood sugar levels and provides longer satiety between meals.

171. B: A 45-degree angle is the appropriate angle to administer a subcutaneous injection in an infant's anterior thigh. Choices *A, C,* and *D* are incorrect because these are wider angles and increase the risk that the injection will reach the muscle instead of the subcutaneous tissue. This would result in the injection being delivered by the incorrect route, which is a medication error.

172. B: Choice *B* is correct because the abbreviation "TID" means the patient should take their medication three times per day. Choice *A* is incorrect because the patient is taking this medication twice daily, or "BID." Choice *C* is incorrect because the patient is taking the medication as needed, or "PRN." Choice *D* is incorrect because the patient is taking the medication every other day, or "QOD."

173. C: The pancreas produces hormones to regulate blood sugar, and it assists with the production of digestive enzymes to assist in digestion. Choice *A* is incorrect because this describes the function of the liver. Choice *B* is incorrect because this describes the function of the small intestine. Choice *D* is incorrect because this is a description of the function of the kidneys.

174. C: A growth chart is used by physicians to track a child's growth, including their percentile in relation to others who are the child's age and sex. Choices *A, B,* and *D* are incorrect because they do not describe metrics that are recorded with a growth chart.

175. C: Verbally assaulting, criticizing, and using language to make a victim feel worthless, insecure, fearful, and belittled are examples of emotional/mental abuse. This abuse should be monitored, investigated, and reported through proper channels.

176. C: Choice *C* is correct because the handgrips should align with the top of the pelvis. This allows for relaxed, upright posture while also preventing pressure injuries from the crutch pads pressing against the underarm. Choice *A* is incorrect because the hip flexor is located at the bottom of the pelvis, which would cause the patient to be at increased risk of orthopedic injury to the spine and back due to forward-leaning posture. Choice *B* is incorrect because the waist (the narrowest point between the ribs and the hips) would be too high and would push the top pads of the crutches into the underarm, which would increase the risk of discomfort and pressure injury. Choice *D* is incorrect because the greater

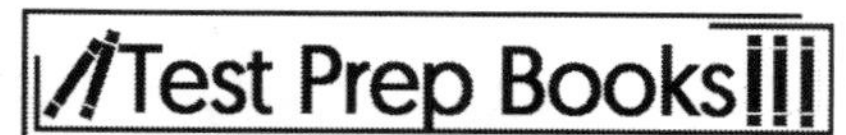

trochanter is located below the pelvis. This position would lead to a deeply forward-leaning posture, which would increase the risk of posture-related injuries.

177. B: A pulse rate of 56 beats per minute is the correct answer because this may indicate that the patient's metoprolol dose needs to be decreased, as this medication can cause bradycardia. Choice *A* is incorrect because a temperature of 99.9 degrees Fahrenheit is nonfebrile and is not indicative that metoprolol may need to be decreased. Choice *C* is incorrect because a blood pressure of 180/110 would indicate an increase in blood pressure medication as opposed to a decrease in metoprolol dose. Choice *D* is incorrect because a respiratory rate of 22, which is mildly elevated, would not inherently indicate that a decrease in metoprolol is necessary.

178. C: This type of seizure with muscle rigidity, convulsions, and unconsciousness is called a grand mal seizure. An absence seizure involves a brief loss of consciousness where the patient may stare into space. A myoclonic seizure involves the body making jerking movements. A tonic seizure is characterized by rigidity and stiffness of the muscles.

179. D: The patient is most likely experiencing a stroke, as evidenced by the difficulty with speech and facial drooping. A migraine is a severe headache that can sometimes mimic stroke symptoms but is less severe. A stroke should be suspected until it is proven otherwise in order to get the patient timely and effective treatment. A seizure is characterized by muscle rigidity, convulsions, and loss of consciousness. Meningitis is an inflammation of the meninges and does not fit the description of symptoms here.

180. B: E-prescribing is the process by which a healthcare provider uses electronic communication to send prescriptions directly to the pharmacy. Choice *B* is correct. Choice *A* is incorrect because most prescription refills require an in-person appointment to determine if the medication has an appropriate effect on the illness. Choices *C* and *D* are incorrect because pharmacies and healthcare providers do not operate at that level of electronic integration.

181. D: When interviewing patients, the best approach is to use a mix of closed- and open-ended questions to get a range of information; listen carefully to each answer and ask probing questions when necessary to clarify the information. Focusing only on closed-ended questions could prevent patients from sharing certain relevant information, so Choice *A* is incorrect. Using mainly open-ended questions could encourage patients to ramble excessively about irrelevant information, so Choice *B* is incorrect. Probing questions should be used when necessary to narrow down facts, but general questions are also useful to include, so Choice *C* is incorrect.

182. B: In emergency departments, there is often not enough time to perform formal informed consent with patients, who may be in need of prompt life-saving treatments. Thus, implied consent is often used in such situations, assuming that any reasonable person would consent to the types of emergency treatment being provided. Choice *A* is incorrect because informed consent is the type of formal, signed consent that is regularly obtained from patients for their treatment plans in nonemergency situations. Before giving such consent, patients must be provided with educational information about the planned treatment. Choice *C* is incorrect because expressed consent is a type of verbal, nonverbal, or written consent that a patient gives to receive certain care. Unlike informed consent, educational information might not be provided. Choice *D* is incorrect because emergency consent is not an actual name for any type of patient consent.

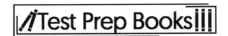

183. B: A patient's social history, which is one aspect of the documentation of care, should include such items as alcohol, smoking, and recreational drug use; living accommodations and arrangements; marital status; occupation; and baseline functioning. Choice *A* is incorrect because the number of friends and relatives and types of social activities are features of social behavior, but they do not accurately represent a medically relevant social history. Choices *C* and *D* are incorrect because chief complaint, review of symptoms, past medical history, family history, occupation history, compliance with treatment, and test and examination results are other aspects of the documentation of care.

184. A: Advanced beneficiary notices (ABNs) of non-coverage apply only to patients with original Medicare. Whenever Medicare determines that the standard of care for a particular service is not met for such patients, the CMA must provide the patient with an ABN and document the notification in the patient's electronic health record. Choice *B* is incorrect because patients with Medicare Advantage receive notices of Medicare non-coverage, rather than ABNs, if their claims are denied. Choices *C* and *D* are incorrect because ABNs are not used for non-coverage notices for private insurance.

185. B: The Papanicolaou (PAP) test is useful for reducing the incidence and mortality of cervical cancer, and doctors generally recommend that women between the ages of 21 and 65 get the test performed once every three years. Choice *A* is incorrect because the human papillomavirus (HPV) test, which is performed to detect a virus that may lead to cervical cancer or genital warts, is generally recommended for women over age 30, though it is also given to some men to detect the virus on the penis or scrotum. Choice *C* is incorrect because a colonoscopy is generally recommended for women and men once every 10 years to screen for colon cancer or polyps. Choice *D* is incorrect because a mammogram is generally recommended once a year for women over age 40 to screen for breast cancer.

186. B: Disinfection is a cleaning process that kills or inactivates most harmful, infectious bacteria and viruses on hard surfaces—most importantly, those microorganisms that are listed on the product label. Disinfectants are the only cleaning agents that are approved by the Environmental Protection Agency to kill viruses on hard surfaces. However, this process does not destroy all bacteria, viruses, and other microorganisms. Choice *A* is incorrect because sanitization is a cleaning process that reduces the number of bacteria on surfaces, but it does not actually kill or inactivate bacteria or viruses. Choice *C* is incorrect because sterilization is a cleaning process that kills all bacteria and viruses, as well as all other microorganisms. Choice *D* is incorrect because medical asepsis is the general term used to describe any cleaning process that reduces the number of infectious agents in a patient's environment.

187. C: Professional liability refers to legal obligations that CMAs and other healthcare professionals have in being responsible for their actions and, if found seriously negligent in these actions, to face legal penalties. Such penalties may include paying compensation to injured parties or even losing one's license to practice. Choice *A* is incorrect because tort is a general legal term that refers to any civil wrong that causes a claimant to suffer some loss or harm. Choice *B* is incorrect because libel refers to a tort that involves documenting something false about another person in order to damage that person's reputation. Choice *D* is incorrect because slander is a tort that involves intentional verbal harm to another person, such as spreading lies to supervisors about the person.

188. B: Medicaid is a federal (but state-run) health insurance program that covers people who have incomes below a certain level, as well as people in certain population groups that have historically experienced disparities in accessing healthcare services, such as racial minorities and the LGBT (lesbian, gay, bisexual, transgender) community. Choice *A* is incorrect because Medicaid is not limited to people who have incomes below a certain level. Choice *C* is incorrect because Medicaid is not limited to people

in certain historically disadvantaged racial or ethnic groups. Choice *D* is incorrect because it describes requirements for Medicare, not Medicaid.

189. C: Caution signs, which are used to identify hazards that pose risks of minor-to-moderate injuries (such as very hot water), are typically made with black letters on a bright yellow background. Choices *A* and *B* are incorrect because they show incorrect colors for caution signs. Choice *D* is incorrect because caution signs are typically standardized as yellow and black for easy and quick identification; they rarely vary in color.

190. B: For a childhood fever to be accommodated with a same-day appointment, the child's temperature must typically be over 102 °F or 103 °F. Choices *A*, *C*, and *D* all describe conditions that can typically be accommodated with a same-day appointment.

191. D: Warning signs in healthcare settings, which are typically orange and black, are used to indicate the potential of serious harm or even death. Examples include signs warning of exposure to x-ray radiation, a quarantine in progress, and biohazards. Choices *A* and *B* are incorrect because they refer to specific purposes of certain warning signs rather than to the general purpose of warning signs. Choice *C* is incorrect because warning signs are used to indicate serious risks; moderate-level risks are typically indicated by caution signs.

192. C: In people with diabetes, insulin deficiency causes hyperglycemia (high blood glucose levels), which, in turn, leads to salt and water depletion—not excess salt. Thus, Choice *C* does not offer a valid explanation for delayed wound healing. Choice *A* does offer an accurate explanation for delayed wound healing because hyperglycemia does adversely affect the immune system. Choice *B* offers an accurate explanation for delayed wound healing because hyperglycemia does cause blood vessel constriction, which reduces the circulation of blood and oxygen to the feet; wounds require blood and oxygen to heal. Choice *D* offers an accurate explanation for delayed wound healing because reduced blood circulation can cause neuropathy (nerve damage) in the feet, preventing a person from being aware of the presence of wounds and, thereby, causing the wounds to worsen over time.

193. D: In many cases of terminal illness, it may be better to, instead of searching for something meaningful or helpful to say, just give a hug or hold hands with the patient as a way of offering some comfort. Choice *A* is incorrect because saying anything at all to the patient may come across as insincere and phony. Choice *B* is incorrect because it is good to offer compassion but not false hope to the patient. Choice *C* is incorrect because acting cold and showing no emotion may come across as uncaring.

194. B: In normal development patterns, an infant typically begins to recognize familiar faces at the age of about six months. That's also when the infant starts to make consonant sounds, put objects in their mouth, and roll over both ways. Regarding Choice *A*, infants at three months may look at faces, but they do not seem to recognize them yet. Regarding Choice *C*, infants at nine months tend to exhibit fear of strangers. For Choice *D*, infants that are one year old tend to cry when their parents leave, and they can wave "hi" and "bye."

195. A: The hematopoietic system, a division of the lymphatic system, is the specific system of the body that is responsible for the continuous production of blood cells. It consists mainly of the bone marrow, spleen, tonsils, and lymph nodes. Red bone marrow is the primary site of blood cell formation from stem cells; yellow bone marrow is less active but can also produce blood cells. Choice *B* is incorrect because the cardiovascular system consists of the heart, blood vessels, and blood. Choice *C* is incorrect because the lymphatic system consists of—in addition to the hematopoietic tissues—the vast network of lymphatic vessels and the lymph. Choice *D* is incorrect because the circulatory system is the general name for all tissues and organs involved in the circulation of blood and lymph throughout the body.

196. A: The best general definition of a patient portal is a secure website that gives patients convenient 24-hour access to their personal health information, such as recent doctor visits, discharge summaries, prescribed medications, and lab results. Choices *B*, *C*, and *D* are incorrect because they all describe specific activities that may be available with some, but not all, patient portals.

197. D: With subcutaneous injections, medications are absorbed slowly and gradually because of the limited supply of blood in the fatty tissue beneath the skin. Choice *A* is incorrect because the main reason for giving Z-tract injections is to avoid skin irritation or discoloration with certain medications, which are injected into muscles where the drugs can be rapidly absorbed. Choice *B* is incorrect because medications that are given orally will be rapidly absorbed into the bloodstream through the mucous membrane of the gastrointestinal tract. Choice *C* is incorrect because intramuscular injection ensures rapid absorption of medication into the bloodstream.

198. A: Because the patient is upset that the nurse has not brought his pain medication despite repeated requests, it would be best for the CMA to call the nurse while he is in the room with the patient so that the patient can see that action is being taken. Choice *B* is incorrect because simply promising to tell the nurse may not give the highly agitated patient much comfort. Choice *C* is incorrect because telling the patient to calm down may make him angrier and more agitated. Choice *D* is incorrect because the CMA cannot know for sure that the nurse is aware of the patient's request.

199. B: MedWatch is the Food and Drug Administration's system for both healthcare providers and the public to report medical errors, drug reactions, product quality problems, and drug failures, as well as problems with medical devices, dietary supplements, foods, and cosmetics. Choice *A* is incorrect because MedWatch is not only for the public. Choices *C* and *D* are incorrect because MedWatch is not a program of the National Institutes of Health, and the stated purposes of the program are inaccurate.

200. D: The Centers for Disease Control and Prevention (CDC) publishes the Vaccine Information Statements. Providers obtain these documents from the CDC, and they then must supply them to patients before administering the vaccines. Choices *A*, *B*, and *C* are incorrect because, although all of these federal agencies perform important medical- and health-related work, none of them are tasked with publishing and providing the Vaccine Information Statements.

CMA Practice Tests #3, #4, & #5

To keep the size of this book manageable, save paper, and provide a digital test-taking experience, the 3rd5th practice test can be found online. Scan the QR code or go to this link to access it:

testprepbooks.com/bonus/cma

The first time you access the tests, you will need to register as a "new user" and verify your email address.

If you have any issues, please email support@testprepbooks.com.

Index

Dear CMA Test Taker,

Thank you for purchasing this study guide for your CMA exam. We hope that we exceeded your expectations.

Our goal in creating this study guide was to cover all of the topics that you will see on the test. We also strove to make our practice questions as similar as possible to what you will encounter on test day. With that being said, if you found something that you feel was not up to your standards, please send us an email and let us know.

We would also like to let you know about another book in our catalog that may interest you.

CNA

This can be found on Amazon: amazon.com/dp/1637757832

We have study guides in a wide variety of fields. If you are looking for one, then try searching for it on Amazon or send us an email.

Thanks Again and Happy Testing!
Product Development Team
info@studyguideteam.com

FREE Test Taking Tips Video/DVD Offer

To better serve you, we created videos covering test taking tips that we want to give you for FREE. **These videos cover world-class tips that will help you succeed on your test.**

We just ask that you send us feedback about this product. Please let us know what you thought about it—whether good, bad, or indifferent.

To get your **FREE videos**, you can use the QR code below or email freevideos@studyguideteam.com with "Free Videos" in the subject line and the following information in the body of the email:

a. The title of your product

b. Your product rating on a scale of 1-5, with 5 being the highest

c. Your feedback about the product

If you have any questions or concerns, please don't hesitate to contact us at info@studyguideteam.com.

Thank you!

Made in United States
Orlando, FL
30 April 2025